Preferences and Well-Being

ROYAL INSTITUTE OF PHILOSOPHY SUPPLEMENT: 59

EDITED BY

Serena Olsaretti

CAMBRIDGE
UNIVERSITY PRESS

PUBLISHED BY THE PRESS SYNDICATE OF THE UNIVERSITY OF CAMBRIDGE
The Pitt Building, Trumpington Street, Cambridge, CB2 1RP,
United Kingdom

CAMBRIDGE UNIVERSITY PRESS
The Edinburgh Building, Cambridge CB2 2RU, United Kingdom
40 West 20th Street, New York, NY 10011–4211, USA
477 Williamstown Road, Port Melbourne, VIC 3207, Australia
Ruiz de Alarcón 13, 28014 Madrid, Spain
Dock House, The Waterfront, Cape Town 8001, South Africa

© The Royal Institute of Philosophy and the contributors 2006

Printed in the United Kingdom at the University Press, Cambridge
Typeset by Michael Heath Ltd, Reigate, Surrey

Library of Congress Cataloguing-in-Publication Data applied for

Contents

List of Contributors

Richard Arneson, University of California, San Diego, USA

Johan Brännmark, Lund University, Sweden

John Broome, University of Oxford

Daniel M. Hausman, University of Wisconsin-Madison, USA

Serena Olsaretti, University of Cambridge

Philip Pettit, Princeton University, USA

Christian Piller, University of York

Mozaffar Qizilbash, University of East Anglia

Connie S. Rosati, University of California, Davis, USA

Robert Sugden, University of East Anglia

Cass R. Sunstein, University of Chicago, USA

Richard H. Thaler, University of Chicago, USA

Alex Voorhoeve, London School of Economics and Political Science

Introduction

SERENA OLSARETTI

In a number of debates in contemporary moral and political philosophy and philosophy of economics, philosophers hold the conviction that preferences have normative significance. A central assumption that underlies this conviction is that a cogent account of preference-formation can be developed. This is particularly evident in debates about well-being. Those who defend subjective accounts of well-being, on which a person's life goes better for her to the extent that her preferences are satisfied, often qualify that account so that it does not include malformed or adaptive preferences (that is, preferences formed in non-autonomous ways, or humble preferences tailored to stifling circumstances), the satisfaction of which does not seem to contribute to well-being. This assumes that there is a normative standard of preference-formation with which to identify those preference that are malformed or adaptive in the relevant sense. An account of preference-formation is also important for philosophers who uphold an objective theory of well-being, on which well-being consists of the pursuit of objectively valuable goals, but who also believe in the value of freedom and thus emphasise the importance of respecting individuals' choices among various goals. For they, too, in extolling the importance of respect for choices, assume that these choices are not distorted by inauthentically formed preferences, and thus also need an account of preference-formation to help distinguish those cases in which we ought to respect people's choices from those in which we do not. In the vast literature on preferences, however, relatively little attention has been devoted to the explicit discussion of candidate accounts of preference-formation. The aim of the 2004 annual Royal Institute of Philosophy conference, which constitutes the basis for the present volume, was to foster such a discussion.

The papers collected here can, broadly speaking, be seen to address three main sets of questions on the topic of preference-formation and well-being. The first main set of questions concern the formulation of normative and descriptive accounts of preference-formation. The former are especially important, as they provide a standard by which we can discriminate between

1

preferences that do, and those that do not have, prudential value. The papers by Richard Arneson, Connie Rosati, Johan Brännmark, and Mozaffar Qizilbash all start with the two-fold assumption that the satisfaction of preferences has some normative significance, where this significance is thought of specifically in terms of the relevance of preference satisfaction for our well-being; and that this significance varies depending on what the preferences in question are, or how they have been formed, so that it is possible that with respect to some preferences their satisfaction has little or indeed no prudential value. These papers then seek a standard with which we can discriminate between the prudential values of different preferences.

Arneson's "Desire Formation and Human Good" considers the three main families of theories of well-being or the human good—the desire or preference satisfaction account, the objective list account, and the hybrid account—with a view to identifying and examining their implications about which preferences it would be good for individuals to form. Arneson argues that the desire satisfaction account is committed to the problematic implication that people should form the desires that they can satisfy most easily, and that any attempt to avoid this implication from within the premises of the desire satisfaction account is unsuccessful. Ultimately, Arneson suggests, what underpins our unease with this implication of the desire satisfaction account is our implicit evaluation of some desires as more objectively valuable than others, an evaluation that requires the abandonment of the desire satisfaction account. The objective list account, and the hybrid account, fare better than the desire satisfaction account, in that they have the resources to offer a discriminating view of what desires people should form: both accounts suggest that individuals should form desires for goods that are objectively valuable. However, Arneson suggests that there is a tension between two different claims these accounts make. They may imply either that it is good for individuals to form desires that track what is of value, and thus reflect proper appreciation of it; or that it is good for individuals to form desires that make the pursuit of the good *effective*. These two things are not the same. For example, it may be that a disproportionately positive evaluation of the value of a particular goal one sets oneself—say, that of succeeding in one's career—can more effectively lead a person to achieve that valuable goal than a fitting and more moderate appreciation of its value. Arneson suggests that objective list theorists should adopt the second, rather than the first, view of what preferences people should form. Hybrid accounts of the good life, by contrast, will also emphasise the importance of there being a proper fit between people's preferences and the objects of those preferences, since on these accounts the *attitudes* that people have towards objectively valuable goods is an essential component of the good life.

Like Arneson, Qizilbash is interested in teasing out the implications of the central competing accounts of well-being for the formulation of a standard for discriminating between preferences. Moreover, he, too, doubts the capacity of purely subjective accounts to provide such a standard. Qizilbash proposes that a standard for discriminating between preferences should be able to identify adaptive preferences as problematic from the point of view of well-being, without positing an overly demanding set of conditions that preferences must meet in order to have prudential value. In particular, these conditions should reflect human limitations in forming preferences, including, for example, the constrained capacity to gather and appreciate information about the various options we may face. This limitation is ignored by desire satisfaction accounts which hold that the only desires whose satisfaction contribute to a person's well-being are those that person would have if she were fully informed about all the alternative options she faces.

In his "Leading a Life of One's Own: On Well-Being and Narrative Autonomy", Brännmark is also concerned that the standard for identifying which preferences have prudential value not be an overly demanding one. His suggestion is that we adopt the criterion of narrative autonomy as such a standard. Narrative autonomy is the autonomy an individual enjoys when she lives a life of her own, and is both protagonist and author of her own life. She must be a protagonist of her own life, as opposed to merely playing the role of a supporting character, and she must be author of her life, in the sense of having a certain independence of judgement about what she wants. Those preferences that hinder our leading lives that exhibit narrative autonomy, then, are problematic from the point of view of well-being. Narrative autonomy, according to Brännmark, constitutes a relatively undemanding standard of prudential value which can be satisfied by people with very different plans of life, and is more plausible than competing standards for discriminating between preferences, such as a standard that deems only idealised preferences which survive critical reflection as prudentially valuable. An important implication of Brännmark's argument, like Arneson's, is that we should abandon subjectivism about well-being, since arguably the theory of well-being within which narrative autonomy can play a role is an objective one that identifies the narrative meaning of lives as objectively valuable.

In contrast with the objective list and hybrid accounts examined by Arneson and Qizilbash, Rosati suggests that we discriminate between preferences by looking, not to the value of the objects of preferences, but to whether those preferences would be formed by individuals who have the capacity to form preferences well. To be good formers of preferences, individuals must have certain dispositions, which are best thought of as those they develop when successfully parented. Successful parenting, on Rosati's view, will exhibit, first, a concern for the agent-neutral value of children that fosters a robust sense of self-worth; second, a regard for the child as an autonomous agent, which fosters the capacity to respond to reasons, deliberate on desires, and engage in self-reflection; and third, a regard to the individuality of the child. In short, then, Rosati suggests that good formers of preferences have the dispositions that successful parenting promotes in children, and good preferences are those which we would form if we were ourselves guided by the regard towards ourselves which successful parents are guided by. Rosati's proposal casts new light on why adaptive preferences are sometimes problematic. For Rosati, adaptive preferences are problematic because the individuals who form them lack the dispositions that are necessary for them to be good formers of preferences. She can thus account for what seems deeply troubling about the paradigmatic cases of adaptive preferences, namely the adaptive preferences of "the hopeless beggar" or "the dominated housewife".

Finally, turning from normative to descriptive accounts of preference-formation, Daniel Hausman's paper argues that economists offer an account of preference-formation despite their claiming not to do so. More specifically, Hausman's main contention is that game theory can be seen to offer an account of how some preferences (namely, preferences over strategies) are formed, taking people's preferences over outcomes as given, and that moreover, in those cases where people's preferences over outcomes are affected by features of the game form other than its results (such as, for example, how a certain result is brought about), then even preferences over outcomes are not just given, and economists tacitly construct them. The claim economists often make, namely, that they do not and should not have anything to say about preference-formation, is therefore unjustified.

The second main set of issues explored by papers in this volume concerns whether preferences conform with requirements of rationality, and what types of reasons we have to prefer certain things rather than others. In "Preference, Deliberation and Satisfaction", Philip Pettit defends a "value-serving" view of deliberation, on which the aim of deliberation is to find criteria with which to assess our goal-pursuing activities. On this view of deliberation, we deliberate not just *from* goals or desires, but also *about* them; we form our desires or goals in light of the desirability features of their objects, where these features could include the extent to which our desires cohere with one another, or the degree to which we are likely to be able to satisfy them. Desires are not just cravings which must be taken as givens, but are the objects of deliberation, and the significance of satisfying them, both from the first-person and the third-person perspective, will be a function of the desirability features of what is desired.

Christian Piller's paper also allows for the fact that the desirability features of the objects of desire may determine whether we have reasons to desire those objects. But his main concern is with whether we may be said to have reasons to desire something that track, not the desirability features *of the objects of desire*, but rather, *of the having of the desire* itself. In Piller's language, the question is whether we have "attitude-related", as well as "content-related", reasons to prefer or desire something, that is, whether the fact that having a desire for something makes it more likely that we will achieve something that is good for us is a reason to desire that thing (so that, for example, if preferring a saucer of mud over a pot of gold ensures that you will receive two pots of gold, you would have a reason to prefer a saucer of mud). Piller's answer to this question is affirmative for desires (while granting that the answer may be negative for other attitudes, like beliefs). If Piller is right, it can be rational to have preferences for what is (in terms of the desirability features of the objects of those preferences) worse, because to have such preferences can be better for us.

Even if we assume that there are requirements of rationality that our preferences must satisfy, there is a further question as to how we come to meet these requirements. In his contribution to this volume, John Broome asks whether we can come to meet those requirements by reasoning our way to them. Such reasoning could either start from the requirements themselves as premises (as the "second-order model" supposes), or proceed by considering the content of one's preferences (as suggested by the "first-order model"). Broome argues that the first-order rather than the second-order model of reasoning is more apt as an account of reasoning with preferences, where these are narrowly understood as desires, rather than, broadly, as dispositions to choose.

The third and final question addressed by papers in this volume concerns the normative significance of preferences that do not meet requirements of rationality or which do not seem to have prudential value, and, in particular, the significance of such preferences for the purposes of designing various policies (such as policies concerning what goods and services should be made available to people). Here the arguments by Robert Sugden on the one hand, and Cass Sunstein and Richard Thaler on the other, point in opposite directions. Both papers cite recent research in psychology and behavioural economics that points to systematic evidence of people's preferences being arational or irrational. But while Sugden believes that, in spite of this, a case can still be made for the presumption in favour of respecting people's choices, even when these reflect unconsidered preferences (preferences that do not meet the relevant requirements of rationality), Sunstein and Thaler suggest that there is a sense in which talk of the presumption in favour of "respecting" these preferences is altogether misleading here. More precisely, Sunstein and Thaler show that people's preferences are shaped by the context of choice people face, so that the setting up of that context determines what preferences people form. So, for example, there is evidence that more employees choose to commit to a savings plan if they are automatically enrolled into one and are given the option to opt out than if they have to opt in (where the savings plans are otherwise identical), thereby displaying a status-quo bias. This means that any policy inevitably affects people's preferences. Once we recognise this, it seems reasonable to suggest that we should so set up the context of choice as to promote preferences that it is rational or good for people to have, rather than setting up the context of choice in a way that leads people to have irrational preferences, or preferences that do not promote their well-being. Sunstein and Thaler grant that so setting up the context of choice is paternalistic, but insist that paternalism is inevitable, and that the paternalism they favour is *liberal* paternalism, in that it does not act by removing options, but by making an unavoidable decision concerning *which* options people should be offered.

The last paper in this volume, by Alex Voorhoeve, points to a problem with taking preferences as the relevant standard for policy that arises with both unconsidered and considered preferences.

Introduction

Voorhoeve's concern is specifically with welfarism, understood as the view that we should take the degree to which people's preferences are satisfied (as opposed to just respected, or not interfered with, which Sugden and Sustein and Thaler focus on) as the standard by which to evaluate people's situations for the purposes of policy. Voorhoeve points out that people's preferences, including their preferences about what preferences they have, change over time. For example, someone may now prefer to be, in the future, a struggling artist with artist's preferences over a successful banker with banker's preferences, but, if he becomes a banker and his preferences change, he will prefer to be a banker with banker's preferences. There is then an irresolvable tension between satisfying people's unchanged preferences on the hand and their changed ones on the other, in light of which, Voorhoeve suggests, it is desirable to abandon preference-satisfaction as a standard for policy.

Although a number of the papers in this volume are sceptical about allowing preferences to play too large a role in determining how it is prudent or rational for us to act, and what we owe to others, they all agree that respecting and satisfying preferences will play *some* role in how well a life goes, and in deliberation both from the first-person and the third-person perspective. If we share this starting point, the discussion of how preferences should be formed in order for them to have normative significance, which the papers in this volume make a contribution to, is of fundamental importance.

Acknowledgements

Acknowledgements are owed to the Royal Institute of Philosophy for sponsoring the conference that was the basis for this volume. Thanks also to the Analysis Committee and the Faculty of Philosophy, Cambridge, for further financial support, to St. John's College, Cambridge, for hosting the conference, and to Ross Harrison and Katherine Harloe for their contribution in organising the conference.

Desire Formation and Human Good

RICHARD ARNESON

In *Wuthering Heights* a man and a woman fall in love and their passion for each other wreaks havoc on several lives, theirs included.[1] Long after his beloved is dead, Heathcliff's life revolves entirely around his love for her. Frustrated by events, his grand romantic passion expresses itself in destructive spasms of antisocial behavior. Catherine, the object of this passion, marries another man on a whim, but describes her feelings for him as like superficial foliage, whereas 'her love for Heathcliff resembles eternal rocks beneath.' 'I *am* Heathcliff,' she declares, shortly before dying at the age of nineteen.

As a reader of the novel, I confess to an impulse to preach little sermons on bourgeois prudence to the main characters.[2] In my family, adolescents caught in romantic turmoil are told, 'Men are like buses—If you miss one, another will come along in ten minutes.' Buses are heterogeneous, and differ from one another in ways that make them differentially charming, but in important ways they are fungible. It can make sense to become passionately attached to a person or a bus, but not so attached that one is in thrall to that particular attachment and cannot withstand its demise. The love of Heathcliff and Catherine looks to be an instance of the vice that Robert Adams calls idolatry, caring for a finite good to an extent that would be appropriate only for an infinite good.[3]

In the rural neighborhood depicted in this novel, competition for romantic partners takes place on what economists call a thin market. Each person has few options, few potential partners for interaction. From an individual's perspective, the gap in value between his first choice and his next-best choice may be enormous. However, the degree of adequacy of a given option set depends on

---

[1]   Emily Bronte, *Wuthering Heights*, ed. David Daiches (Harmondsworth, Middlesex: Penguin Books, 1963). Originally published 1847.

[2]   For a far more affirmative view, see Martha Nussbaum, '*Wuthering Heights*: The Romantic Ascent,' *Philosophy and Literature*, vol. 20 (1996), pp. 362–382. See also my discussion toward the end of this essay.

[3]   Robert M. Adams, *Finite and Infinite Goods* (Oxford: Oxford University Press), 1999, p. 200.

one's tastes. The reader is tempted to the conclusion that Heathcliff and Catherine are done in by their desires, which are presented as elemental and wild forces of nature. But this suggests an engineering problem. Dams channel the energy of wild and powerful rivers. *Wuthering Heights* presents a resolution of sorts to the problem of wild desires breaking apart social conventions and social bonds, but the resolution appears to depend on the natural fact that the desires of the children of the next generation are milder and more conventional and hence a better fit with social norms and conventional practices. This resolution has struck critics as evasive, as though one could solve the problems posed by wild rivers by pointing to the existence of tame streams.

The ideology of romanticism suggests another tidy resolution of the tragedy of Heathcliff and Catherine. 'Find your deepest impulse, and follow that' is precisely what Catherine fails to do.[4] She passes up the person she loves to marry the person she does not love and thereby triggers melodramatic disruption. But one of the strengths of this novel is that it shows the forces of passion to be enormously powerful, amoral, and capable of destroying social ties in a way that reveals the romanticist creed just quoted to be, if not silly, then one-sided. Nothing guarantees that your deepest impulse will be nice rather than nasty, productively cooperative rather than monstrously destructive. Anyway the notion of one's 'deepest' impulse is a metaphor that resists interpretation—what sort of depth are we talking about? If shallow impulses are those that tend to be short-lived or to be easily extirpated, it's hard to see why desires that are deeper (more entrenched) should just for that reason be regarded as better. The same is true if the shallow is what is socially implanted. In the end the novel declines to draw normative conclusions and just carefully observes a case study in fanaticism, attractively distorted desire.

I shall return later in this essay to the assessment of the desires of Heathcliff and Catherine. This essay explores the normative standards that might guide the formation of desire.

Consider the problem of a social planner whose task is to devise institutional arrangements and changes in practices to maximize some function of human well-being. A part of her task is to consider the impact of proposed changes in institutions and practices on education and socialization of individuals. A part of

---

[4] The quoted words are those of D. H. Lawrence, as cited by Bernard Williams in *Morality: An Introduction to Ethics* (New York: Harper and Row, 1972), p. 86.

this subtask is to devise education and socialization arrangements that will influence the formation of desire so as to boost people's well-being. Finally, a part of this component of the task is to propose policies that will alter the formation of each individual's preferences in such a way as to boost the well-being of that very person. This essay explores how three different accounts of well-being would generate standards for assessing the work of the social planner engaged in the project just described.

A similar problem must be solved by the parents or guardian of a child if they are concerned to promote the lifetime well-being of the child and seek to mould the child's preferences to this end. How does one determine which preferences are maximally conducive to well-being? To some extent, of course, responsible parents will seek to induce prosocial preferences in their offspring that will be conducive to the well-being of other people whose lives might be affected by interaction with the child. For purposes of this essay I set this problem of balancing the good of one's child against the conflicting good of other people to the side and confine attention to what must be done to promote the well-being of one's own child so far as this is a legitimate goal. (In a variant of this problem, an individual might consider self-culture, strategies she might pursue that would alter her desires with the aim of making her life go better.)

I assume that to some extent feasible changes in social and parental policy can predictably influence the formation of desires, so that preference formation in a desired direction can become the object of policy. Of course preference formation is a hit and miss operation, at best, and the lore that we possess about how to mould the desires of people may largely reflect wishful thinking rather than empirical knowledge. The assumption I am making is not obviously and uncontroversially correct, and if it is false, no one should take any interest in the following discussion.

1. Desire satisfaction accounts of human good and preference formation.

According to a subjectivist view, human good is satisfaction of basic (noninstrumental) desires. The greater the extent to which a person satisfies her basic desires (weighted by their comparative importance as rated by that very person), the more she gains what is good. The more she gains what is good over the course of her life, the greater the degree to which her life goes well for her. The idea of a desire here combines two elements. If I have a basic desire for x, I am disposed to some extent to choose x or pursue it if it is obtainable, and I am also disposed to some extent to feel attracted to x. The basicness of the desire consists in the fact that I am disposed to choose x and feel attracted to x for itself, independently of any further consequences.

A straightforward implication of a desire satisfaction view of human good is that one can increase a person's well-being by bringing it about that her present basic desires are satisfied to a greater extent or by bringing it about that she acquires different basic desires that are easier to satisfy and that are satisfied to a greater extent than her initial desires would have been. In principle the one strategy is as good as the other. Either one can achieve the same effect: the person's basic desires are satisfied to a greater extent. If I desire drinking expensive wine and attaining Olympic-quality sports achievements, you can improve my well-being by increasing my means for obtaining the wine and the sports excellence, or you can achieve the same end by inducing me to switch my basic desires toward cheap beer and easy-to-satisfy minimal competence at shuffleboard.

This implication of the desire satisfaction view might strike some of us as counterintuitive, but this sense of unease arises from the belief that the satisfaction of some basic desires is inherently less valuable than the satisfaction of others. This way of thinking presupposes that some things we might desire to do or get are objectively more valuable than others. This just asserts what subjectivism denies, so the subjectivist should not attempt to tinker with the desire satisfaction view in order to render the view less counterintuitive in this respect.

The claim that each person seeks to maximize the satisfaction of her own desires does not entail that anyone, much less everyone, seeks to maximize the satisfaction of whatever desires she might come to have. In fact my present desires might include a desire that if I were to develop a dominant desire to skateboard, this desire should be frustrated. I might abhor the skateboarding lifestyle. Moreover, the claim that each person seeks to maximize the satisfaction of her own desires could be true even though no one believes that the good is constituted by desire satisfaction and everyone believes that her own desires uniquely track objective good.

These points may help explain that it will strike many people as incorrect that one can improve the quality of someone's life by inducing her to develop cheap tastes, so that with given resources she can attain a higher level of desire satisfaction. But they are strictly irrelevant to what I am concerned to assert: that if human good or well-being is the satisfaction of desire, then a person's lifetime well-being level can be raised either by changing the world so that it conforms to her desires or by changing her desires so that they conform to the way the world is. By either route, desire satisfaction increases, and thus well-being rises. Developing cheap, easy-to-satisfy tastes is a way of changing one's desires so that they more readily and easily conform to the way the world is.

It is only contingently true that one can improve a person's lifetime well-being prospects, according to the subjectivist view, by changing her desires so that they are cheap, in the sense that with a given level of resources, a higher ratio of satisfied to unsatisfied desires (weighted by their importance to that individual) can be attained. For one thing, there may well be cases in which the level of resources the individual can expect to command over the course of her life will vary depending on the kind of desires she comes to have. The desire for complex work, taken by itself, may be hard to satisfy, but having the desire may increase the chances that one will obtain complex work, and since (if) complex work tends to be lucrative, developing this expensive taste may improve one's lifetime prospects of desire satisfaction, all things considered. Here is another example: Suppose that if I shed my plebeian taste for plonk and reality TV shows and acquire in their place patrician tastes for fine wine and opera, I will attract a network of wealthy friends, interact with them, and significantly increase the amount of wealth at my disposal over the long run. One might then be raising one's lifetime well-being prospects according to the subjectivist view. The general point is that if well-being is lifetime desire satisfaction, a person who cares for the well-being of another and strives to increase it can sometimes accomplish this task by bringing it about that her desires change in ways that increase lifetime desire satisfaction.

Another possibility to consider is that a person may come to embrace her desires with varying degrees of confidence and wholeheartedness, and other things being equal, the satisfaction of confidently and wholeheartedly held desires contributes more to a person's well-being. One might put this point in terms of higher-order preferences.[5] One person may desire to surf, but has

---

[5] Conflict between lower-order and higher-order preferences cannot be all there is to less than wholehearted embrace of a lower-order preference. One might have an unconfident and halfhearted preference for

no desires concerning this desire. Another person wants to surf, wants to want to surf, and so on. The latter we may regard as confident and wholehearted embrace of first-order desire. If the two persons are otherwise exactly alike and lead exactly similar lives, with equal satisfaction of the desire to surf, the person with higher-order desires that are themselves satisfied arguably obtains more desire satisfaction overall. Acquiring higher-order desires to have particular lower-order desires and satisfying those higher-order desires might be difficult or easy depending on the case. In some cases higher-order desires can be cheap tastes, like a taste for beer rather than champagne. Being a good philosopher or physicist may be hard but coming to desire being the sort of person who desires to be a good philosopher or physicist and satisfying this higher-order desire may be by comparison quite easy. Socratic achievement may be hard while desiring to desire to be a Socratic rather than foolish person and satisfying the desire to desire to be Socratic may be almost as easy as falling off a log.

One might then speculate that coming to believe in the desire satisfaction account of human good and striving to become a prudent person by its lights by themselves tend to diminish the degree to which one's embrace of one's own desires is confident and wholehearted. If true, this speculation implies that people will be better off, other things being equal, if they do not believe the desire satisfaction account of human good and try to be prudent by its lights. Notice that this speculation does not gainsay the claim that one can generally improve the lifetime well-being of a person in desire satisfaction terms if one can induce him to acquire more easily satisfied desires.

John Rawls invents the term 'bare person' to describe a person who accepts the desire satisfaction view of human good and aims to be prudent in its terms—to maximize her lifetime total desire satisfaction weighted by the importance to her of the satisfied desires. Such persons, he observes, 'are ready to consider any new convictions and aims, and even to abandon attachments and loyalties, when doing this promises a life with greater overall satisfaction, or well-being.' A society with a public commitment to justice as the maximization of desire satisfaction (he is specifically considering an ordinal version of utilitarianism) he describes as committed to a 'shared highest-order preference.' He writes, 'The

---

a thing, supported by an unconfident and halfhearted second-order preference concerning it, and so on, up the hierarchy.

notion of a bare person implicit in the notion of shared highest-order preference represents the dissolution of the person as leading a life expressive of character and of devotion to specific final ends and adopted (or affirmed) values which define the distinctive points of view associated with different (and incommensurable) conceptions of the good.'[6] Rawls has a point. Suppose I am married to Sam, committed to particular family and friends, dedicated to philosophy and mountain biking, and I am then offered a pill that will immediately and costlessly change my tastes, so that my former desires disappear, and I desire only casual sex, listening to sectarian religious sermons, mindless work, and TV watching. I am assured that taking the pill will increase my lifetime level of desire satisfaction. If I accept the desire satisfaction view of human good and aim to be prudent in its terms, I will have good reason to take the pill and no good reason not to ingest it.

If my desire, say, to mountain bike is stronger than my desire to be prudent (to maximize my lifetime well-being), then I might not take the pill. But still in the scenario as described I have no reason not to take the pill that is not outweighed by stronger reasons. The fact that I will not achieve satisfaction of my mountain biking desire if I take the pill is outweighed by the consideration that other desires will be satisfied to a greater extent. This claim assumes that according to the desire satisfaction view of the good, a person has most reason to do what will bring her most good over the course of her life. One might deny the assumption and tie the idea of what one has reason at a time to do to the idea of what one desires at that time to do.[7] On this suggestion, one might have no desire to be prudent (to maximize one's lifetime well-being) or a weak desire to be prudent, in which case, since what one has reason to do is tied to what one desires here and now to do, one has no reason to be prudent. However, it is plausible even on a subjectivist view of good and well-being to detach the idea of reason for choice from current basic desires. A reflective person who accepts the desire satisfaction view of good will see that she will be better off by her own standard if her present desires shift to become more satisfiable, provided that shift results in an increase in overall desire

---

[6]   John Rawls, 'Social Unity and Primary Goods,' reprinted in *John Rawls: Collected Papers*, ed. Samuel Freeman (Cambridge: Harvard University Press, 1999), 359–387; see pp. 382–3.

[7]   The best analysis of these issues regarding reasons and prudence is still in Derek Parfit, *Reasons and Persons* (Oxford: Oxford University Press, 1984).

satisfaction. Reflecting on this, she has reason to act to change her present desires just in case this will yield larger lifetime desire satisfaction, regardless of whether or not an actual desire blossoms now from the recognition of this reason.

Sometimes it is claimed that large-scale changes in basic desires break personal identity.[8] If taking the pill that alters my desires would literally make me a different person, then I would not be better off taking the pill, for I do not survive as the post-pill person. This claim introduces a large topic. A short response is that if spatio-temporal bodily continuity is the right criterion of personal identity, desire change cannot bring it about that Dick Arneson at a later time is not identical to Dick Arneson at an earlier time, but if sufficient psychological continuity is the criterion, desire change can do this.

I have conceded that according to subjectivism, a person might be better off if she does not adopt the mind-set that would make her a bare person. But of course, becoming a bare person or ceasing to be a bare person is not a feat I can achieve by an act of will, so given that I am a bare person, I will recognize I have decisive reason to take the pill. And if you are sincerely and strongly concerned to advance my well-being, you would do well to slip the desire-transforming pill in my coffee if your choice is either to give me the pill or to refrain (if you refrain, my desires do not shift).

Does the thought that conceptions of the good are incommensurable free the desire satisfaction view of its commitment to the bare person notion? Suppose we say that the more a person's desires are satisfied, the better her life goes for her. If a person's basic desires change, there is no way to compare her well-being level prior to the change and afterward. On this view, taking the pill could neither improve one's life nor diminish its value. The choice to take the pill or not would have to be seen as a 'don't care.' If we discovered that a friend accidentally ingested such a pill and suffered involuntarily transformed desires, we should on balance be neither glad nor sad, for the friend's sake, that this occurred. If the bare person idea involves the dissolution of the person as leading a life expressive of character and of devotion to specific final ends' (Rawls's words), the amended bare person idea joined to a thesis of incommensurability does not block the dissolution.

---

[8]   Philip Bricker considers this idea in 'Prudence,' *Journal of Philosophy*, vol. 77, no. 7 (July, 1980), pp. 381–401. My analysis of the 'bare person' issue generally is indebted to this excellent essay.

Repeating myself, I maintain that what fuels resistance to the idea of a bare person implicit in subjectivism is the thought that a basic desire can be mistaken insofar as it is directed toward an object that is not truly worthwhile. If my central life ambition becomes counting the blades of grass on courthouse lawns (Rawls's example), many would say I have suffered misfortune. My main desires fail to track what is truly valuable. The advocate of the desire satisfaction account of human good should not attempt to accommodate this objection, which amounts to blanket denial of subjectivism. The response should rather be that the objection draws its considerable plausibility from the assumption that we can vindicate the idea that some basic aims can be shown to be objectively more valuable than others. The subjectivist denies that this assumption is supportable.

The subjectivist can also point out that human desires form themselves in ways that are to a large extent impervious to voluntary choice and resistant to deliberate manipulation. One cannot just choose to desire to count blades of grass on courthouse lawns, and if one discovers one has such a desire, it may well be inexorable. Even if romantic desires tend to do to our lives what Heathcliff's desire for Catherine did for his, we cannot simply abjure them. Moreover, even if one could instill in one's child a dominant easily satisfiable desire such as the desire to count blades of grass on public property, to organize one's life around this desire would predictably attract scorn and bewilderment on the part of significant others, so the expected satisfiability of the instilled desire must be balanced against the resultant expectable loss in the child's desire for recognition and acceptance by other people. A better bet is to try to induce one's child to develop desires and ambitions that others in one's community esteem. These responses say that there are limits to the extent to which one can deliberately manipulate the formation of preferences and that inducing a cheap, easy-to-satisfy preference in a person may not be to his advantage all things considered. These remarks do not challenge the claim that acceptance of the desire satisfaction view of well-being implies acceptance of the bare person notion that some find repellant.

Another strategy for driving a wedge between subjectivism and the bare person appeals to the inadequacy of simple desire satisfaction accounts of human good. Unrestricted desire satisfaction accounts count as enhancing a person's well-being the satisfaction of some of her preferences that intuitively do not seem connected in this way to her well-being. For example, one might desire that strangers live good lives, even at cost to oneself, but the satisfaction of this desire would seem to contribute to the strangers' well-being, not one's own. This line of thought inspires restricted desire satisfaction accounts of human good. But this intramural dispute among desire satisfaction theorists does not alter substantially the nature of the theory's recommendations regarding desire formation. Much the same holds if we shift from a simple desire satisfaction view to the view that satisfaction of desire enhances well-being to the degree that the actual desires satisfied would withstand critical scrutiny with full information. One should then seek to instill whatever desires will facilitate the person's gaining as much lifetime informed desire satisfaction as possible.

Another strategy responds more directly to something in the vicinity of the bare person worry. The strategy distinguishes autonomous and nonautonomous desire formation and holds that the satisfaction only of autonomously formed desires contributes to well-being. A weaker version of this view holds that the contribution that satisfaction of a desire makes to a person's well-being varies with the extent to which the desire was autonomously formed, so other things being equal, autonomously formed desires have more weight in determining the degree to which a person leads a life that is good for her.[9]

To the degree that the person is autonomous in the process by which a particular preference of that very person is formed, we count the preference as autonomous and its satisfaction counts for more.

According to this account, a subjectivist account of human good properly conceived should be associated not with the conception of the person as bare person but rather with the conception of person as autonomous bare person. Consider the example of the desire to count blades of grass on courthouse lawns (assumed to be extremely easy to satisfy). If one brings it about that one has this desire by a process of autonomous character formation, the value of satisfying this desire is accordingly amplified, and if the desire is intense, its satisfaction can make a great contribution to one's well-being. In contrast, if some other agent sets in play some causal process that induces the grass-counting desire in a way that bypasses the individual's own faculties of deliberation and

---

[9] Jon Elster takes this line in 'Sour Grapes,' reprinted in his *Sour Grapes: Studies in the Subversion of Rationality* (Cambridge: Cambridge University Press, 1983), pp. 109–140. Elster distinguishes autonomy and utility and seems to regard both as enhancing an individual's quality of life.

reflection and choice, the value of satisfying the desire is accordingly dampened, and even if the resultant desire is intense, its satisfaction counts for little toward the individual's well-being. Insofar as the agent actively directs the course of her life, in part by choosing the processes by which her present desires will be further formed, if she accepts the autonomous desire satisfaction view of human good, and seeks to maximize her well-being, then she ought autonomously to select modes of desire alteration that contribute to this end. This will mean that, other things being equal, she should prefer to extirpate any present desire no matter how intense and heartfelt if she can substitute for it a desire that is more easily satisfied and thus contributes more to her lifetime well-being.

Echoing Rawls, the critic will say that conceiving oneself and one's good in this way 'represents the dissolution of the person as leading a life expressive of character and of devotion to specific final ends and adopted (or affirmed) values.' Once again, I suspect the critic's objection is toothless unless an objective account of human good can be justified.

As a bare person, I aim to maximize my lifetime well-being, and I interpret well-being as desire satisfaction (or desire satisfaction qualified in some way). It might be thought that in so conceiving my aims, I am conceiving my desires as mere means to some further goal, the maximization of desire satisfaction. If my desire is to be loyal to my friends, what I really care about (according to the critic) is not that per se, but only as abstract desire satisfaction. This emerges when it is noticed that I would not regard it as any sort of loss if my desires suddenly shifted and the loyalty-to-friends desire were replaced by some substitute that promised to be equally or more conducive to boosting my overall desire satisfaction level. The substitute could be the desire to be disloyal to friends.

Granted that the bare person stands in a somewhat alienated or detached relation to her own desires, I note that something similar will be true if one adopts an objective list account of human good. If I am committed to maximizing my well-being, I will from this perspective regard as equally satisfactory the state of affairs in which my satisfied desire for some object that is an entry on the objective list is eliminated and replaced by any satisfied desire for any other entry on the objective list with the same objective value.

If I seek x as partly constitutive of my good while recognizing that there are equivalents for x, this is not to regard x as mere means to what is valuable. What is replaceable is not valueless in virtue of its replaceability. I might desire the taste of honey for itself, while recognizing that if my taste buds were to alter so that I came to desire the taste of sour pickles instead, then that taste would be desirable for itself.

2. Objective list accounts of human good and preference formation

An objective list account of human good or well-being merely denies subjectivism. According to the objective list account, a life goes well (for the person whose life it is) to the extent that the individual attains items that occur as entries on a list of objectively intrinsically valuable things. If one gets some item on the list, one's life thereby goes better, independently of one's subjective attitudes or opinions toward getting that thing. If sexual pleasure appears on the list, then getting it adds to one's well-being, even if one is of the opinion that sexual pleasure is worthless or has no desire for sexual pleasure. A more developed account would specify an index, so that for any combination of instances of items on the objective list, one could in principle determine what the total value of the combination is. For my purposes in this essay I do not need to take any stand on the possibility of interpersonal comparisons of well-being, though I do assume the possibility of cardinal comparisons of well-being across temporal stages of the same person.

The status of desire satisfaction according to the objective list account depends on whether or not desire satisfaction can or should appear as one entry on the objective list. My sense is that desire satisfaction should be excluded. The core of the objective list idea is that there are desires whose satisfaction contributes nothing at all to well-being. Consider an example suggested by Richard Kraut: A boy forms the desire to throw a rock at a duck. One might hold that satisfaction of this desire contributes nothing at all to the boy's well-being.[10] This judgment is compatible with holding that desire satisfaction is intrinsically valuable provided some condition or conditions are satisfied. (The whole consisting of the desire satisfaction plus its fulfilled conditions is intrinsically valuable.) I suppose it is coherent to maintain that the satisfaction of a desire (with the necessary conditions satisfied) is valuable in itself,

[10]   Richard Kraut, 'Desire and the Human Good,' *Proceedings and Addresses of the American Philosophical Association,* vol. 68, no. 2 (November, 1994), 39–54.

independently of the individual's subjective attitudes or opinions toward getting that desire satisfaction. Compare Parfit's characterization of the objective list account: 'According to this theory, certain things are good or bad for people, whether or not these people would want to have the good things, or to avoid the bad things.' My strained loose interpretation of this claim holds that (given the satisfaction of some condition) the satisfaction of desire can be among the certain things that are good or bad for people, whether or not they desire them. Desire satisfaction is then good, contributes to your well-being, whether or not you desire the desire to be satisfied. But this gambit, besides committing the sin of splitting hairs, looks to be implausible. I might want to desire taking heroin, without desiring at all that this desire should be satisfied. So if I succeed in getting myself to desire taking heroin, it hardly follows that it is good for me that this desire be satisfied even if all along I don't desire it to be satisfied. So let's suppose that desire satisfaction does not appear on the objective list. (Another qualification is discussed below, when we consider whether desiring what is in itself good might be in itself good.)

According to the objective list account of the good, so interpreted, desire and for that matter desire satisfaction contribute to the desirer's well-being, if at all, only as helps or hindrances to the attainment of items on the objective list.

Looked at from a certain angle, the view that desire satisfaction and frustration in and of themselves have nothing to do with well-being is just as paradoxical and opposed to common-sense as the subjectivist view that desire satisfaction is the alpha and omega of well-being. If one describes a person's life by noting that all of her most deeply cherished lifelong ambitions were fully satisfied, it sounds odd to add that this of course has no bearing on the question of well-being—to what extent the person's life went well for her.[11]

Ordinary common-sense lore on happiness and well-being probably allows that desires can be mistaken in the sense that they are directed toward inappropriate objects. Common sense surely affirms that desires can become disproportionate and in that way lead the desirer to become self-destructive. A desire may become

---

[11] There may be problematic slippage here. Satisfying one's desires is one thing and fulfilling one's life aims or ambitions is another. The latter involves a commitment, an orientation of the will, in a way the former does not. The theory of the good might treat desire satisfaction and aim fulfillment differently.

bloated and crowd out all other desires, but common sense does not then say that the person's life goes well for her provided the single dominant desire is satisfied. But the objective list account as I interpret it goes further in downgrading the status of desire. That I desire x may cause me to seek x. If my desire for x indicates that there is something valuable about x, the desire can be an indicator of reasons that have a bearing on what I should do. But the mere fact of desiring per se does not establish that there is any value at all in satisfying the desire and hence does not establish that there is any reason to choose to pursue what one desires. Even if my desire is persistent, strong, deeply entrenched, heartfelt or whole-hearted as we might say, that is all consistent with there being no reason whatsoever for me to act on the desire or to think that other things being equal I am better off if the desire is satisfied rather than frustrated.

If one cares about a person and wants him to enjoy a life that is good for him, accepts an objective list account of human good, and believes one can influence to some degree the formation of his desires, what sorts of desires should one seek to instill? What sorts of desires should one want for oneself, insofar as one is concerned about the impact of one's desires on one's prospects for one's own well-being? The abstract answer is that one should seek to influence the formation of desires so as to maximize the person's lifetime well-being. Since having a desire tends to induce the desiring person to behave in ways that bring about its satisfaction when he believes that is feasible, one should want to instill desires for what is valuable.

In constructing a plan of life with the aim of amassing over the course of one's life the largest feasible weighted sum of objective goods, one will have to attend carefully to one's basic desires—their actual and expected future character and the extent to which these are alterable by actions one might take. One seeks a mesh between one's enduring strong basic desires and goods one can achieve. Someone who has mathematical talent, but finds that she is deeply and irremediably averse to doing mathematics, would be ill-advised to form a life plan in which doing mathematics looms large. To understate the point, one is unlikely to accomplish anything significant that requires sustained dedicated effort over the long haul against the grain of one's desires.

Desiring what is valuable in proportion to its objective value is appealing, but may get in the way of attainment of objective value in the course of one's life. Desires animate action toward what is desired, and it is better for a person if her desires point her toward the best goods she can achieve, or has a realistic chance of achieving. If ballet is ten times more valuable than square dancing, and my desire for ballet achievement is correspondingly ten times stronger than my desire for square dancing achievement, then proportioning my desires to the values of their objects may simply lead to the situation in which I hopelessly pine after achievements I cannot reach and have insufficient psychic energy at my disposal for seeking the achievements that are within my reach.

One's value judgments may function as helps and hindrances to the attainment of value in much the same way. Overvaluing an activity may help to rouse desire for succeeding in that activity, and if the activity is the best that one can reasonably hope to engage with any prospect of success, overvaluing what one can get can help one to get it.

A variant on the fable of the fox and the grapes illustrates the point. Suppose there are wondrous grapes clearly beyond the fox's reach, and acceptable grapes that are just barely within the fox's reach if she musters a supreme effort. If the fox correctly assesses the relative merits of the grapes beyond reach and the grapes marginally within reach, and proportions her desires for these goods to their objective merits, she may find her desire for the reachable grapes insufficiently motivating. If on the other hand she forms an exaggerated estimation of the barely reachable grapes and thereby comes to have an urgent desire to attain them, she may be motivated to put forth the extreme effort that is necessary to give herself the best chance of gaining the maximal good she can achieve.

There may be other ways in which correct appraisal and correspondingly appropriate desire may inhibit maximal attainment of items on the objective list. If superlative grapes for once in the fox's life are barely within her reach, correct appreciation of her situation may lead to fright or exhilaration that impedes putting forth her best effort. Undervaluation or desire that is weaker than the object deserves on its merits may increase the prospects for gaining as much objective good as is feasible (maximizing rationally expected good). These discrepancies between the desires that are a proper evaluative fit with their objects and the desires that are most helpful to the attainment of maximal objective goods may occur not just in specific situations but globally over the course of an individual's life.

These strategic considerations are usually not in tension with the ideals of correct appraisal and proportionate strength of desire and aversion. We usually suppose that training an individual to

23

appreciate and love correct values will help that individual orient herself in the world so as to achieve these values. But thinking about possible cases in which, as it were, one hits the target by aiming away from it, reveals that there are two different and sometimes opposed ideals that require somehow to be reconciled or integrated.

What kinds of desires should we want to have, so far as our aspiration to attain our own well-being is concerned? On the one hand, desires are means to achieving valuable goods. They should be selected so as optimally to facilitate achievement. On the other hand, desires can be intrinsically good or bad. They should be selected so that the ensemble of our desires is intrinsically best.

Thomas Hurka has suggested that desires and aversions are intrinsically good when they are the appropriate or fitting attitudes to their objects. Loving for itself what is intrinsically good is intrinsically good, as is hating for itself what is intrinsically evil. Loving the good is being for the good, having a positive orientation to it. Hurka explains, 'One can love x by desiring or wishing for it when it does not obtain, by actively pursuing it to make it obtain, or by taking pleasure in it when it does obtain.'[12] Perhaps with respect to pursuit it is better to say that one form of loving something is being disposed to act to bring it about (for itself, not for any further consequences) when the agent believes such action can be efficacious. We can fold all of this into the notion of desire if we say that the appropriate, intrinsically good attitude toward an intrinsic good is desiring that it obtain when it does not exist and desiring that it be sustained and increased when it does, adding that, as G.E.M. Anscombe once noted, a primitive sign of wanting is trying to get.

There is a rich world of goods spanning a wide range of degrees of value. The acme of scientific achievement is intrinsically good, and so is enjoying the taste of ketchup on a hamburger. The appropriate attitude toward the diversity of goods (and evils) is to love (hate) them in proportion to their comparative objective value. There does not seem to be any absolute normative ceiling to the degree of attitudinal enthusiasm with which it is appropriate to respond to any good or type of good. If there were a being that responded with incredible heights of ecstasy to an infinitesimal good, that would not amount to defective desiring provided the

---

[12] Thomas Hurka, *Virtue, Vice, and Value* (Oxford: Oxford University Press, 2001), p. 13.

being's responses to greater goods was proportionately greater. It is intrinsically good to divide our love in proportion to the objective value of the goods that there are.

Alongside the ideal of loving the good (and hating the bad) proportionately one should set the ideal of loving the good (and hating the bad) effectively. Loving the good effectively is loving it in such a way as to maximize one's attainment of good.

These two ideals often run together. Loving romantic marriage-like commitment more than casual sex in proportion to the greater comparative value of the former, Randy and Tom are thereby rendered more likely to achieve the better good rather than rest content with the inferior one. But the two ideals are different, and they can and probably do conflict. Sometimes getting more of the one leads to getting less of the other, so tradeoffs are necessary. It is plausible to think that desiring to achieve Olympic-quality athletic achievement with disproportionate excess is instrumentally advantageous, for some people in some contexts, and conduces to maximizing their athletic achievement. Here loving the good proportionately is at odds with loving the good effectively.

According to the objective list account of human good, the desires we should wish to have for our own good are those that constitute the proper mix of desires that are intrinsically good, as just characterized, and the desires that are instrumentally good.

The tradeoff between loving the good proportionately and loving the good effectively stands in the background as a regulative norm when one considers vices of fanaticism. Our condemnation of the fanatic who loves some good disproportionately should be tempered by the consideration that loving excessively in this way might also be loving to exactly the right extent if what we are measuring is effective love of the good. Although plausible examples seem to me to be harder to find, in principle we should also see the phenomenon of tempering the impulse to negative judgment on someone who has desires that significantly impede his achievement of good to the extent that those desires exhibit the virtue of loving the good proportionately.

It seems to me that people generally are quite tolerant even of significantly distorted evaluation on the part of an individual when the distortion is harmless to others and works to enhance the individual's achievement of significant goods. It is also sometimes uncertain how seriously to take a profession that the segment of the world of goods in which one's life is engaged is superior to all others. A person may be wildly enthusiastic about soccer and hold it to be the world's greatest sport but also recognize that if she had

25

been raised in another country or culture she would have come to have loved and esteemed, say, rugby, to the same great extent that she actually loves and esteems soccer. Here perhaps the person does not seriously affirm a distorted assessment. What is happening is that intense desire is coloring evaluation and exerting a psychological pressure to magnify positive evaluation of what is so strongly desired—a pressure that the person does not reflectively endorse.

Regarding the ideal of loving the good effectively, we should give full credit to a person whose desires are prudent in that they are well adapted to maximizing her expected well-being given available knowledge at the time of desire formation. We should not criticize people for having expected well-being maximizing desires even if things turn out badly.

Consider Heathcliff and Catherine, the characters in *Wuthering Heights*, in the light of this discussion. If we regard their romantic passion for each other as fanatically excessive, are we measuring their desires against the standard of intrinsically good desiring (loving the good proportionately) or instrumentally good desiring (loving the good effectively) or both? One view is that each of these characters' intense passion is an appropriate response to the nobility and sex appeal of the beloved, hence an intrinsically good desire. The problem is in the arena of bourgeois prudence: a different constellation of desires, moderation all around, would be a set of desires with higher expected well-being than the intrinsically good desires they end up holding.

We might even refrain from rendering a negative prudential judgment: not all fanaticism or extremism is irrational. If achieving a life together would be a sufficiently great good, and if other options are bleak, then a life plan that yields even a small chance of achieving this great good may be the one that maximizes their expected well-being, and their hyper-intense love may be an expected-well-being maximizing desire. Even if speaking of their choice of life plan is a misdescription, because their lives are driven by inner forces beyond their power to control, we can still affirm their unchosen life plan as one that would have been reasonable to choose.

The question arises whether the ideal of proportionate love of the good is really desirable, and has any weight at all in competition with the ideal of effective love of the good. If someone loves the good effectively, is there any defect at all present if effective love involves some strategically disproportionate love? Here what is called into question is the ideal of loving the good proportionally that Hurka affirms and that I have been accepting so far in this section.

For any position that embraces moral cognitivism, there will be an intellectual flaw in a person whose evaluations of goods and bads are incorrect. If the sport of judo is three times better than the sport of wrestling, it would be a failure of moral knowledge in a wrestling fan to overvalue the relative merits of her favored sport, compared to those of judo.

It is not clear that disproportionate desiring per se is defective. There is a universe of diverse goods. Any individual has limited capacities for coming to appreciate and crave particular instances of goods and also kinds of goods. Beyond some point, which may differ for each person, further attempts to broaden the scope of one's desiring of the good would dilute the quality of one's sensitive and nuanced desirous response to goods in the limited scope. If we conceive of different persons, and the same person at different times, as varying in their total capacities to desire, one question is whether or not it is intrinsically better to have the capacity for greater rather than lesser desires in the aggregate. Another question can be posed: for any finite stock of capacity to desire is it intrinsically better to divide the stock of desire in proportion to the values of the things desired? Once the intellectual apprehension issue is distinguished from the strength of desire issue, I see no reason to affirm the idea that it is intrinsically better that desire should vary in strength with the goodness of its object.

The rejection of the ideal of proportionate desiring might seem most plausible when the goods in question are particular persons who might be selected as friends or associates. Sally might desire friendship with Sue a lot and with Samantha hardly at all even though she sees clearly that Sue's merits are not greater than Samantha's. The same goes perhaps for categories of goods. Someone might desire to become accomplished at painting but not at philosophy or physics without being tempted to claim that painting is an inherently more excellent kind of activity than the undesired others.

Even if proportionate desiring were intrinsically desirable, it might be perfectly acceptable all things considered for Sally to desire friendship only with Sue and for someone to desire only to pursue painting achievement, not other kinds. This is so because the disproportionate desires might be strategically valuable, aids to maximizing well-being. So to fix on the question that concerns us, we need to suppose that instrumental considerations are not in play.

Richard Arneson

Suppose my total stock of desires will be deployed effectively in any case, whether I proportion my desires to the value of their objects or not. Suppose I can bring it about that I love painting, philosophy, and physics in strict proportion to their objective merits or disproportionately. To repeat, there is no loss or gain in expected well-being from choosing one or another of these constellations of desires, so there is no trade-off issue to consider. Nor will the aggregate amount of desire alter with one or another choice.[13] The only difference is in the distribution of fixed stock of desire. In this scenario, is proportionate desiring intrinsically better than disproportionate desiring? I'm unsure, but I have no strong impulse to answer affirmatively.

Perhaps a decisive reason for an affirmative answer emerges once one notes that desiring the good can be intellectualized or simple. An intellectualized desire for something that is intrinsically good is a desire for it as good. As Hurka notes, discussing this point, 'here one's love derives from a prior judgment of intrinsic value.'[14] In contrast, a simple desire for something that is intrinsically good is a direct positive emotional response or orientation, 'direct' in the sense that it is unmediated by any value judgment.

Consider intellectualized desires for goods. If one's desire for x proceeds from a value judgment that x is intrinsically good, then if this value judgment is accurate, it will register the comparative merits of goods. If chess is intrinsically better than checkers, the value judgment that is ingredient in one's intellectualized desire for chess will register that fact. It would be odd to say the least, and perhaps defective, if one's intellectualized desires fail to be

[13] Is it intrinsically better to have more rather than less desire in the aggregate (I assume desire is being conceived in such a way that its total amount per person varies)? In *On Liberty*, John Stuart Mill suggests that having strong desires is potentially instrumentally better than having weak desires. He seems to envisage that one person may have more, and more intense, desires than another person, in total: 'To say that one person's desires and feelings are stronger and more various than those of another, is merely to say that he has more of the raw material of human nature, and is therefore capable, perhaps of more evil, but certainly of more good. Strong impulses are but another name for energy' (chapter 3, paragraph 5). I don't understand the 'perhaps' and the 'certainly' in the first quoted sentence, but having more and stronger desires surely can be instrumentally valuable to maximizing one's expected well-being if the desires are well-aimed. But I don't see that it is intrinsically better or worse to have more rather than less desire in the aggregate.

[14] Hurka, *Virtue, Vice, and Value*, p. 14.

proportionate to their objects. Can one reasonably love chess as valuable without loving it more or less, according to the extent of its intrinsic value?

This question does not strike me as rhetorical. For any intrinsic good or type of good, it is better that one's desire for it be based on correct judgments, so that one appreciates the good properly. Still, the desire so based might be disproportionate, as when one knows full well that Hong Kong action movies are not an excellent aesthetic type but loves the type anyway. Moreover, even if it were true that intellectualized desires ought to be proportionate, there does not seem comparable reason why simple desires should be the same. There can be different mixes of intellectualized and simple desires in one's overall affection for any good, and so far as I can see no practical imperative that the mix should include any particular ratio of one type than the other. So there does not seem to be an imperative of practical reason prescribing that other things being equal one ought to have desire for goods proportionate to their intrinsic excellence.

An objective list account of human good or well-being implies that insofar as one aims to increase the well-being of a person (the person might be oneself) by influencing the character of her desires, one should strive to alter or form desires with a view to inducing a set that is maximally efficient for the goal to maximizing the person's lifetime achievement of the entries on the objective list. This aim should perhaps be balanced against the aim of altering desires so as to maximize the extent to which having those desires is itself intrinsically good. But the ideal of proportionate desiring looks problematic under scrutiny, whereas the ideal of effective desiring should be uncontroversial.

3. Hybrid accounts of human good and preference formation.

A hybrid view holds that nothing that an individual does or gets contributes in itself to her well-being unless the thing is both objectively valuable and positively engages her subjectivity.

Richard Arneson

Derek Parfit mentions such a view.[15] Robert Adams suggests that well-being is constituted by enjoyment of the excellent.[16] Stephen Darwall comes close to asserting a similar view.[17] Ronald Dworkin urges that nothing can contribute to a person's well-being that fails to elicit the endorsement of that very person.[18] I focus on Adams's suggestion.

The hybrid view's recommendations regarding policies of desire formation will be broadly similar to those of objective list accounts.

The enjoyment that according to the hybrid view is required for well-being must be enjoyment taken in what is objectively valuable. One must enjoy not merely what is in fact excellent, but an excellent aspect of it. So if I am a defensive end and play football at a high level of excellence, but enjoy nothing about this achievement except the sensation of smashing my body into opponents' bodies, this does not suffice. One must enjoy the excellent as excellent. This enjoyment might be intellectualized, mediated by a value judgment to the effect that what one is doing or having is excellent, or simple and direct, unmediated by any such value judgment.

An objective list view can grant that other things being equal, it is better that one's objectively valuable achievements and attainments be accompanied by pleasure, since this adds to the overall well-being boost that one gains thereby. In a similar way, since knowledge is better than confusion or ignorance, a person who does or gets what is excellent and understands what about it is excellent and to what degree is gaining more well-being, other things being

---

[15]   Derek Parfit, *Reasons and Persons* (Oxford: Oxford University Press, 1984), pp. 501–502.

[16]   Adams, *Finite and Infinite Goods*, chapter 3. Adams backs away from the view by the end of the chapter, so his position is not that enjoyment is necessary for it to be the case that excellence adds to the well-being of the one who does or gets it, but rather that the well-being value of excellence without enjoyment and of enjoyment without excellence are steeply discounted. So understood, Adams's position is close to Darwall's. Serena Olsaretti has developed another version of the hybrid view. According to her position, no achievement however great adds to the well-being of the person unless that very person has some pro-attitude toward the achievement itself (regarded apart from its further consequences).

[17]   Stephen Darwall, *Welfare and Rational Care* (Princeton and Oxford: Princeton University Press, 2002), last chapter.

[18]   Ronald Dworkin: *Sovereign Virtue: The Theory and Practice of Equality* (Cambridge: Harvard University Press, 2000), chapter 6.

equal, than someone whose attainment of the excellent is unaccompanied by these correct beliefs.

The disagreement between the objective list view and the hybrid view emerges clearly in cases where the individual could be induced either to achieve a greater weighted sum of entries on the list or a smaller sum when only the lesser attainment satisfies the enjoyment condition. Suppose that Smith could be brought to lead one of two lives. The lives are identical except that in the first, Smith gains lots of pleasure from reading trashy novels (of nil excellence) and attains lots of excellent but purely mercenary achievement as a scientist (so the achievement is accompanied by nil enjoyment), whereas in the second life there is far less pleasure and less achievement overall but the two are integrated–the scientist enjoys his modest achievements. No matter how great the shortfall in the total pleasure and achievement registered in the second life, the hybrid view will rate the second life as greater in well-being, whereas the objective list view disagrees, and depending on the sums, will sometimes favor the first life. Notice, however, that the difference between the hybrid view and the straight objective list view need not be that the former but not the latter holds that it is a condition of one's life counting as good for the one who lives it that it must contain enjoyment. A version of the objective list view might hold that no life counts as good for the one who lives it unless some threshold level of enjoyment (and perhaps other goods) is achieved. The difference is that the hybrid view holds that no achievement, however great, adds to one's well-being unless it is enjoyed and no enjoyment however great adds to one's well-being unless it is directed at what is excellent.

The upshot, if we are considering how we should try to shape people's desires, is that the hybrid view as described above takes a sterner line than the objective list view against cheap thrills, trashy pleasures, the enjoyment of the nonexcellent.[19] The hybrid view urges more decisively than the objective list view that we should train people, if we can, not to desire the cotton candy of life. Regarding excellence, the hybrid view, like the objective list view,

[19] But the extent of disagreement here depends on one's views on the nature of the excellent. Adams's theistic Platonism appears to understand the *excellent* to be a broadly encompassing category, so that simple ordinary pleasures such as scratching one's nose might qualify as an instance of the excellent. For Adams, finite goods are fragmentary shards of the infinite, and what constitutes them as excellent is their greater or lesser resemblance to infinite good.

favors the training of desire so that desire is maximally instrumentally efficacious for the attainment of well-being. The difference is that the hybrid view sees no point in inducing desire for excellence that can be achieved but that cannot (or, one foresees, will not) be enjoyed, and no point in bringing about enjoyment if enjoyment is taken in what is nonexcellent. So besides counseling against developing basic desires for the nonexcellent just on the ground that doing so will lead to enjoyment of the nonexcellent, the hybrid view will by the same token counsel against seeking and even desiring excellent achievements if those excellent achievements will certainly never be enjoyed. The hybrid view seeks an overlap. At least, this will be the recommendation if the task is to shape an individual's desires in ways that are conducive to the well-being of that very individual.

Preference-Formation and Personal Good[1]

CONNIE S. ROSATI

As persons, beings with a capacity for autonomy, we face a certain practical task in living out our lives. At any given period we find ourselves with many desires or preferences, yet we have limited resources, and so we cannot satisfy them all.[2] Our limited resources include insufficient economic means, of course; few of us have either the funds or the material provisions to obtain or pursue all that we might like. More significantly, though, we are limited to a single life and one of finite duration. We also age, and pursuits that were possible at earlier points within a life may become impossible at later stages; we thus encounter not only an ultimate time limit but episodic limits as well. Because we must live our lives with limited resources—material and temporal—we are pressed to choose among and to order our preferences. Without some selection and ordering, few if any of them would be satisfied, and we would be unable to live lives that are recognizably good at all. Moreover, we would be unable to function well as the autonomous beings that we are. Our practical task then is to form a coherent, stable, and attractive ordering of aims—to develop a conception of our good.[3]

[1]   This paper was presented at the annual conference of the Royal Institute of Philosophy, St. John's College, Cambridge, on July 15, 2004. Many thanks to fellow presenters and audience members for their helpful questions and comments.
[2]   Strictly speaking, the notion of preference is comparative as the notion of desire is not. A person prefers one thing *to* another. But in most instances, a desire can be recast as a preference of one among at least some small class of alternatives, and a conflict of desires is, in this respect, also a conflict of preferences. For this reason, I follow what I take to be common practice in using the terms 'desire' and 'preference' for the most part interchangeably.
[3]   I assume, of course, that we are not talking about aims (or desires or preferences) that one has only insofar as one is concerned about the requirements of morality. I roughly follow Rawls in treating a conception of the good as an ordered scheme of final ends, together with a story about what makes those ends appropriate or worthwhile, though Rawls' idea has seeming moral elements which I want to leave to one side. See John Rawls,

Connie S. Rosati

The task is a complex one, for many of our conflicting preferences represent not merely the different things we might happen to want but the different selves we could become and the different lives we might lead. The choice among our preferences—actual and possible—can thus have far reaching consequences. If we fail to choose and order our aims well, we may find ourselves living lives that disappoint us or, worse, lives self-deceived, resigned, or riddled with regret.

If we are to form a coherent, stable, and attractive ordering of aims, however, we must first have something suitable to work with. A moment's reflection tells us as much, and those who have explored the phenomena of adaptive and deformed preferences have aptly illustrated their distorting effects.[4] The person whose preferences tend toward the self-destructive may coordinate her preferences however much one might please; she will still end up leading a self-destructive life. The person whose preferences have been stunted by her social conditions or by indoctrination may organize her aims as carefully as one might wish; a diminished life will yet be all that she achieves.[5] If we are to understand how it is possible for us to lead good lives, then, we cannot merely inquire about how it makes sense to organize our aims or preferences. We must also inquire about how to form our preferences in the first place.

Now it strikes me as an interesting fact that some people are especially good formers of their own preferences. What I mean by this is that they are particularly adept at forming preferences for

---

'Kantian Constructivism in Moral Theory: The Dewey Lectures 1980,' *Journal of Philosophy* 67 (1980): 515–72, p. 544. I explore the ideas in this paragraph in greater detail in 'Mortality, Agency, and Regret' (forthcoming, Sergio Tennenbaum, ed., *New Trends in Philosophy: Moral Psychology*, Rodopi, Amsterdam). For extended discussion, of practical reason and the need for intrapersonal coordination of aims and activities, see Michael Bratman, *Intention, Plans, and Practical Reason* (Cambridge: Harvard University Press, 1987).

[4]   See, e.g., Jon Elster, *Sour Grapes: Studies in the Subversion of Rationality* (Cambridge: Cambridge University Press, 1983); Amartya Sen, *On Ethics and Economics* (Oxford: Basil Blackwell, 1987); and Wayne Sumner, *Welfare and Happiness* (Oxford: Clarendon Press, 1996), pp. 162–171. See also Martha C. Nussbaum, 'Adaptive Preferences and Women's Options,' Symposium on Amartya Sen's Philosophy: 5, *Economics and Philosophy* 17 (2001): 67–88.

[5]   Barring intervention, of course.

things that seem, at least over time, to benefit them, and to this extent, they seem to be particularly successful at achieving good lives. Others, as we all know—even leaving to one side the more extreme problems of deformed and adaptive preferences—are notoriously poor preference formers. If they do not gravitate towards things that are positively bad for them, they at least seem to flounder and stumble their way through life far more than most of us do.

Of course, none of us comes into the world fully equipped from the outset either to order or to form our own preferences. Instead, our parents, or those responsible for raising us, must do the ordering on our behalf, at least until we have the maturity and skill to do it on our own, and they must also serve as the primary formers of our preferences.[6] Since parents are the original formers of our preferences and presumably influence how we go on to form preferences in the future, it would seem to follow that some parents do especially well at equipping their children to become effective preference formers. Let's say, speaking roughly, that good or effective parenting is parenting that produces effective formers of preferences, that is, formers of preferences the satisfaction of which is at least more likely to yield a good life for the person whose preferences they are. My suggestion will be this. If we want to arrive at an adequate theory of preference-formation, at least that part of a theory that concerns our welfare, we should study the efforts of those who are both most experienced in shaping our preferences and most strongly motivated to advance our good.[7] If we want to understand the connection between preference-formation and personal good, we should try to understand the

---

[6] I will talk throughout in terms of parents, but my points should be understood to pertain to any primary caregiver.

[7] Throughout this essay, my interest will lie with the good, welfare, or well-being of individual persons—what I will most often refer to as 'personal good.' The value at issue in talk about a person's good is nonmoral, relational value, where our concern is with what makes a person's life go well for her. So when I talk, as I have been, about leading 'good lives,' I mean lives good for the persons living them, as opposed to lives good for others. I have elsewhere explained my preference for the expression 'personal good' over more common expressions like 'welfare,' 'well-being,' and 'flourishing' and have also made a preliminary stab at providing an analysis of the *good for* relation. See Connie S. Rosati, 'Personal Good' Mark Timmons and Terry Horgan, ed., *Metaethics After Moore* (Oxford: Oxford University Press, 2006), pp.107–131.

impact that parenting has on preference-formation when it is done well; we should try to understand how parenting might *be* effective.

One might be inclined to say that what our parents do, in raising us well, is simply raise us to form preferences that are in keeping with our good.[8] As a first approximation, this claim is surely correct, though as we will see, the story to be told about what effective parenting accomplishes is far more complex. I will try to cash out what this claim might come to and to do so in a way that does not require us to take a position on the question of whether personal good itself just is the satisfaction of well-formed and well-ordered preferences.[9] The ideas I want to advance about preference-formation should in fact be compatible with a variety of theories of welfare, even if they lend special support to certain ways of thinking about our good. This means, of course, that what I have to say will leave a gap between preference and personal good, and I make no attempt here to close it. My aim, I want to stress, is not to offer a theory of preference-formation but simply to lay some of the groundwork for such a theory.

Good Parenting

We should begin then by considering what characterizes good parenting and return later to explore any implications for a theory of preference-formation. In setting out features of *good* or *effective*

---

[8]   I leave mainly to one side the moral and social dimensions of raising us well—that is, raising us reasonably to conform our behavior to the requirements of morality and to social roles and expectations—so as to focus on the relationship between preference-formation and personal good. I briefly address this incompleteness in my account later in the text.

[9]   My own view is that while preferences may have some interesting role to play in fixing our welfare, personal good does not consist merely in satisfaction of well-formed and well-ordered preferences. For criticisms of informed-desire theories of personal good, see, e.g., J. David Velleman, 'Brandt's Definition of ''Good,'' *Philosophical Review* 97 (1988): 353–371; David Sobel, 'Full Information Accounts of Well-Being,' *Ethics* 104 (1994): 784–810; Don Loeb, 'Full-Information Theories of Individual Good,' *Social Theory and Practice* 21 (1995): 1–30; and Connie S. Rosati, 'Persons, Perspectives, and Full-Information Accounts of the Good,' *Ethics* 105 (1995): 296–325, 'Naturalism, Normativity, and the Open Question Argument,' *Nôus* 29 (1995): 46–70, 'Brandt's Notion of Therapeutic Agency,' *Ethics* 110 (2000): 780–811, and 'Agency and the Open Question Argument,' *Ethics* 113 (2003): 490–527.

parenting, I mean, of course, to articulate an ideal of parenting, though one that I hope will have intuitive appeal and fit well with those examples of actual parenting that strike us as particularly successful.[10]

What makes parenting optimal, I have been supposing, is its special effects. And presumably good parenting succeeds in achieving its effects not wholly owing to good fortune but also to its being a properly guided activity. I have already mentioned the idea that parents, in raising us well, raise us to form our preferences in keeping with our good. But if we want to understand how they might succeed in this, we must first try to understand not how our parents raise us to be guided but how they are themselves guided in raising us.

One might suggest, in accordance with our original idea, that a parent's efforts at preference-formation must be guided by his own regard for his child's good; and one might think that means that what guides his efforts is the perceived value of the objects of his child's possible preferences or at least his prediction of the benefit those objects will yield in relation to her. No doubt our parents shape our preferences in keeping with their perceptions of what has genuine value, though we will still want to understand precisely why, when, and how they should attend to those perceptions, given their interest in our welfare. And no doubt our parents shape our preferences in keeping with their best judgments as to how we might benefit from our engagement with various goods, though we still need to understand, as theories of personal good aim to tell us, the precise nature of this 'benefit.' But the key to understanding effective parenting and what it accomplishes in shaping preferences is to recognize that parents are guided in the first instance not by a regard for the child's good but by a regard for the child herself.[11] And this suggests, as I will explain, that preference-formation ought to be guided not so much by the nature and value of the

[10] I will often talk simply in terms of parenting rather than good parenting, but it should be understood that I mean throughout to articulate a normative account.

[11] Stephen Darwall has recently suggested that welfare just is what one ought to want for a person insofar as one cares for her or for her sake. On this analysis, the direct object of care or concern for another is the person herself. See Stephen Darwall, *Welfare and Rational Care* (Princeton: Princeton University Press, 2002). I have argued elsewhere that Darwall's rich and appealing theory does not in fact offer us an analysis of welfare. See Connie S. Rosati, 'Darwall on Welfare and Rational Care' (forthcoming, *Philosophical Studies*). But I believe something is deeply

objects of preferences or even their value in relation to a particular person but by the nature and value of the person whose preferences are at issue.

In what sense, though, is parenting guided by a regard for the child herself? It is guided by a regard for the child herself, I want to suggest, in at least three related senses: first, a parent has regard for the child's agent-neutral value; second, he has regard for the child as a being with the capacity for autonomous agency; and finally, he has regard for the child as the distinct individual that she is. These respects in which parenting is guided by a regard for the child are importantly related, for they reflect those factors that must be borne in mind if parenting is to succeed in its fundamental aim, namely, producing happy, autonomous agents—beings who both fare well and function well.[12]

Regard for the Value of Children

Good parenting is, first and foremost, an activity in which a person responds appropriately to the value of children.[13] The acts a loving parent performs on behalf of his child both honor and express the child's value. These acts obviously include, though they go well beyond, nurturing the child, protecting her, and providing her with basic discipline and education.[14] What is especially important about

---

right in what I take to be the insight that underlies Darwall's analysis, namely, that goodness for a person is importantly related to the goodness of persons.

[12] Again, I leave out the component of producing morally decent agents. See note 8. I explore the deep connection between autonomy and personal good and the role of parents in simultaneously seeing to it that we fare well and function well in 'Autonomy and Personal Good: Lessons From Frankenstein's Monster' (manuscript). My use of the word 'happy' should not be construed hedonistically. Rather, I use the word merely to connote a positive or flourishing state of existence, however we should best understand what that is for a person.

[13] It is thus an example of what Darwall has recently called a 'valuing activity.' See Darwall, ch. IV. See also Elizabeth Anderson, *Value in Ethics and Economics* (Cambridge: Harvard University Press, 1993), pp. 8–16, for discussion of how goods differ in kind and of how different modes of valuing are appropriate to different goods.

[14] For exploration of this and related ideas, see Tamar Schapiro, 'What is a Child?' *Ethics* 109 (1999): 715–738, p. 716.

the sundry acts a good parent undertakes for his child's sake, out of his regard for her value, is that they effectively convey to the child a sense of her worth or value.[15]

The sense of one's worth that good parenting conveys should not be confused with self-esteem. Although some complex connections surely hold between having self-esteem and having a sense of one's worth, the underlying attitudes differ in at least three critical respects. First, whereas self-esteem rests in large measure on an assessment of merit—one's sense of one's own apparent excellence or of what one has accomplished through one's own (seemingly) worthwhile activity—a sense of one's own worth does not properly rest on achievement, either actual or perceived.[16] Instead, a sense of one's worth properly rests only on an accurate perception of one's value, a value one has in common with all persons.[17] Second,

---

[15]   Throughout, I use the terms 'worth' and 'value' interchangeably.

[16]   In this regard, the distinction between self-esteem and a sense of one's worth corresponds to the distinction Darwall has drawn between 'appraisal respect' and 'recognition respect.' See Stephen L. Darwall, 'Two Kinds of Respect,' *Ethics* 88 (1977): 36–49. I explore the parallel a bit more in 'Autonomy and Personal Good: Lessons From Frankenstein's Monster.' As Darwall explains the distinction, whereas appraisal respect rests on a person's perceived merit—her apparent possession of features which are excellences of persons, recognition respect, where its object is persons, does not rest on merit and is owed to all persons as such. Kant refers to recognition respect, Darwall says, when he writes of persons that 'Such a being is thus an object of respect and, so far, restricts all (arbitrary) choice.' See Immanuel Kant, *Foundations of the Metaphysics of Morals*, trans. L.W. Beck (Indianapolis: Bobbs-Merrill Co., 1959), p. 428. Darwall discusses this passage and further connections to Kantian ethics at pp. 45 ff.. A sense of one's worth or value, in my view, inclines one toward recognitional self-respect but also to a variety of other self-directed attitudes, including self-concern. In the text this note accompanies, I have expressed the contrast between a sense of worth and self-esteem in a way that draws on Darwall's suggestions regarding the connection between self-esteem and merit in Darwall, *Welfare and Rational Care*, p. 96. See also Rosati, 'Personal Good.'

[17]   And, perhaps, with all valuable beings. Complex questions arise, to be sure, about what it means and how it is possible for persons (or other beings) to have value, and theoretical efforts to untangle and defend this essentially Kantian idea have not fared especially well. For recent critical discussion, see Donald Regan, 'The Value of Rational Nature,' *Ethics* 112 (2002): 267–91. See also David Sussman, 'The Authority of Humanity,' *Ethics* 113 (2003): 350–366, replying to Regan. I make no attempt here to address these questions.

Connie S. Rosati

whereas self-esteem admits of degrees and can properly be enhanced by one's own activities and efforts at self-improvement, or diminished by one's own failures and faults, a sense of one's worth is not something to be earned or forfeited. It is an internalized apprehension of a value inhering in oneself, rather than a response to one's assessment of how one stacks up relative to certain external standards. A sense of one's worth can, to be sure, be weaker or stronger. When incorrectly rooted or confused with self-esteem, it can also be inflated, as in the thought of the egotist or of the high achiever that 'I am worth more than anyone else.' But it cannot be more or less deserved. Finally, whereas self-esteem seems to be something one feels, a sense of one's own worth is best understood, I suspect, not as a distinct feeling or emotion at all but as a basic orientation one has when parented well. The most ordinary way in which it manifests itself is in the absence of doubt that one is entitled to be cared for or loved, and what it involves is therefore most conspicuous, and most debilitating, when it is absent.[18]

[18] My notion of a sense of one's worth has affinities with the notion of self-respect. For helpful discussion and useful references to the substantial literature on self-respect, see Robin S. Dillon, 'How to Lose Your Self-Respect,' *American Philosophical Quarterly* 29 (1992): 125–139, 'Respect and Care: Toward Moral Integration,' *Canadian Journal of Philosophy* 22 (1992): 105–131, and 'Self-Respect: Moral, Emotional, Political,' *Ethics* 107 (1997): 226–249. Like Dillon, I have found Darwall's distinction, in 'Two Kinds of Respect,' helpful in isolating the notion I take to be of most interest. And my characterization of a sense of one's value or worth comes close to Dillon's characterization of self-respect: 'reflection on fine-grained descriptions of self-respecting individuals urges that self-respect is not a discrete entity but is rather a complex of multiply layered and interpenetrating phenomena that compose a certain way of being in the world, a way of being whose core is a deep appreciation of one's morally significant worth.' Dillon, 'Self-Respect: Moral, Emotional, Political,' p. 228. Dillon in fact distinguishes a number of senses of self-respect, and corresponding ways of losing it. The sense of worth that interests me seems most closely related to what Dillon calls 'recognition self-respect.' As Dillon, drawing on Darwall, describes it, recognition respect 'is a matter of taking appropriate account of the fact that something is a person. It involves (a) recognizing that something is a person; (b) appreciating that persons as such have intrinsic moral value; (c) understanding that the fact that this being is a person morally constrains our actions in connection with her; and (d) acting or being disposed to act only in fitting ways out of that recognition, appreciation,

I am, in fact, tempted to describe what a child acquires in acquiring a sense of her worth as a piece of knowledge. Insofar as it is properly so described, when parents behave in ways that communicate to the child a sense of her own value, they operate not only as caretakers but as moral teachers, for they impart an important bit of self-knowledge that is itself a bit of moral knowledge.[19] Those who maintain that nothing but states of affairs have value will no doubt insist that a sense of one's worth, even assuming that it involves a belief in one's worth, couldn't possibly constitute an item of knowledge. Indeed, they will deny having any belief in their own value or worth, however much they might actually feel loved and enjoy feeling loved.

Defending the idea that we have a piece of knowledge in having a sense of our worth would obviously require far more argument than I could possibly undertake to give here. But let me offer a quick observation and then a qualification. Whatever one thinks is the correct account of the metaphysics of value, it would misdescribe both our psychology—our inner experience—and our ordinary moral convictions to deny that, as a general matter, people tend to believe that they have value and that other people do, too. We well appreciate the difference between merely being loved and being worthy of love and our grasp of the distinction shows itself in common emotional states. People who are seriously depressed,

---

and understanding. *Recognition self-respect*, then, is responding appropriately to one's own personhood.' See Dillon, 'How to Lose Your Self-Respect,' p. 133. Still, a sense of one's worth is not, I think, the same thing as self-respect. Rather it is an orientation that underpins a great many attitudes one can take toward oneself—love, sympathy, and concern, as well as respect. I suspect that Dillon's characterization of self-respect may incorporate too theoretical a view of one's worth, a view that ordinary agents may lack and that many otherwise self-respecting agents might reject, however mistakenly.

[19] This claim depends, of course, on the truth of the claim that persons have value. Those who reject this idea will need to account for features of moral discourse that presuppose that persons do have value, as well as for the basic psychological phenomena connected to talk about a person's value. As I go on to explain, people certainly tend to see themselves and those they care about as having value, and a host of psychological maladies reflect a basic absence or erosion of a person's sense of her own worth. I discuss the latter point in 'Autonomy and Personal Good: Lessons From Frankenstein's Monster.' See also Darwall, *Welfare and Rational Care*, p. 6.

for example, may not be ignorant of the fact that they are loved by others, they just do not feel worthy of that love; they feel worthless, that they are not appropriate objects of others' care or concern.

In any case, and this is the qualification, although I will continue to talk about it as a piece of knowledge or information, nothing I shall say requires that a sense of one's worth amount to an item of knowledge; it is enough that the orientation I mean to point to is familiar. Think of it, if you prefer, as a sort of confidence akin to the kind of confidence Wittgenstein describes us as having that we are not now dreaming, say, or that there really are hands in front of me typing on this keyboard.[20] Like those other items of belief in which we have such confidence, it is among the 'hinges' on which a great deal turns. For as we will see later, a sense of one's worth, whether it is a bit of self-knowledge or not, helps to prepare the way for broader and deeper forms of self-knowledge, and in this and other ways, it plays a critical role in preference-formation.

Of course, the information about our worth that good parenting conveys to us is not transmitted in the same way as, say, facts about the natural sciences or history. Instead, we acquire this knowledge in much the way that we acquire knowledge of other valuable things. We learn the value of a piece of sculpture, for instance, not by being told that it is a valuable or important work of art. Instead, we receive training or at least relevant exposure—in particular, exposure to how others respond to its value—and this training or exposure enables us to come to grasp and appreciate the value that it has. Consider the debate in recent years about how properly to clean Michelangelo's David so as to preserve its aesthetic value. Participants to this debate both expressed, through their actions and arguments, the value of that work of art and modeled how properly to respond to it. Through the acts our parents perform in nurturing us, providing for our needs and so on, they likewise model how we are to be valued. In seeing to our needs and helping us to make our way in the world, our parents prepare us to grasp or sense our own value, and we absorb the information their actions convey, more or less unconsciously, through our interactions with them.

---

[20] Ludwig Wittgenstein, *On Certainty* (New York: Harper and Row, Publishers, 1972/1969).

Raising Autonomy Agents

In responding appropriately to the value of their children, parents respond to the value of a special kind of being. To respond appropriately to the value of a child is not merely to recognize that she has physiological needs as a particular sort of organism but to recognize also that she is a person, a being with the capacity for autonomous agency who must eventually shape her identity and her good on her own. Since good parenting is guided by a regard for the child as a being with the capacity to become an autonomous agent, much parenting consists, unsurprisingly, in training a child in autonomous functioning. As a preliminary matter, parents must help their children to develop those skills that provide the necessary foundations for genuine self-governance. To begin with the obvious, they must help their children learn to control their impulses and delay gratification. Unless they succeed in their efforts, their children will be unable to evolve from wantonness to agency or to develop the capacities for the long-term intentional action and planning that we associate with full autonomous functioning. Good parents impart these and other 'skills in living' not only by correcting and structuring the child's behavior but by behaving themselves in ways that model these skills for the child. For instance, children learn to control their anger and express it in constructive ways, at least in part, by watching how their angry parents manage their own feelings. As part and parcel of their efforts to guide their children in becoming autonomous, parents will also allow their children to practice at being autonomous by engaging in more or less supervised experimentation, appropriate to their developmental stage.[21]

Just what our autonomy consists in remains a perplexing question, and I can't undertake to develop an account of autonomy here. We needn't, in any case, settle the question for present purposes. Whatever the proper analysis of autonomy might turn out to be, autonomous functioning will require the successful exercise of those capacities that render us self-governing, that help to free us from the immediate grip of our desires so that we are not simply moved by whichever first-order desire is presently strongest. The relevant capacities are no doubt varied but almost certainly include these: the capacity to engage in self-reflection and so to understand, to varying degrees, what we are doing; to exercise imagination and so to envision possibilities; to reason and be moved

---

[21] For related ideas, see Schapiro.

by reasons and so to look for warrant for our actions; and to form and act on higher-order desires and so to guide our own conduct by what we reflectively support.[22]

22 The idea that certain motives and capacities are either constitutive of or at least essential to agency has been suggested by a number of writers. Velleman has argued, that intrinsic desires for self-understanding and self-awareness, or more recently, an inclination toward autonomy, are constitutive of agency. See J. David Velleman, *Practical Reflection*, and 'The Possibility of Practical Reason,' *Ethics* 106 (1996): 694–726. In *Practical Reflection*, Velleman argues that the motives constitutive of agency are intrinsic desires for self-understanding and self-awareness, but he shifts to talk about an inclination toward autonomy in 'The Possibility of Practical Reason.' See J. David Velleman, 'Deciding How to Decide,' in *Ethics and Practical Reason*, ed. Garrett Cullity and Berys Gaut (Oxford: Clarendon Press, 1997), p. 41, n. 20, on why these formulations are supposed to come to roughly the same thing. Michael Smith has argued that a disposition toward coherence is constitutive of rational agency. See Michael Smith, 'A Theory of Freedom and Responsibility,' in *Ethics and Practical Reason*, pp. 293–320. Richard Brandt has argued that humans happen to have standing desires for their own long-term happiness and for desires that are consonant with reality, and these standing desires enable them to act (against a present desire) in favor of their longer-term interests. See Richard Brandt, *A Theory of the Good and the Right* (Oxford: Clarendon Press, 1979), pp. 156–57 and 85. See also Rosati, 'Brandt's Notion of Therapeutic Agency', for discussion of this aspect of Brandt's views. Finally, Rawls has argued that the possession of certain moral powers (the capacity for an effective sense of justice and the capacity to construct, revise, and rationally pursue a conception of the good) and corresponding highest-order interests in exercising them is constitutive of persons on a Kantian ideal and renders persons autonomous in the original position. See Rawls, 'Kantian Constructivism in Moral Theory,' p. 525. Numerous philosophers have discussed the importance of capacities for self-reflection and the formation of higher order desires, while taking differing positions on their relation to free will or autonomy. See Gerald Dworkin, 'Acting Freely,' *Nous* 4 (1970): 367–83; Harry Frankfurt, 'Freedom of the Will and the Concept of a Person,' *Journal of Philosophy* 68 (1971): 5–20; Wright Neely, 'Freedom and Desire,' *Philosophical Review* 83 (1974): 32–54; and Gary Watson, 'Free Agency,' *Journal of Philosophy* 72 (1975): 205–220. See also Charles Taylor, 'What is Human Agency?' in *Human Agency and Language: Philosophical Papers I* (Cambridge: Cambridge University Press, 1985); Thomas Nagel, *The View from Nowhere* (New York: Oxford University Press, 1986), ch. VII; and Sarah Buss, 'Autonomy Reconsidered,' *Midwest Studies in Philosophy* XIX (1994): 95–121.

Developing and exercising these capacities is no small task, and so if we are to exercise them successfully and function well as autonomous agents, we must presumably have some motivation to do so. It seems plausible to think that autonomous agents are intrinsically motivated to persist as the sort of creature they are; as a consequence, we would expect them to develop standing desires or dispositions to exercise those capacities the successful exercise of which renders them autonomous.[23] These considerations suggest that beyond cultivating those 'autonomy making capacities' that are the basic preconditions for the development of deeper forms of self-governance, parents must also foster development of the 'autonomy making motives.' Parents can presumably nurture or squelch motivational tendencies to be self-reflective, to reason and act for reasons, to consider the possibilities before acting, and so on, much as they can help to develop a child's capacity for self-control.

We have been considering the character of good parenting with an eye to its effects on preference-formation in relation to our good. But it might seem that this fact about us—that we are autonomous agents as well as creatures of a certain biological type—means only that valuing a person requires that one show respect for her autonomy as well as concern for her welfare. And so one might think that this fact has little bearing on our original inquiry, but I believe that would be a mistake. Respect and care are indeed distinct attitudes one can take toward persons, and parents owe their children both respect and concern. But the relationships that hold among respect, care, and our good are more complex than it might seem. Our being autonomous agents bears not only on the respect that is owed us but on the very nature of our good.[24] For

---

[23] We find expression of something akin to the idea that autonomous agents want to persist as such in John Stuart Mill's famous observation that a discontented Socrates wouldn't consent to become a happy fool. See John Stuart Mill, *Utilitarianism* (Indianapolis: Hackett, 1979). The other desires or dispositions we acquire, in having a motive to persist as autonomous agents, will likely be of greater or lesser strength, depending upon an individual's upbringing, aptitude, and personality.

[24] Darwall seems to rely on a fairly sharp distinction between care and respect in his efforts to address what he calls the 'scope problem,' which was first raised for desire theories by Mark Overvold. See, e.g., his discussion of the case of Sheila in Darwall, *Welfare and Rational Care*, pp. 43–45. According to Darwall, what is good for a person is what one ought to want for her insofar as one cares for her. Both care and respect are attitudes toward a person, but whereas care responds to her as a being with a welfare, respect responds to her as a being with dignity. Darwall might

45

one thing, we clearly fair better to the extent that both others and we ourselves treat us with due respect. More deeply, though, what is good for us must presumably fit the sort of creature we are, and since we are beings with a capacity for autonomy, our good must fit us as autonomous agents. It would seem to follow that for creatures like us, important connections must exist between our well-being and our autonomy and, therefore, between what our parents must do to ensure that we fare well and that we function well.

One such connection takes us back to our consideration of how good parenting conveys to the child a sense of her own worth. Just as having a stable sense of one's value seems indispensable to leading a good life, so it seems indispensable to autonomous functioning. The most basic way to see this, I think, is to consider the fact that the vast bulk of the actions a person performs are self-regarding, though the balance between self- and other-regarding actions may vary at different points in a person's life. We feed, clean, and clothe ourselves; we pursue our hobbies and pass time with our friends; we educate ourselves and try to pursue work that we will love. In the ordinary case, we take ourselves to have reason—to be justified—in performing these acts. Arguably what best explains how we could take ourselves to have reason to act in self-regarding ways—and, thereby, how we could autonomously so act—is our sense of our own worth, something we ordinarily do not question.[25] Indeed, it is just at those times when a person feels worthless, as we see in cases of severe depression, that she sees little reason for doing anything, least of all for herself. In the latter cases,

---

suggest, in response to my remarks in the text, that among that things one ought to want for a person insofar as one cares for her is that she be treated with respect. This would be to count respect among the substantive goods for a person, while treating care as part of the analysis of goodness for a person. Because I find reason to doubt Darwall's analysis of welfare (see note 11), I'm not inclined to accept this response. I merely register here my sense that the interactions among care, respect, and welfare stand in need of much fuller exploration.

[25] A number of philosophers have recently suggested that the normativity of welfare depends on the value of persons, that what is good for us matters only if we matter. See especially J. David Velleman, 'A Right of Self-Termination?' *Ethics* 109 (1999): 606–620 and Darwall, *Welfare and Rational Care*. See also Anderson. I here make the related point that one wouldn't see oneself as having reason to do anything, at least that part of what we do that is self-regarding, without a sense that one matters.

as well as in many cases commonly regarded as paradigmatic instances of failed or diminished autonomy, the problem seems rooted in a lack of adequate self-regard. A sense of one's worth thus seems to be indispensable both to living good lives and to autonomous functioning.[26] By treating us in ways that impart a sense of our worth, our parents see to our development as happy *and* autonomous agents.

Adequate development of the autonomy making motives and capacities ordinarily requires many years of effort. Training in autonomous functioning must, in any case, go a step further. It is not enough that children learn to control their impulses or to exercise their reason and imagination. To develop well, children must not only be stopped from acting in certain ways and taught how to exercise self-control; they must also be given positive reasons for acting in some ways rather than others. One might doubt that parents need to supply reasons for acting on the grounds that children will themselves have desires which will supply them with reasons. But even if our desires or, better, the fact that we desire something, could supply us with reasons, recall that our desires or preferences are the source of the practical problem we face. As already observed, the task we each confront in living a life arises because we have many conflicting desires, desires that may pull us toward different life paths and different future selves. Moreover, not just any desires or preferences will supply positive reasons for acting; that is precisely why we wonder how our preferences ought to be formed and why we would seek a theory of preference-formation in the first place. If we are successfully to make our way in the world we will require some means of reflecting

[26] See 'Autonomy and Personal Good: Lessons From Frankenstein's Monster' for more extended discussion and defense of this claim. Paul Benson has made an apparently similar claim about the relationship between autonomy and self-worth. See Paul Benson, 'Free Agency and Self-Worth,' *Journal of Philosophy* 91 (1994): 650–668. But Benson appears to mean something very different by a sense of self-worth. For Benson, it is evidently a sense of one's competence to respond to the various demands one thinks others could appropriately make. So whereas I have in mind a sense of one's own inherent worth or value, Benson's sense of self-worth has as its focus a feature of one's status in relation to others and to standards of conduct. A person could regard herself as competent in the way that interests Benson, while lacking a sense of worth as I understand it. Perhaps both senses of self-worth must be present if a person is to function autonomously, but I leave the question whether that is so for another time.

on and ordering our preferences, and this must amount to more than just opting for some desires over others, more than just acceding to those that happen to be strongest. Rather, we will require some framework for ordering desires—ordinarily, a set of rules, principles, and basic commitments—and such a framework will shape the formation of our preferences, extinguishing some desires, inducing others, and enabling us to settle conflicts among them. In these ways, the framework will itself favor certain preferences over others and, when well constructed, it will do so in a way that affords positive reasons for acting.

Insofar as our capacity for autonomy consists in the capacity to act for reasons, our ability to function autonomously partly depends on our having some such framework for ourselves. Since children cannot develop a framework for shaping their preferences all on their own, a critical part of how parents aid in the development of autonomous agency is by giving their children such a framework until they have developed the ability to decide for themselves what rules, principles, and commitments to embrace. Early on and well into adolescence, our parents must not only structure our time and activities; they must also directly supply us with rules and principles and discipline us to conform to them. In so doing, they shape the formation of our preferences rather directly. Parents commonly provide a framework for their children through a variety of devices, making use of extended family and of a host of existing social structures, including religious and educational institutions and moral and political associations. In so doing, they provide their children with a provisional or 'working' conception of their good and a provisional 'self-ideal'; they give their children a life to live and someone to be until they are able to choose a life and form an ideal for themselves.[27]

---

[27] This may well amount to endorsing the ideal they have been given. See Connie S. Rosati, *Self-Invention and the Good* (doctoral dissertation, 1989) on the importance of a self-ideal. See also Rosati, 'Persons, Perspectives, and Full-Information Accounts of the Good' and 'Naturalism, Normativity, and the Open Question Argument.' For related ideas, see Christine Korsgaard's discussion of practical identities in, *The Sources of Normativity* (Cambridge: Cambridge University Press, 1996). See also David Velleman's discussion of a person's self-conception in J. David Velleman, *Practical Reflection* (Princeton: Princeton University Press, 1989).

Attending to Individuality

Although our parents must give us someone to be they obviously cannot make us into whatever sort of person they might like. We each come into the world with a basic physical and psychological makeup, and the bundle of features we each possess not only creates opportunities for but sets limits to our future development. This brings us to the third sense in which good parenting is guided by a regard for the child: it is guided by a regard for the individual that she is. Children's preferences cannot be shaped in just any way at all if they are both to flourish and to function well. After all, they may not have the ability to undertake certain aims and pursuits. Or they may have the ability, but given their personality, circumstances, and capacity for change, they may never find those aims or pursuits rewarding. When children are pressed into pursuing unachievable aims or engaging in activities they find unrewarding, they tend to lead less satisfying lives and find themselves unable to act in the whole-hearted manner characteristic of fully autonomous engagement in the central activities of one's life.[28] Thoughtful parents attend to their child's personality and circumstances and will be guided in what they do for their child partly by the child herself. They will take notice of their child's strengths and weaknesses; they will be alert to what their child finds stimulating or frustrating. Of course, while good parents must be guided by what the child herself enjoys, they must also steer her away from those things that she may enjoy but must learn to shun, as well as toward those she must learn to enjoy (or at least not to mind). Still, in having a regard for their child as a distinct individual, parents seek to foster their child's interest in activities that do or can, with the proper effort, 'suit' or 'fit' her.

In this last way, a parent's acts on behalf of his child most conspicuously and directly promote her good. For a person's good would seem to consist, intuitively speaking, in just those things that suit or fit her. If this is right, then an analysis of what it is for something to be good for a person ought to elucidate this normative or reason-generating relation of fit or suitability; we would then understand, to return to an earlier aside, the nature of 'benefit.'[29]

---

[28] See Harry Frankfurt, 'Identification and Wholeheartedness,' in *The Importance of What We Care About* (Cambridge: Cambridge University Press, 1988), pp. 159–76

[29] I explore the notion of fit while attempting to spell out the *good for* relation in 'Personal Good.'

Connie S. Rosati

Although a parent most conspicuously promotes his child's good by attending to her as a distinct individual, he also sees to her welfare, though more indirectly, by having due regard for her agent-neutral value and her capacity for autonomy. As we have seen, in having regard for the child as a valuable being, a parent helps to impart information and an orientation critical both to flourishing and good functioning. And in having a regard for the child as a budding autonomous agent, a parent helps to equip her to build a life.

Normative Implications

I hope that this account of good parenting will strike you as just so much common sense. As mundane as these considerations may sound, however, they have quite interesting implications for our efforts to theorize about preference-formation. A theory of preference-formation has both normative and explanatory import. I shall focus on the normative implications of the approach I have taken to laying the groundwork for a theory of preference-formation—the strategy of looking to how a person might come to be an effective former of preferences.

Thus far I have suggested that insofar as parents succeed in the goal of raising their children to be happy, autonomous agents, they thereby raise their children to be good regulators of their own future preference-formation. Let me stress that in making this suggestion, I do not mean to claim that well brought up children will infallibly form self-regarding preferences the satisfaction of which advances their welfare. I want to claim only that however one analyzes what it is for something to be good for a person, and whatever one might plausibly think comprises an individual's substantive good, satisfaction of a well-parented person's self-regarding preferences is, on the whole, more likely to advance and less likely to undermine her welfare. Of course, I have been supposing that effective parenting produces persons who regulate well their future preference-formation. But I do not mean thereby to be making a stipulative claim; rather, my claim is partly conceptual and normative, partly empirical, and I will offer further support for it as we proceed.

The normative import of the foregoing account of good parenting might be expressed, at least as a first approximation, in the following way: properly formed preferences are those preferences that a person would form for herself at a time insofar as she viewed herself and her situation from the standpoint of an ideal parent. What this would mean is that properly formed preferences are those a person would acquire or retain were she guided by a regard for her agent-neutral value, by a regard for her status as an autonomous agent, and by a regard for herself as the individual that she is. In being well-brought up, I am suggesting, a person will tend to deliberate, choose, and act *as if* guided in this way. But of course, she does not do so precisely by contemplating her actual position from the standpoint of an ideal parent. Nor does she, at least not in the ordinary case, think to herself, 'What honors me as the valuable being I am?' or 'What would promote my functioning as an autonomous agent?', though she may well ask what suits her. Rather, she comes to be guided as if she had adopted the standpoint of an ideal parent by virtue of possessing a certain orientation toward herself and by the operation of the complex set of motives and capacities that good parenting has fostered in her. To add a twist to Freud's insight about the superego, she has, in effect, internalized the parental standpoint. This does not mean that she has internalized her parents' particular substantive views about a good life—their values, religious beliefs, and such—though she may have done that, too. It also does not mean that she treats herself in the particular ways parents treat a child, since she is obviously no longer in the condition that warrants and, indeed, calls for the special care and guidance parents give to children.[30] Rather, she has internalized, and so, in effect, has adopted with respect to herself, the normative stance toward children that makes for effective parenting. It is worth considering in more detail why having internalized this standpoint would produce a tendency to form preferences satisfaction of which is more likely to yield a life good for the person whose preferences they are.

I indicated earlier that the many acts a loving parent performs out of a regard for the value of his child and on her behalf effectively convey to the child a sense of her own value. In raising us well, our parents are guided by our value and impart a sense of our value which guides us in turn. Now having a regard for one's own value is not itself having a regard for one's welfare, and yet it is far from irrelevant to whether one fares well. Compare responding to the value of a work of art. When we appreciate the value of a work of art, we endeavor to protect it and preserve its aesthetic integrity, though of course a work of art does not have a welfare. Persons, unlike paintings, do have a welfare, and what is good for persons is not unrelated to the goodness of persons. When we

---

[30] See Schapiro.

appreciate the value of a person, we endeavor to protect her and to preserve her integrity as the valuable creature she is. This will mean, among other things, seeing to her good functioning as well as to her basic needs, and while her good does not consist just in her good functioning or in satisfaction of her basic needs, both are critical to whether in fact she fares well. Through their experience of being cared for, persons learn to grasp and respond appropriately to their own value, and they learn to act successfully in ways that tend to their benefit by seeing to their needs and supporting or at least not undermining their successful functioning.

A person's sense of worth, I have claimed, most ordinarily manifests itself in a basic absence of doubt that she is loveable, but it manifests itself in other important ways as well. First, it shows itself in a certain resilience, an ability better to handle what life might throw her way. In acknowledging our value and in providing us with a sense of our worth, our parents foster in us an emotional stability that provides a firm basis from which to act. Our having a sense of our worth is not only essential to our flourishing, it is also essential to our autonomous functioning. Insofar as autonomous action depends on our authority to speak and act for ourselves, that authority depends not merely on our being in an especially good position to know ourselves and our good, but on our nature as beings whose worth grounds their authority to act and justifies them in acting on their own behalf. A person's sense of her worth better enables her to fare well and to function well and so to manage well even when life does not go as she might wish.[31]

Second, a person's sense of her worth reveals itself in her having both the tendency and capacity to resist those who disrespect her or who would disregard her needs and interests.[32] She will tend to prefer the company of those who value her or at least do not leave her feeling diminished or in doubt about her basic worth. More generally, she will tend to prefer not only people but those activities and pursuits engagement with which supports or at least does not erode her sense of her own worth. This is obviously not to say that

[31] It helps to equip her, borrowing Aristotle's words, to 'bear[] with resignation many great misfortunes.' Aristotle, *The Nicomachean Ethics*, trans. David Ross (Oxford: Oxford University Press, 1926), 1100b.

[32] I have already suggested that persons who have a sense of their own worth will manifest self-respect. As Dillon has emphasized, persons with a sense of self-respect will also be disposed to certain emotional responses to their treatment by others, such as a sense of indignation or resentment of others' disregard of them. See Dillon, 'Self-Respect: Moral, Emotional, Political,' p. 230.

she will shut out or ignore legitimate criticisms or that she will not be stung by negative remarks or assessments of her failings. But experience suggests that a person's ability to take in and respond to legitimate criticism is greater when she has a stable sense of her own value. Greater, too, is her ability to take risks and to recover and learn from her failed experiments.

More generally, a person's sense of her worth manifests itself in her acquired habits of looking out for herself, of seeing to her own needs, of treating herself with care. She will naturally prefer those things that she can see as consistent with her needs and interests. None of this should be mistaken for being self-centered or narcissistic. Nothing in her orientation or habits of self-concern preclude her caring for others. Indeed, having been cared for and having learned how to respond to her own value, it is plausible to think that she will be better able to appreciate and respond appropriately to the value of others. The fact that being the product of effective parenting should have such moral effects in addition to its effects on a child's own flourishing and functioning should not surprise us. In being guided by apprehension of a person's worth, preference-formation, whether effected by us or by our parents acting for us, is guided by a foundational moral value, and this is so whether or not the preferences a person forms are themselves peculiarly moral.[33]

Preference-formation will be guided, too, by a person's status as an autonomous being. Parents attempting to raise a child have as a principal task creating an autonomous agent—they must shape a self-governing being out of a mass of impulse and desire—and so much of their effort is directed at developing the autonomy making motives and capacities. The person who has been well-raised, whose parents have succeeded in this process of shaping, now has a set of internalized motives and capacities at her disposal. Her preference-formation will reflect this and will, as a consequence, tend to redound to her benefit in a number of ways.

First, her preferences, at least as regards the major aims, undertakings, and relationships in her life, will have been formed in the course of ongoing operation of her capacities for imagination, reason, and reflection. What that means is that she will tend to form preferences for those possibilities attraction to which survives her

---

[33] This is most obviously the view of those who accept broadly Kantian approaches in ethics. But some suitable notion of the value of persons (which is not to say of persons alone) is arguably critical to ethics in general and so would have to be a part of any plausible moral theory.

imaginative reflection and consideration in light of reasons. Her 'native preferences,' those arising from the autonomy making motives, are, we might say harnessed in shaping her preferences. Second, since her preferences are formed through and in keeping with the exercise of her autonomy making motives and capacities, we have reason to predict that acting on them will tend to support or at least not undermine her autonomy. Finally, notice that the self-control a person achieves through the operation of these motives and capacities is itself a form of self-concern. The person who effectively governs her own choices and conduct protects herself, at least to some degree, not merely from the outward consequences of acting on unreflective desires or impulses, but from disruption of her efforts to live out her self-ideal and her conception of her good.

Among the things a person will consider in forming her desires are the facts about herself and her circumstances, at least as she knows them at the time. A person ordinarily comes to know herself partly as a consequence of her parents coming to know her as the individual she is and helping to foster her self-awareness. But in addition, effective parents teach their children how and when to draw on their feelings as a source of self-knowledge. They teach their children to exploit effectively the natural mechanisms that operate in the formation of desires and preferences—the feedback we receive in the form of states such as pleasure or satisfaction and pain or frustration, feedback that requires interpretation in light of a person's features and circumstances.[34]

It is important to appreciate the role that inculcating a person's sense of her own worth plays in facilitating the growth of

---

[34] My discussion at this point was prompted by Phillip Pettit, who I here thank for pressing the question of how my account interacts with what he called 'internal norms of preference formation.' I want to say just a bit here to address his question more directly than I have in the text. I am uncertain which norms count as those internal to preference formation. If we understand them to be, or to include, norms of consistency, transitivity, responsiveness to information, and so on, then surely effective parents will shape their children's preferences in keeping with those norms; to do otherwise would, for obvious reasons, subvert the aim of producing happy, autonomous agents. The internal norms may also include ones connected to the natural mechanisms that seem to be at work in preference formation. I have tried to make clear how effective parenting facilitates successful exploitation of these mechanisms in our efforts to achieve good lives. I hope to have said enough here and in the text to allay any worries that my account may be in tension with such internal norms of

self-knowledge. People who lack a stable, appropriate sense of their own worth, who are deeply insecure, notoriously do not see themselves or their circumstances accurately, and they have difficulty accurately gauging what they want and feel.[35] They are less able to recognize when their perceptions are distorted, and they lack the confidence to form and trust their own judgments and self-assessments. They also have a diminished ability to envision genuine possibilities for themselves or to see obvious options as within their reach. People who lack a sense of their own worth tend to be especially defensive and sensitive in the face of legitimate criticism or too willing to acquiesce in the face of unjust criticism; either way they may miss out on the kind of self-learning and the opportunities for growth and change that help to make for success in living a life. These are rough, common sense generalities, of course; some people who lack a sense of their own worth engage in self-scrutiny and self-transformation for that very reason. But a concentrated effort, a sustained act of will, is involved in what they do that isn't necessary for the person who can, even if with some discomfort or pain, simply face the facts about herself.

Insofar as these generalities hold, we should not be surprised that preference-formation under conditions in which a person lacks a basic sense of her own worth would regularly lead to departures from her good. For she will tend to overestimate (or underestimate) her faults, to underestimate (or overestimate) her abilities, and to operate with inaccurate perceptions of her circumstances and possibilities. Not equipped to sort out her feelings, not feeling comfortable with herself, she will tend not to take appropriate care or ferret out what matters most to her and will matter most to her over time. When a person has been well-raised and has a firm sense of her own worth, when she has acquired the kind of self-knowledge that good parenting helps to make possible, she will be more likely to form preferences in line with her real feelings and accurate self-perceptions. To that extent, satisfaction of her preferences will be more likely to reflect and advance her good.

---

preference formation as may exist. No doubt far more needs to be said, but filling out the details is, I think, work for those whose aim is to construct a theory of preference-formation.

[35] This sort of common sense observation has been explored in some of the literature on self-respect. See Dillon, 'How to Lose Your Self-Respect,' p. 131.

Connie S. Rosati

Questions

I want to consider briefly certain questions that might be raised about my account of parenting and its effects on preference-formation. These questions chiefly concern ways in which the account may seem incorrect or in need of modification. I turn last to the issue of its incompleteness.

A first question concerns the account of good parenting and whether it accurately distinguishes the parental role from other roles, such as that of a teacher. After all, though I have often made reference to the acts of loving parents, my discussion makes no mention of what may seem critical to ideal parenting, namely, unconditional love for the child.[36] In my view, the role of parent and teacher are not so utterly distinct. It is no accident that we describe teachers as acting and expect them to act 'in loco parentis,' and that means showing regard for the child in the ways a parent ought, at least compatibly with meeting the other demands of the teacher's position and with observing the limits on what a teacher may appropriately do with a child not his or her own. Furthermore, I suspect we think teachers of children ought to have something like unconditional love for their students; they simply ought not to develop the affection and attachment of a parent, since this might (among other difficulties) lead to disruption of the primary caretaking relationship. So I want to insist that good parenting is guided by a regard for the child in all the ways that I have described even if not only 'official' parents or primary caretakers ought to be so guided.

But recognizing that others appropriately guide their interactions with children as effective parents do leaves unaddressed the more basic issue of whether the account stands in need of modification. What then of unconditional love? I suspect that many people view unconditional love as unique or at least essential to the parent-child relationship, and certain apparent counterexamples would seem to support their view. For instance, many believers maintain that God has unconditional love for mankind. But we are not God's children, not literally anyway, and so God's unconditional love would seem to be a counterexample. But God's unconditional love is often said to be for all of 'his children,' and this common form of expression apparently links unconditional love with the specifically parental role. Still, I believe that other examples show that unconditional love is not unique to the parent-child relationship. To be sure,

[36] I am grateful to Christian Piller for pressing this point.

56

when I describe the unconditional love I feel for my nieces and nephews, I find myself saying that I love them 'as if they were my own kids'—or, as we say, 'no matter what.' But I love a great many people 'no matter what.' I feel this way about my own parents and siblings, for example, but I would not be at all inclined to say that I love *them* as if they were my own kids.

One might nevertheless urge that unconditional love remains essential. But I doubt this, too. I in no way mean to challenge the claim that parents ought to feel unconditional love for their children, at least assuming some plausible understanding of its 'unconditional' character. In my view, however, a parent's unconditional love for his child is merely the form his appreciation of the child's value takes.[37] It may well be that for reasons having to do with the contingencies of human nature, a parent's apprehension of the value of his child finds expression in unconditional love; and it may also be that for reasons having to due with our human nature, a parent can effectively impart to the child a sense of her own unconditional value only by loving her unconditionally. In these ways, unconditional love might plausibly be essential to effective parenting. But we shouldn't confuse the form in which parents (or others) manifest a regard for the value of children for a distinct condition of good parenting.

Having said all this, let me stress a more basic point in response to this first question, and that is that I have been appealing to an ideal of parenting as a heuristic device.[38] My aim has not been to characterize fully 'the parental role' or the parent-child relationship; it has been to lay some of the groundwork for a theory of preference-formation by studying good parents insofar as they are expert at producing effective preference formers. Unconditional love makes no independent contribution, as far as I can see, to how good parents succeed in this. Even if unconditional love properly motivates a parent's actions on behalf of his child, it isn't what

[37] This is not yet to say that unconditional love just is a regard for the value of the child. See J. David Velleman, 'Love as a Moral Emotion,' *Ethics* 109 (1999): 338–374, for defense of the idea that love is an 'arresting awareness' of value in another person, an awareness that 'arrests our tendencies toward emotional self-protection from another person, tendencies to draw ourselves in and close ourselves off from being affected by him' (360–361).

[38] This response applies, of course, to the next two objections that I consider, but I won't repeat the point. The additional replies I make in the text are compatible with treating the appeal to good parenting as purely heuristic.

properly guides his actions. So a reference to unconditional love need not figure in an ideal of good parenting, at least insofar as that ideal bears on preference-formation.

A second question concerns whether the account places sufficient normative restrictions on how effective parents are guided. I have claimed that parents must provide their children with a framework of basic rules and principles that provide them with a source of reasons, that give them a life to live and someone to be until they are able to choose for themselves. The natural candidate for this framework would seem to be a parent's own value system or his conception of the good. Yet certain value systems and conceptions of the good seem at odds both with a child's welfare and with the development of her capacity to choose and decide for herself. One might insist that parents can exhibit due regard for their children's well-being and for their status as beings with the capacity for autonomy, only if they refrain from imposing or seeking to inculcate their own values, religious beliefs, and fundamental commitments. It has been suggested to me, for instance, that parents who hold religious views that tend to instill feelings of guilt, shame, or self-loathing must refrain from raising their children to accept those views.[39]

I don't doubt that some value systems and conceptions of the good may be absolutely damaging to children, and others, while not outright damaging, may in various ways impede efforts to raise children who will, as adults, both fare well and function well. Perhaps then one cannot be even an adequate parent while accepting the former sort of value system; and one cannot be an effective parent, in our sense, while endeavoring to inculcate the latter sort of value system.

I am inclined to believe, however, that such value systems and conceptions of the good aside, a great many frameworks may be accepted by parents and employed in raising their children compatibly with having due regard for their value, their capacity for autonomy, and their individuality. In any case, the fact that accepting or imparting certain value systems may be incompatible with effective parenting does not require a modification of the model I have offered. Rather, that fact simply follows as an implication of the model, together with empirical considerations about the effects of raising children with differing sorts of rules and principles. And acknowledging it amounts to recognizing, as we already do, that *we* ought not to adopt certain value systems and

[39] Thanks to Andrew Williams for pressing this line of objection.

conceptions of the good or to shape our preferences by them—at least not if we want to fare well and function well.

Finally, I have stressed three senses in which effective parents have a regard for the child, but one might remind us that these cannot be the only senses. After all, a parent must have a regard for the child as a prospective occupant of social roles within the community and a regard for her as a prospective moral agent. My account does omit direct examination of the social and moral dimensions of effective parenting. A partial explanation for the omission lies in my focus on the relationship between preference-formation and personal good—that is, an individual's intrinsic, nonmoral good. But the explanation is only partial for our positions as occupants of social roles and as moral agents bear not only on our social and moral obligations, which may be at odds with our good, but on our good itself.

I have nevertheless set to one side consideration of the social and moral dimensions of parenting for the following reason. My aim herein has been to lay some of the groundwork for a theory of preference formation rather than to offer such a theory, and, as just noted, to lay the groundwork for such a theory only insofar as it concerns well-being. Difficult questions exist about the precise ways in which behaving well within social roles and behaving morally benefit an individual, and I have deliberately sought to sidestep these particular complexities in the interest of advancing a more general idea about preference-formation. My suggestion has been that we must look not so much to the nature and value of the objects of preference—though we must consider these things, too—as to the nature and value of the individual whose preferences are at issue. Insofar as that suggestion is correct, it should remain central to our thinking even when we begin to attend—as we must in constructing a full theory of preference-formation—to the individual's position as moral agent and member of society. So attention to these additional dimensions of parenting would augment rather than upset the account I have offered.

What I have said up to this point is not, in any case, wholly unrelated to the social and moral dimensions of effective parenting. The questions of how parents must raise children to equip them for moral and social life and of how their doing so bears on preference-formation merit more direct, philosophical investigation. But while we must be careful not to exaggerate the moral impact of good parenting, as I have described it, I find it plausible to believe, as already suggested, that children who have been well cared for and who have learned to respond to their own value will be at least better able to recognize and respond appropriately to other valuable beings. Insofar as parents convey to their child a sense of her worth—a value she has in common with all other persons—they begin to lay the foundations for proper moral conduct and social interactions.

'Mind the Gap'

I have been examining the links between good parenting, preference-formation, and personal good. Insofar as my claims and conjectures seem plausible, they help to display some of the sundry connections between what good parents do in seeing to our welfare and in seeing to our development as autonomous agents. By attending to their children's nature and value, effective parents help, in all the ways we have considered, to make their children into more effective formers of their own preferences.

In saying, as I have, that persons who have been well raised will be *more likely* to form preferences the satisfaction of which results in good lives for them, I make note of the residual space that exists between a person's good and the preferences she would form if well raised. Presumably that space exists whether or not one thinks personal good just consists in satisfaction of well-formed and well-ordered preferences, and it exists for a number of reasons.

Before making note of them, we must distinguish this gap from a very different one. This other gap arises because a parent can have a regard for his child in all the ways that I have described, while failing to produce the expected effects. Actual parents, however well they approximate to the ideal we have considered, must work with the children they've got. A child's intellectual capacities and emotional makeup may impede in sundry ways a parent's best efforts; the child may be unable, for instance, to internalize a stable sense of her worth. In such cases, although the child may be better off for having been so raised and may be a better former of preferences than she would otherwise have been, her preferences may still routinely fall far a field from what would, intuitively, benefit her. I have, it seems, presented not only an ideal of parenting but of its effects. Yet these 'ideal effects' are just what should interest us for purposes of theorizing about how preferences ought to be formed—they ought to be formed, I have been suggesting, as if the effects of ideal parenting had been realized. So our real interest at this juncture lies, not with the gap between ideal and actual effects of properly guided parenting but with the gap between a person's good and the preferences she would form if *successfully* well-raised.

Even if parenting has achieved its effects, then, even if a person has acquired a firm sense of her worth and is a self-knowing, well-functioning autonomous agent, she may, simply lack critical, nonevaluative information needed to choose well, information that would alter her preferences.[40] And even if a person forms preferences after imaginative reflection and consideration in light of reasons, her actual reflection may just fall short. In addition, an individual may fail to recognize or properly assess the value of the objects of her preferences. Of course, if a successfully well parented person is just as we've imagined, we can reasonably predict that she will, over time, make efforts to compensate for deficiencies in her own reflective capacities by, say, consulting others. We can also reasonably predict that once she acquires critical information she previously lacked, her preferences will undergo a shift toward ones more consonant with her sense of her own worth, more in keeping with her autonomous functioning and with what she knows more generally about herself and her circumstances. We might also predict, though perhaps with somewhat less confidence, that she will learn over time to distinguish worthless from worthwhile pursuits and undertakings. Nevertheless, for all of the reasons we have just considered, and no doubt others besides, satisfaction of a well-raised person's preferences may depart from her good.

Still, by studying the effects of good parenting, we go some important way toward understanding proper preference-formation, even if we require independent theoretical work to close the gap between preference and personal good. Having gone this far, however, we can better understand and explain what has gone wrong at least in many cases of deformed and adaptive preferences and, more generally, in cases in which our preferences intuitively depart from our good. When the problems with people's preferences arise from limited deprivation, like a lack of adequate education, distortions can often be easily remedied.[41] But the

---

[40] This is, of course, true whether or not one holds an ideal preference or informed-desire theory of welfare.

[41] Martha Nussbaum describes a case involving a village with no reliable supply of clean water. The women had experienced no anger about their physical situation, because they had no recognition that they were malnourished and living in unhealthy conditions. Once adequately

problems commonly arise from more pervasively adverse material and social conditions. Consider the condition of most men and women in Afghanistan under the Taliban. In many such cases, I want to suggest, the deprivation that leads to malformed preferences may be due not simply to desperate circumstances but, more deeply, to the way in which these alter the prospects for a good upbringing.[42]

We can also better appreciate the appeal of certain theories of welfare in light of their resources for addressing the problems with

---

informed about their situation, through government sponsored consciousness raising programs, they began to demand a host of changes. This is just the shift in preference we would expect, a shift toward preferences more consonant with their own value, as well as the value they attach to their children. Nussbaum, p. 69.

[42] Nussbaum describes the case of Vasanti, who stayed in an abusive marriage for a number of years. While disliking her abuse, Nussbaum tells us, she also thought of it as something women simply must tolerate as a part of their role in life once they marry and move into the home of their husbands. Nussbaum, pp. 68–69. We might plausibly explain this case in the following way. Vasanti lives in a culture in which women are not properly valued, and so in being raised, they do not acquire a sense of their own worth but instead are taught that their value is instrumental to the needs of their husbands and children. Moreover, autonomous functioning is not encouraged, and so neither the autonomy making capacities nor the concomitant motives are adequately nurtured. Not having been encouraged to reason and be moved by reasons, not having been encouraged to reflect, not having been stimulated to imagine possibilities, it is no wonder that women like Vasanti may lack a sufficiently critical perspective on their life circumstances and may have trouble envisioning how their circumstances might be better. Whether people are better off for having adjusted their preferences to their limited life prospects is, of course, a complex question. In some cases, we may be inclined to say that a person is better off with her diminished preference scheme; in others, we may judge that the preferences that suit her circumstances deprive her, sadly, of a good life. Whatever we say about a particular case, thinking prospectively, a person arguably fares better if her preferences not adapt, at least not fully, to her difficult circumstances; for she does better to be prepared for the possibility of changed circumstances. Women who illicitly educated girls while the Taliban remained in power presumably took the view that, rather than raise their daughters to accept fully their limited circumstances, they would ready them for a better day. Doing just that, I would suggest, is in keeping with the foregoing account of good parenting and its relation to preference-formation and personal good.

our actual preferences.[43] Consider informed-desire theories, which identify a person's good with what satisfies her informed desires. These theories of welfare rightly stress that we often need far more information than we may have if we are to form preferences satisfaction of which enhances our lives. Fuller information surely would go some way toward offsetting the conditions that lead to deformed, adaptive, or otherwise problematic preferences. But perhaps the most significant information we require concerns ourselves. Unsurprisingly, self-knowledge especially well equips a person to form preferences for those things she can well live with. Unfortunately, self-knowledge can be especially elusive; our actual upbringings—and both our idiosyncratic and shared psychologies—can make it especially difficult to acquire. Any plausible 'reality requirement' on preference-formation would surely include such information, as well as information about a person's character as an autonomous agent, and this may partly explain the appeal of informed-desire theories.[44]

One piece of information informed-desire views, at least as forms of naturalism, must preclude is information about a person's own worth. To be sure, they may include facts about how an individual's life is affected when she has a stable sense of her own worth, but for all the accounts say, that sort of knowledge plays no special role in the formation of preferences. This omission may help to explain the attraction of some sort of 'objective value requirement,' even if one finds perfectionism or objective list theories otherwise unappealing. Theories of welfare that adopt such a requirement would maintain that satisfaction of a person's preferences enhances her life only insofar as she prefers those things that have genuine value.[45] Attention to and recognition of

---

[43] I do not mean to suggest that all welfare theorists see themselves as addressing these problems, though proponents of preference or desire theories of welfare surely do.

[44] I borrow the term 'reality requirement' from Sumner, pp. 158–65, where he contrast a reality requirement with what he calls an 'objective value requirement.'

[45] As Sumner explains, an objective value requirement takes one of two basic forms, depending on whether welfare is thought to have a subjective component. See Ibid., pp. 163–166. The first form holds that a person benefits only from satisfaction of her preferences for objective values, and she benefits regardless of whether she finds engagement with those values satisfying. The second adopts a hybrid approach, maintaining that a person benefits only from satisfying engagement with objective values.

those things that have real worth surely would help to shape more beneficial preferences. For the achievement of a good life does seem to depend on engagement with objective values—most critically, on engagement with one's own value as a person.[46]

Conclusion

I have relied heavily throughout this essay on an ideal of parenting, an ideal that I acknowledge not everyone will accept. But it is an ideal, I want to insist, that matches the sort of creature that we are, and so what it might suggest about preference-formation in turn will tend better to match the sort of good that must be ours as creatures of this kind. I have not attempted to offer a theory of preference-formation, and what I have said will not by itself answer a great many questions that remain. I have not attempted to address the broader roles of information or of objective values in the formation of preferences, for instance, and I have not attempted to address complex questions about the place of our moral and social upbringing. My suggestion has simply been that efforts to construct a theory of preference-formation should be guided by what guides effective formers of our preferences, namely, attention to the nature and value of persons.

[46] The difficulty arises when proponents of objective value requirements attend only to the value of the objects of preferences and not to the value of the preferring individual. Of course, some who reject the idea that persons have value also reject the notion of anything being 'good for' a person in favor of the idea of 'good occurring in the life of' a person. See Thomas Hurka, "'Good' and 'Good For,'" *Mind* 96 (1987): 71–73 and Donald H. Regan, 'Against Evaluator Relativity: A Response to Sen,' *Philosophy & Public Affairs* 12(1983): 89–132. In a more recent essay, in which he criticizes attempts to show the value of rational nature, Regan suggests that Mooreans can accept a picture that comes pretty close to what 'good for' theorists have in mind. See Regan, 'The Value of Rational Nature.' For his most recent discussion of 'good for,' see Donald H. Regan, 'Why Am I My Brother's Keeper?' in R. Jay Wallace, Phillip Pettit, Samuel Scheffler, and Michael Smith, ed., *Reason and Value: Themes From the Moral Philosophy of Joseph Raz* (Oxford: Oxford University Press, 2004).

Leading a Life of One's Own: On Well-Being and Narrative Autonomy

JOHAN BRÄNNMARK

We all want things. And although we might disagree on just how significant our wants, desires, or preferences are for the matter of how well we fare in life, we would probably all agree on some of them having some significance. So any reasonable theory about the human good should in some way acknowledge this. The theory that most clearly meets this demand is of course preferentialism, but even pluralist theories can do so. However, then they will at the same time bring aboard a classical problem for preferentialism, namely that of discriminating among preferences. Not all preferences would seem to make contributions to our well-being and there should be some set of criteria which at least makes it intelligible why there is such a difference and that perhaps can even be used in order to evaluate hard cases.

In what follows here I will start with a brief overview of the kind of approach to the human good that I find most reasonable, namely a holistic one, and I will then go on to discuss how one should, given such an approach, discriminate between different preferences. I will start by explicating why some preferences might, because they have the wrong kind of structure, never contribute to our well-being and I will then go on to account for how even among those that can, many preferences still have this capacity lessened because of an impaired autonomy in the holder of them. Finally, I will conclude with a brief discussion of how such deficient preferences should be treated.

1. Holism about the Human Good

Most philosophical theories about the constituents of the human good are atomistic, or at least they seem to be (since most theorists in the field do not even raise the question of whether one really can, even ideally, judge the quality of lives by assigning values to discrete parts of lives and then simply run these through some function, preferably a simple additive one, to arrive at overall values of the lives—they just proceed as if that is the way to do it). But

Johan Brännmark

even if we were to find, at the end of the day, that atomism is correct, it is not at all obviously the case. Lives are after all not just heaps of events, they are meaningful wholes, and if we look at the way that we judge the quality of other such wholes, like novels, it is clear that there is another possibility: we can judge wholes holistically. This is not the same thing as saying that we judge them by some mysterious form of intuition, it may in fact take quite a bit of analysis in order to get the judgment right; but it does mean that there is a gap between having analyzed the role played by the different parts constitutive of the whole and the estimate of its value, a gap that must be filled by judgment of the whole as a whole.

I am not going to argue for the holistic approach here[1] and much of what I will say is not dependent on such a framework, but it is still the background theory from which I will proceed and there are a few things that should be pointed out about it. To begin with, being a holist is compatible with theorizing about the human good. Take a list like the one presented by James Griffin as the constituents of the human good: (a) accomplishment, (b) the components of human existence (which include such things as autonomy of choice, working limbs and senses, freedom from great pain and anxiety, and political liberty), (c) understanding, (d) enjoyment, and (e) deep personal relations.[2] Griffin seems to be an atomist, but even a holist can acknowledge that one can produce some kind of list like this. There are certainly things that generally are more worthwhile objects of pursuit than others—and, indeed, if we really were unable to say anything of substance about them then we could at any rate hardly be in possession of the kind of discrimination required for judging well about the quality of lives. Compared to traditional conceptions of the human good, holism is most akin to what is sometimes called the objective-list approach. The main difference, which is also what provides the rationale for judging lives holistically, lies in the treatment of meaning; not 'meaning' in the sense of there being an overarching point to life, but in the sense that parts of any given life have a significance that depends on how they are situated within that particular and

[1] I have tried to provide some arguments in 'Good Lives: Parts and Wholes', *American Philosophical Quarterly* 38 (April 2001): 221–31, and 'Leading Lives: On Happiness and Narrative Meaning', *Philosophical Papers* 32 (November 2003): 321–43.
[2] *Well-Being* (Oxford: Clarendon Press, 1986), p. 67.

concrete life. This is why any list of goods is always incomplete since such lists are necessarily formulated in the abstract.

Meaning, or significance, is not just another item on a list—it is a pervasive phenomenon. Since lives are temporally extended wholes, the most obvious analogue to them is, as already hinted at, that of the novel and narrative meaning is probably the most important form of significance involved in determining how well our lives are going, although there is no reason to presume that all relevant forms of significance can be squeezed into this category. Sequencing of events and balancing of thematic threads are however among the kind of phenomena that are most clearly of relevance in this context. Now, the idea that human lives have a narrative structure is one that quite a few philosophers have found appealing,[3] but it is also an idea that one has to treat with some caution. The reason is that it is one of those ideas that can be interpreted both very weakly, in which case it is trivially true, and quite strongly, in which case it is considerably more controversial. The risk is that one will lean towards the weak interpretation when arguing for the position and shift towards the strong one when drawing out the implications. In order to safeguard against this tendency (which can certainly be found in connection with other philosophical ideas as well), it is probably a good idea to emphasize a couple of disanalogies between human lives and novels.

(i) The person leading a life is a mix of author and protagonist, which is something that has no real parallel in the case of literary fiction. We are not quite like literary protagonists in that when they reflect on their lives, they still do so within the confines of their story, whereas we do it from the perspective of someone who *really* can make a difference as to how events will turn out. But more importantly, we are not like authors in a number of respects. Above all we just have to accept a certain world as the more or less given context in which we are to lead our lives. Additionally, most of the major events that shape our lives are partly under the control of others, which

---

[3] Some examples are Alasdair MacIntyre, *After Virtue,* 2nd *Ed.* (Notre Dame: University of Notre Dame Press, 1984), Charles Taylor, *Sources of the Self* (Cambridge, Mass.: Harvard University Press, 1989), Mark Johnson, *Moral Imagination* (Chicago: University of Chicago Press, 1993), Owen Flanagan, 'Multiple Identity, Character Transformation, and Self-Reclamation' in *Self-Expressions* (New York: Oxford University Press, 1996), and David Velleman, 'Well-Being and Time' in *The Possibility of Practical Reason* (Oxford: Oxford University Press, 2000).

means not just that we can fail because others hinder us, but also that many of our accomplishments involve the help of others and that just how much of an accomplishment something is depends on what our share in it is. And it is not just others; blind nature can often play a crucial role in shaping our lives, not merely in determining how long our lives will be, but also in setting limits on the kind of roles that we effectively can play: we can train and reshape ourselves in a variety of ways, but in the final analysis biology has still dealt us certain cards that we can only try to make the best of.

(ii) Whereas novels are there for the readers to enjoy, lives are not there for the bystanders in any analogous way. And this means that lives cannot be evaluated simply as stories. *Madame Bovary* is a fantastic novel and it portrays a great drama, but Madame Bovary did not lead a particularly good life. Even though we evaluate lives as wholes, the goodness of good lives is still goodness *for* some particular person. This does not mean that lives are good to the extent that the people leading them find them good—we can be wrong about the quality of our own lives—but even if we are not privileged in determining how we fare, it is still we, and no-one else, that are faring more or less well. This also means that we must not confuse the admirability of certain lives with prudential goodness. As a bystander I might be in awe when faced with how some people struggle against insurmountable obstacles, but were I to wish something for their sake I might want them to lead altogether different lives.

(iii) Although there is a certain basic narrative structure of birth-aging-death in human lives, they are otherwise rarely characterized by the coherence of novels or even of collections of short stories. This does not mean that narrative categories are not relevant to the details of our lives; in fact, most of the things we do are performances in accordance or contrast with some kind of script of how situations of different kinds are normally played out. Whether courting a love interest, trying to publish a scientific article, or going to a restaurant, there are certain sequencings of events that we tend to follow and the fact that we follow them is vital in coordinating ourselves with others. In order to be interpersonally intelligible we need to play by the same rules, to know that if we make this move, then we can expect that in return. Scripts ensure this and the existence of them also provides a background of normalcy against which certain deviations acquire specific meanings that our actions can be imbued with—which in some cases might be precisely what we want, but in others might be something that we will have to live with in spite of what we would ideally want to be the case. This fragmented narrativity is indeed one important reason why it is preferable to speak of a holism about the human good, rather than a narrative conception of it.[4] Narrative structures are of paramount importance and human lives always have at least some narrative unity; but when we judge the goodness of lives, we should judge them as wholes with strong narrative elements rather than as narratives proper.

(iv) Even though it does make sense to understand our lives narratively and even though there is a possibility of leading one's life to a lesser or greater extent as one big story, this does not mean that it is better to lead one's life as if it were some great quest or artistic challenge. And it is not just that we are not fully authors of our lives, even to the extent that we are authors our task is not obviously an aesthetic one. Of course, one might certainly have a substantive vision of the human good that is quest-like,[5] but then that is something that one must provide separate arguments for, it is not anything that simply follows from the holistic, or narrative, approach as such.

(v) Unlike novels, human lives are not even moderately self-contained. This means that the significance of particular events in any given life is something determined not just by the way that they are situated in that particular life, but also on the larger context in which that life is situated. The narrative categories we employ are cultural constructs, not only the scripts in accordance with which we play out certain events, but also the personae that we take on.[6] We inhabit certain social roles and depending on which roles we inhabit what on a surface level can look like the same action might, for instance, be either one of neglect or of courage. And it is not just roles

---

[4] The latter is the line taken by Timothy Chappell in *Understanding Human Goods: A Theory of Ethics* (Edinburgh: Edinburgh University Press, 1998).

[5] Alasdair MacIntyre, *ibid.*, p. 219, and Charles Taylor, *ibid.*, p. 48, both embrace this idea of life as a form of quest.

[6] I borrow both of these notions from Richard Nisbett & Lee Ross, *Human Inference: Strategies and Shortcomings of Social Judgment* (Englewood Cliff, N.J.: Prentice-Hall, 1980), pp. 32–5.

like being a parent, a teacher, and so on, that matter; we also understand each other in terms of character types and while such types are usually oversimplifications they still shape the expectations of others and through our sensitivity to these expectations and our tendency to roughly conform to them certain social niches are carved out for us and define who we are. This also means that if we accept that the meaning of the constituents of our lives bear on how well our lives are going, we can never judge the quality of a person's life without taking into account the cultural constructs that are relevant to it. So holism will tend to lead to a weak form of relativism. This does however not preclude that there are substantial things to say on a structural level, and perhaps even to some extent on the level of concrete content, that hold for the human good in general; it is just that such a picture can never give us a complete manual for evaluating lives.

2. Preferences that Matter

One of the perennial problems of theories of well-being that emphasize the role played by preferences or desires is the need to discriminate; not all preferences seem to matter for our well-being and from a philosophical point of view we would want to have a criterion that picks out those that matter and that is able to make sense of this. To begin with, it seems reasonable to say that only intrinsic preferences matter, *i.e.* preferences that do not merely concern means to something else. This much is uncontroversial, although in real life one should perhaps not expect our preferences to neatly fall into the categories of intrinsic and instrumental. Some things (*e.g.* nice-looking kitchen utensils) might be dependent on their instrumental value for us to want them, but they might still have qualities that make us prefer them for their own sake over other potential means. Many things are such that we partly value them instrumentally, partly intrinsically.

The most significant problem in this area is however that it would seem that even among clear-cut intrinsic preferences there are some the fulfillment of which do not make us better off. We might care about the well-being of others, but it does not seem obvious that increases in their well-being would automatically constitute increases in our own. Or we might care for things like saving the mountain gorilla from extinction or that the Darwinian theory of evolution is universally recognized as superior to creationism. Again, even if they are intrinsic preferences, fulfilling them does not seem to make us better off in any direct way. So how do we distinguish between those preferences that matter for well-being and those that do not? The most obvious candidate answer is probably to say that only preferences that are in some way self-referential should count. In order to be able to affect our well-being, they should in some sense be about us, either in the sense that the object of the preference involves us[7] or that we want the thing in question for the sake of ourselves.[8] But the problem is that some selfless preferences might actually be connected to our well-being. For instance, parents want the happiness of their children and they do it not for their own sake, nor are they part of the object of this kind of preferences. But it still seem reasonable to say that if the lives of their children turn out well then that also makes their own lives go better. Or if I really work hard to save the mountain gorilla from extinction, then it does no longer seem unreasonable to say that my life would go better if I succeeded. We are dealing in both cases with successes that are appropriate sources of satisfaction with one's life and if something is such a source then it should surely be understood as a potential source of well-being.

One might perhaps think that the lesson to be learned from these examples is that striving matters. Were I only to idly hope for the preservation of the mountain gorilla then it is more doubtful whether fulfillment of my preference would constitute an improvement in my well-being. Perhaps the key is to demand that preferences that matter should involve effort. But this would be too strong. Even if some things that we want are such that whether we get them is not under our control this hardly means that it would not be good for us were they to land in our laps. For instance, I might throughout my life hope that some rare honor will be bestowed on me while knowing that there is nothing I really can do to ensure that it would happen. Were I then to receive this honor then it seems reasonable to say that it would make my life go better in a way that it would not improve the life of someone who does not care about receiving it. The conclusion to be drawn from

---

[7]   This would be similar to Ronald Dworkin's emphasis on what he calls 'personal preferences' (as opposed to 'external preferences'), see *Taking Rights Seriously* (London: Duckworth, 1978), pp. 234–37.

[8]   This would be a variation on Stephen Darwall's position in *Welfare and Rational Care* (Princeton: Princeton University Press, 2002), Chapter 1, where he emphasizes the dimension concerning *the one for whom* one wants something.

Johan Brännmark

considering this example is that if we are to discriminate among preferences then we will have to look not just at the structure of the preference taken by itself, but rather at the role it has in the life of the person holding it.

Given that our lives are narratively structured one way of examining preferences would be to look at the way that they are narratively embedded. There are two way to go here. One is to look at the having of the preferences, the other to look at the objects. The first alternative would mean that we discriminate among preferences by whether the having of them constitutes a narrative thread or theme in one's life. But if I were to hope for world peace throughout my life, then the realization of world peace would as such hardly make my life go better (although in a variety of indirect ways it probably would). In fact, even if I had done more than idly hope, even if I had taken an active part in the peace movement, it is not clear that the achievement of world peace would make a direct contribution to my well-being. And if we look at the life-narrative I would have in this example there seems to be a problem with regarding the achievement of world peace as directly improving my life since this achievement does not really seem to be a part of *my* life. My taking part in the peace movement is, but not world peace. And, in fact, even if we abstract from the narrative approach, this intuitively seems like a reasonable demand to make: that when considering how well one's life is going, only things that constitute parts of my life are directly relevant for that issue. This suggests that we should opt for the second alternative, to look at the objects of the preferences, or rather to look at whether the events or features that constitute the fulfillment of the preferences also constitute events or features of my life. Only when they do that are they preferences that matter for how well my life is going.

This explanation shows how striving might make a difference for whether a certain selfless preference will matter for my well-being. It is not that the striving as such imbues the preference in question with a special import; it is rather that in some cases the striving might be enough to make the event that would fulfill that preference into an event that is part of my life-narrative. In some cases, such as in the example about world peace, the distance between my striving and the accomplishment is simply too great for it to form a part of my life. In the example with the rare honor being bestowed on me, that event would be part of my life simply because it is something that happens to me rather than being a global occasion. The example with the mountain gorillas lies on an intermediate level and might perhaps go either way. Let us say that

I choose to do something about it. In one scenario I simply donate money to this end, in another I travel to Uganda and work for years in order to achieve it. I think that my desire could be equally strong in both of these scenarios (we can assume that in the first case I have some commitment preventing me from going to Uganda). In the first case success in saving the mountain gorillas would hardly make my life go substantially better, whereas in the second it might very well do so. In both cases I act on my desire, but the difference is that in the first case my doing so is too distanced from the end for the achievement of it to be counted as part of my life. I have helped in making it possible for others to achieve it, but it cannot be said to be partly my achievement. And if we modify the second scenario so that the success would come after my death, again my life would not be made better by it (or at least not in the same direct way that it otherwise would[9]).

Given that there are advantages to this narrative approach, could a strict preferentialist simply borrow the idea that only preferences the fulfillments of which would constitute parts of one's life would be relevant for one's well-being? There is one obstacle to this. It is very difficult to provide exact criteria for when something is a part of a life and when it is not. For a holist this is just what would be expected; he would say that parts and whole stand in a reciprocal relationship and that while the parts constitute the whole, we cannot identify the parts without looking at the whole. And in fact, in order to determine whether something constitutes a part of my life, it is not enough to look at my life in isolation; one must also look at how it is socially embedded. The narrative schemata that are involved in shaping our lives are cultural constructs and the meaning that our pursuits take on is constituted by these schemata, such as the scripts according to which we act and the personae that we take on in our relations with others. So to look at preferences narratively is to take a decisive step towards a position that emphasizes the meaning of constituents of well-being and this is probably a step that strict preferentialists would feel uncomfortable with taking.

[9] Since the meaning of events in my life can be affected by things lying outside my life, my strivings can to a certain extent be made more valuable by posthumous success. Such contributions to how well my life went are however probably not best understood in terms of preference fulfillment and, additionally, are only minor ones (as already Aristotle noted, albeit for quite different reasons). In this case the achievement would still not be a part of my life, but the strivings that are will acquire a different resonance.

Johan Brännmark

The social embeddedness of our lives also means that as holders of preferences we are severely restricted by contingent factors having to do with when and where we happened to be born and by the concrete ways in which we gradually learned to find our way about in the world. In fact, the patchiness of this process of becoming a person raises further doubts about whether all preferences really matter equally, even among those where the events constituting their fulfillment would count as parts of our lives. Even if we can never just choose what to prefer, some preferences still seem particularly suspect in that they are just too heteronomous. Take a slave that has so internalized his master's wishes that he has no real conception of a successful life apart from making his master well off, or take an addict that subordinates everything else to the hunt for some drug—such persons have preferences that might fit the schema suggested above but which are at the same time questionable as sources of well-being for the agent in question. A theory of well-being that includes subjective sources as constituents of a good life should contain a critical potential for assessing the aptness of the subject's own judgments or preferences.

The standard way of appraising our preferences or desires is usually in terms of their structural features or deliberative underpinning. One model for doing this is what might be called the hierarchical affirmation account, which looks at whether our desires are supported by second-order desires, *i.e.* whether the goals that we pursue are also ones with which we identify wholeheartedly.[10] Another, and more popular, model is what might be called idealized preference accounts, according to which the test of our current preferences is what we would prefer if we had all the relevant information and reasoned in a fully rational way. This type of account comes in a great number of varieties and one might distinguish between weak and strong versions of it. Weak versions only offer a test with which we can rule out certain current preferences,[11] whereas strong versions allow the alternative preferences that we would have in this ideal state as bearing on our

---

[10]   A classic piece in which this idea is formulated is Harry Frankfurt's 'Freedom of the Will and the Concept of a Person' in *The Importance of What We Care About* (Cambridge: Cambridge University Press, 1988).

[11]   Richard Brandt's rational desire theory is an example of this approach, see *A Theory of the Good and the Right* (Oxford: Oxford University Press, 1978).

situation now.[12] This is not the place to go into the details, the arguments, and the counter-arguments concerning these accounts; I will only note one general problem with these traditional accounts, namely that they to a far too great extent valorize critical reflection. These accounts so clearly bear the mark of having been formulated by people that have critical reflection as their occupation. Not that critical reflection is a bad thing, but at least in this context we should resist the temptation of a conception of autonomy that emphasizes it, the reason being that such an account would risk being too substantive and perhaps even lead to unacceptably paternalistic conclusions. Take a somewhat simple-minded peasant, one who does not suffer from either oppression or repression, yet for whom his preferences are simply something given. His tastes are unsophisticated and were he to have full information and loose his naivete he would most likely change many of them. Yet, there seems to be no good reason for thinking that his current preferences are unable to contribute to his well-being.[13] One can be unsophisticated and still lead a life of one's own. And so there seems to be reason to articulate a notion of autonomy that is weaker than the standard accounts.

3. Narrative Autonomy

The sense of autonomy that is of interest here is not one that concerns matters of moral responsibility. Rather, what I am interested in is something like the degree to which it makes sense to say of a person that she leads a life of her own. Even though we are social creatures and even though the meaning of what we do is never fully under our control but dependent on the social setting, it would still seem that certain lives are reasonably deemed as being led more autonomously than others. Of course, this might just be

---

[12]   Peter Railton's approach is of this kind, see 'Moral Realism' and 'Facts and Values' in *Facts, Values, and Norms* (Cambridge: Cambridge University Press, 2003).

[13]   Richard Arneson uses a similar line of thought as a general argument against the idea of putting an autonomy constraint on our prudentially relevant preferences, 'Autonomy and Preference-Formation' in Jules L. Coleman & Allen Buchanan (eds.), *In Harm's Way: Essays in Honor of Joel Feinberg* (Cambridge: Cambridge University Press, 1994), p. 65.

an illusion, but here I will at least attempt to formulate a picture of what it means to lead a life of one's own and I will use the phrase 'narrative autonomy' for it.

Now, the most obvious way in which one's freedom can be compromised is when one's choices are dictated by others, for instance by threats of violence or economic sanctions. But while this obviously compromises our freedom, the preferences that arise from such oppression are (normally) not intrinsic ones. The problem then is simply that we do not get what we want or even that we suffer things we positively do not want (and our lives are of course thereby worsened), not that what we basically want is corrupted. The freedom thus compromised is certainly something important, but it is not what is of primary interest here. Narrative autonomy is about wanting things (intrinsically) in the right way. Given a narrative understanding of human lives there are, as already noted, two senses in which we can be positioned with respect to the contents of our lives—one is as something akin to a protagonist, the other as something akin to an author. In neither case should this be understood in strict analogue to the case of literary fiction—already the fact that we are a bit of both precludes this. Yet, it does also seem reasonable that we really should be a bit of both in more than a superficial sense, so these two dimensions are accordingly plausible candidates for being used in order to understand what it means to lead a life of one's own. I will now try to delineate what this would entail.

(i) The Agent as Protagonist

It might seem that one cannot but help being the protagonist of one's life and in a very general sense that is certainly true. But as already noted, few of us lead lives that are in any substantial sense constituted by a single big storyline running from birth to death. Rather, our lives are constituted by a number of narrative threads that are of different lengths, sometimes intertwining, sometimes being resolved, sometimes being left unresolved; some of them are ones that we give much attention to and that we explicitly understand ourselves in terms of, others are simply formed by the way that we happen to act on a sequence of relevantly connected occasions. Additionally, the applicable cultural constructs, such as scripts and personae, which are involved in me playing out my life are always connected to other such cultural constructs. For me to play a certain part requires others playing their parts. And in one sense there is reciprocity in this: we are all the protagonists of our own lives as well as supporting characters in the lives of others. But if we look at the concrete narrative threads of particular lives there are also ways in which this reciprocity might break down.

The first possibility is that we might find ourselves excluded from the very narratives that happen to be the vital ones for the kind of life stories that are central in the communities where we lead our lives. For instance, to be unloved or unemployed over long stretches of time is (at least under normal circumstances) to be standing on the side-line of life and certain preferences that are formed under such conditions thus take on a resonance that raises issues about their relevance for the well-being of the person in question.[14] A person can adapt her preferences so that they suit the circumstances and while adaptation in general is quite plainly just good sense there are clearly situations where we adapt in ways that make the resulting preferences into simply too much of a surrender to one's situation. To be the protagonist of one's life requires a certain amount of supporting circumstances in terms of a positive narrative embedding of the ways in which one leads one's life. One is always a protagonist of one's life in the abstract, but the sense of being a protagonist that is of interest here is that of being it in the concrete, and that is something which presupposes narrative structures in which we are affirmed as protagonists. But this also means that it is quite possible to have in a reasonable way a set of preferences that involves eschewing concerns like love or work, which are usually so central to the construction of meaningful lives, but where these are held in a way that is different from the hardened unemployed or the disillusioned unloved. The life of a hermit or a monk is one that clearly involves abstaining from things that we usually regard as central to a good human life, but given that these lives are chosen in ways that narratively are structured not as settling oneself in a dead end but rather as a spiritual journey then the preferences involved in such lives are perfectly fine as bases for well-being. Here there are perfectly sound scripts which can provide narrative embedding of the relevant preferences. So the lesson is that we cannot simply look at the preferences or even the way that the person has deliberated before adopting them, we must look at the concrete narrative embedding of them. And on a philosophical level we can thus only say certain quite general things

---

[14] I am grateful to Mozaffar Qizilbash for stressing the importance of this type of problem to me.

about what it is that we are to look for (such as whether the person in question is the protagonist of her own life or not).

The second possibility of failure is that in the concrete we might very well lead our entire lives playing the part of supporting characters in the narrative threads that make up our lives and we can do so in two ways: the first is that we might act in accordance with these scripts in bad faith—we really prefer something else but since that is not feasible we still play along; the second is that we have internalized the ideals of these scripts and made them our own and it is this latter possibility that is of interest here because it means that just getting what we want need not make us better off. If we would have a state where half of the population are servants and the other half masters, then even if their preferences would be fully harmonious and fully satisfied, there would still be something prudentially problematic about that situation. And the reason is that even if the servants got exactly what they wanted, that is something that they want as a part of leading lives that are not really their own. Or to put it differently: they would not be the protagonists of their own lives in a sufficiently substantial sense. What I would suggest here is thus that preferences that are of this kind, that are the preferences of supporting characters, are questionable as potential sources of well-being and that they are so because of the way that they are *actually* embedded rather than because of some counterfactuals that happen to be true of them (such as that we would not have had these preferences were the situation ideal in some sense). And if there are too many preferences of this kind, or a few of them that are too central, then there is room for saying that such a person is not really leading a life of her own. It is not a question of false consciousness in the sense that her true interests lie elsewhere while she believes in an illusion. What is needed for an improvement of her situation is not that she understands that some particular things *really* lie in her own best interest, but that she develops preferences for which the grounds that make sense of them will be in the form of scripts and personae that do not reduce her to the constant role of a supporting character. In fact, it might even be the case that the preferences she ends up with will be roughly the same as the ones she holds now, but since their embeddings would not be the same, they would still be different from her present ones—and unlike them they would be able to fully function as potential sources of well-being. In the here and now it is the actual embedding that matters, not what would hold in a better tomorrow or in some never-never land of ideal agency.

(ii) The Agent as Author

Even if one is the protagonist of one's own life, one can still lead it in a way that involves a rift between oneself as a person and the life that one is leading. To have narrative autonomy, one has to be the kind of person that has reached a sense of what to achieve in a way that has involved making up one's own mind. This presupposes a certain self-trust: to a reasonable extent one has to rely on one's own judgment and not just defer to the judgment of others. One of the most insidious ways in which people can be tyrannized is by being made to think that their own judgment is not good enough and that they must defer to others in order to know what to do. Indeed, this might even be the case with extremely privileged persons that have key roles in the central scripts of their societies. Someone can be a king and still be a person that simply wants what people expect of him to want. However, even if we demand that we lead lives that are not just led the way people around us expect them to be led, it should be made clear that for it to be the case that we are to be counted as authors of our lives, far-reaching originality cannot be a requirement. That would be an unrealistic demand to place on human beings—in a world of five billion people, there is precious little we can do or say that has not roughly been said or done already. What is needed is rather an account of authorship that takes as its contrast something akin to a secretary who is simply writing from dictation. What is needed to possess authorship is to create a space of individuality in the intersections of all the general cultural constructs, sometimes even clichés, that structure our lives.

The ideal here is not that of a person explicitly distancing herself from her impulses and asking questions about their grounds, which is the kind of ideal usually put forward by theorists of autonomy in the Kantian tradition. Rather it is an ideal of being a melting pot of influences, of being someone who is not compartmentalized and who does not merely follow influences on a one-by-one basis, but who lets her different influences cast light on each other. Authorship is thus not about making non-influenced choices, it is about influences from different persons and different times blending with each other. It is through that blending of influences that one's own voice and a power of judgment emerges. It involves a kind of wholeness that is similar to the one that is thought to characterize the *phronimos* in the Aristotelian tradition. One need however not be a *phronimos* to be characterized by it. It should also be noted that what we are talking about here is not simply coherence whatever form it might take—since having one's voice comes through a blending of influences, it must be a reciprocal form of wholeness. One might think of a drug addict that is wholeheartedly an addict, but then that is because one side of him has completely subjugated his other sides. Such a person might speak in a single voice, but we are still dealing with the voice of his addiction, not a voice of his own.

Still, although such reciprocal wholeness is important, it would be unrealistic to require that complete wholeness is necessary for possessing authorship in general. We might certainly suffer local breakdowns of this aspect of autonomy without losing authorship in general. And it is quite clear that we sometimes have what might be called 'dangling' preferences, ones that we have with respect to possible events in certain circumstances simply because other people have similar preferences and they thus involve stances that appear to be the natural ones to take. These are preferences that have no real footing in our personalities and they can reasonably be regarded as heteronomous, *i.e.* they are not ours in any interesting sense of the word. Such preferences can be discounted as possible bases for improvements in our well-being. Of course, they are usually quite weak as well, but the point here is that there is something more than their weakness that makes them matter less than other preferences.

But might it not reasonably be wondered whether this demand for wholeness is not too strong; will it not too harshly discriminate against certain kinds of life, ones that are free and impulsive? It must however be remembered that there are impulses and there are impulses. One can certainly follow one's impulses, both external and internal, in a way that results in an existence that amounts to considerably more than the life of a vane. Impulses can spring to mind almost instinctively while still having been mediated by one's experiences. Indeed, if we really followed our impulses without even this kind of previous unconscious mediation, then it really is a bit difficult to see why the satisfaction of them should actually matter that much to us. And the reason is that they simply are not ours in any interesting sense of the word.

None of us is ever fully an author. Human existence is too complex for that. But although it might be difficult to say exactly where the line goes beyond which different lapses in authorship are typical rather than atypical, there is still such a line and most of us are comfortably on the safe side of it. On a general level the demand that we are authors is accordingly a very weak demand, one where failures to meet it require special circumstances like addiction, brainwashing, indoctrinating forms of upbringing, or especially overpowering social pressure. Still, some people do have the misfortune to live under such conditions and the question then becomes how we should behave with respect to them.

4. Moral and Political Implications: Some Brief Comments

Given that there are things that can decrease our narrative autonomy, making the lives we lead not fully our own, the question is what the implications for our well-being would be. The natural conclusion would seem to be that the fulfillment of non-autonomous preferences cannot make our lives go as well as the fulfillment of autonomous ones. Yet there is something like a dilemma here. Since oppressed people are the ones whose preferences will be most distorted, they would be the most likely candidates for having their preferences judged to be not fully their own. Were one then to disregard such preferences, they would seem to be doubly damaged: first by being oppressed, then by being having their wants discounted.

However, from the fact that certain people under present circumstances really cannot have their lives go truly well (for that they would need narrative embeddings in which they are affirmed as protagonists of their lives and/or enabling conditions where they can have the kind of wholeness necessary for being authors), it does not follow that their preferences should generally be given less weight under present circumstances. The Rawlsian distinction between ideal and non-ideal theory[15] is an important one in this context. A theory of the human good is a theory concerning what should ideally be the case, but when we find ourselves in a situation where this ideal is unreachable (at least in the short run), then we should also have non-ideal theory about what to do then. So even if we ideally find it reasonable to fulfill the preferences that yield more welfare than those that yield less, we need not find this standard the relevant one under our present circumstances. Rather, a more attractive approach would be to say that if we find ourselves in a situation where the narrative autonomy of some people is compromised, the appropriate response is to generally give their current preferences the same weight as the preferences of others, while at the same time trying to change the circumstances in which

[15] *A Theory of Justice* (Cambridge, Mass.: Harvard University Press, 1971), pp. 245–50.

these preferences have their basis.[16] Of course, these two objectives can come in conflict with each other and in that case one would have to weigh the importance of the possible gains in improving the situation of the narratively disadvantaged against losses in the fulfillment of current wants. But that is simply a trade-off and we always have to deal with those.

In addition to this, even when our narrative autonomy is compromised it seems overly harsh to embrace the position that our current preferences do not matter at all for our well-being rather than the weaker claim that the prudential value of their fulfillment is lessened. Circumstances might be far from perfect, but as human beings in this world we never lead lives that are so fully not our own that our preferences must be regarded as completely alien. So it seems reasonable to say that, on the whole, to get what we want is always at least a *pro tanto* good for us. It is just that when we are not in possession of narrative autonomy, we could have been even better off had the circumstances been different.

[16] For a similar approach, although framed in terms of identities instead, see Nancy Fraser, 'From Redistribution to Recognition? Dilemmas of Justice in a 'Postsocialist' Age', *New Left Review,* no. 212 (July/August 1995): 68–93.

Well-Being, Adaptation and Human Limitations*

MOZAFFAR QIZILBASH

Introduction

Philosophical accounts of human well-being face a number of significant challenges. In this paper, I shall be primarily concerned with one of these. It relates to the possibility, noted by Martha Nussbaum and Amartya Sen amongst others, that people's desires and attitudes are malleable and can 'adapt' in various ways to the straitened circumstances in which they live. If attitudes or desires adapt in this way it can be argued that the relevant desires or attitudes fail to provide a reliable basis for evaluating well-being. This is, what I shall call the 'adaptation problem'. Nussbaum and Sen have—in different ways used this argument to motivate their versions of the 'capability approach'. However, questions remain about the implications of adaptation for philosophical accounts of well-being.

In considering the way in which the adaptation problem can pose difficulties for various views of well-being, I take there to be a significant constraint on such views. In his more recent works, James Griffin has, I think rightly, argued that there are limitations to a human being's capacities—whether these relate to calculative powers, the acquisition and retention of information or impartiality.[1] Griffin thinks that this is particularly significant for ethics because moral philosophers have tended to work with too abstract a picture of human agents. While Griffin has focused on the implications of this point for accounts of moral norms, it is also relevant to accounts of well-being.

In this paper, I am concerned with adaptation and human limitations in the context of a number of influential accounts of well-being. I consider in turn: various versions of the desire account (including Griffin's version of the 'informed desire account'); Wayne Sumner's view of welfare as authentic happiness; prudential value list views (particularly as articulated in Griffin's

---

[1] See, in particular, his *Value Judgement: Improving Our Ethical Beliefs* (Oxford: Clarendon Press, 1996).

later work); and versions of the capability approach developed by Martha Nussbaum and Amartya Sen.

1. Desires, Human Limitations and Adaptation

An appealing approach to thinking about well-being involves seeing it in terms of the satisfaction of desires. It is well-known, however, that there are serious difficulties with any such account, if it focuses on people's *actual* desires.[2] People's actual desires are too often unrelated to what is good for them or in their *interests*. Yet it is the latter that an account of well-being should provide.[3] Some of the reasons why people's desires might not be closely related to their interests have to do with people's limited human capacities. People's desires sometimes reflect their limited ability to acquire and retain information and the bounds of their rationality.[4] It seems plausible to suppose that if they had all the relevant information and were rational their desires would be closely connected with their interests. This intuition is the basis of 'informed' or 'rational' desire accounts.

There are a number of versions of the 'rational' or 'informed' desire account. On Henry Sidgwick's formulation of it, 'a man's future good on the whole is what he would now desire and seek on the whole if all the consequences of all the different lines of conduct open to him were accurately foreseen and adequately realised in imagination at the present point in time'.[5] On Richard Brandt's more recent and influential account a 'rational' desire is a desire that is not an *irrational desire*: an irrational desire is 'one which would *not* survive, in a given person, in the presence of vivid

[2] See James P. Griffin, *Well-Being: Its Meaning, Measurement and Moral Importance* (Oxford: Clarendon Press, 1986), 1–39.

[3] I set aside well-known problems relating to whether the desire account should focus on a person's 'self-regarding' desires as well as those that relate to the prospective nature of desires. The problems I discuss arise even if those problems could, somehow, be solved.

[4] While weakness of will is very pertinent to human limitations in the context of accounts of well-being, I do not discuss it here since it is already much discussed in the literature. See, for example, my 'The Concept of Well-Being,' *Economics and Philosophy*, 14, No. 1, (April, 1998), 58–61.

[5] Henry Sidgwick, *The Method of Ethics* (Indianapolis: Hackett, 1981), 111–112.

awareness of knowable propositions'. [6] On a fuller formulation of this view, Brandt describes the process of 'confronting desires with relevant information, by repeatedly representing it, in an ideally vivid way, and at an appropriate time' as *cognitive psychotherapy*.[7] A person's desire is then 'rational' if it would survive or be produced by careful cognitive pshychotherapy. Brandt characterises the process of confronting desires with relevant information etc. in this way because 'it relies on available information, without influence by prestige of someone, use of evaluative language, extrinsic reward or punishment, or use of artificially induced feeling-states such as relaxation'.[8] His concern is to rule out 'mistaken' desires of various sorts, whether these be generated by ignorance or social conditioning. Inasmuch as Brandt argues that some desires or aversions generated by deprivation in childhood and 'cultural transmission' would not survive cognitive psychotherapy, his account may address some forms of adaptation.[9] Yet as a number of commentators have pointed out, Brandt's account may not rule out some desires which seem irrational—in the ordinary sense of the term.[10] For example, while a desire to be the centre of attention does not promote any interest of mine, and I know this after years of analysis, it nonetheless survives. Or, suppose that I have an obsessive desire to count the blades of grass on the lawns of Oxford colleges. In this case also, in the absence of factual error and acquaintance with all available information, the relevant desire might persist while its satisfaction does not promote any interest of mine. So while Brandt's 'rational' desire account seems to deal with some reasons why there is a gap between our desires and what is good for us, there are nonetheless cases where satisfaction of 'rational' desires does not seem to be constitutive of well-being.

Close relations of Brandt's account are the informed desire accounts associated with James Griffin and Peter Railton. Griffin's account in his *Well-Being* involves a number of formulations of the information requirement which must be met if a desire is to count as 'informed'. One of these runs: 'an "informed" desire is one

---

[6] Richard B. Brandt, *Morality, Utilitarianism and Rights* (Cambridge: Cambridge University Press, 1992), 40.

[7] *A Theory of the Good and the Right*, 113.

[8] Ibid., 113.

[9] Ibid., 116–120 and 122–126.

[10] See for example, James, P. Griffin, *Value Judgement: Improving Our Ethical Beliefs* (Oxford: Clarendon Press, 1996), 21 and Allan Gibbard, *Wise Choices, Apt Feelings* (Oxford: Clarendon Press, 1990), 18.

formed by appreciation of the nature of its object, and it includes anything necessary to achieve it'.[11] However, Griffin identifies 'the technical sense' of 'informed desires' with desires which avoid all the faults he finds with actual desires[12] and these go beyond those faults which relate purely to a lack of information and rationality in any ordinary sense. Griffin then relates 'information' to 'what advances plans of life' and 'information is *full*' on his view 'when more, even when there is more, will not advance them further.' [13] Griffin's criterion for a desire to be 'informed'—at least in the 'technical sense' of 'informed'—is clearly demanding. It goes beyond Brandt's standard for a 'rational' desire, since some faults in our actual desires may not be corrected in 'rational desires'.

Griffin notes various worries about his version of the informed desire account. One concern is that, if according to the informed desire account what makes for well-being lies in the features or properties of the objects of informed desire, then desire itself does not play much of a role.[14] Griffin himself goes on to present his list of 'prudential values'—i.e. of those things that make a distinctively human life go better. While these are thought of as the objects of informed desire in *Well-Being*, they can, nonetheless, be articulated without any reference to informed desire. Indeed, in Griffin's later work, prudential values remain at the centre of the stage, though they are no longer discussed within the framework of an informed desire account. [15] I shall return to this point in section 3.

The key point to note is that the requirement for someone to have all the information that advances his or her life plan is so strong that it may often be beyond human beings, given their limited capacities for acquiring and retaining information. The strategy of 'idealising' desires so that they match with people's interests may go so far that the idealised desires are hardly *human desires* at all. Of course, informed desires are not supposed to be our actual desires (even if these were fairly well informed), but desires we *would have* if we had full information. However, given our limited capacities, it remains difficult to make sense of this

---

[11]   *Well-Being*, 14.
[12]   Ibid., 12–14.
[13]   Ibid., 13.
[14]   Ibid., 17.
[15]   Wayne Sumner also notes the shift in Griffin's thought in L.W. Sumner, 'Something in Between', *Well-Being and Morality: Essays in Honour of James Griffin* R. Crisp and B. Hooker (eds.) (Oxford, Clarendon Press, 2000), 2–4.

counterfactual. It is worth noting, nonetheless, that when Griffin defines informed desires as those formed with an appreciation of the nature of their object, it is not obvious that the standard he is using is quite as demanding as that implied by his 'technical sense' of informed desire, since such appreciation is often clearly within our grasp. [16]

A related line of criticism can be found in Connie Rosati's work. Her critique of some informed desire accounts does not focus on Griffin's formulation but on others, including Peter Railton's. On Railton's view we are to imagine an idealised version of the person. Suppose we are concerned with A. We must give him 'unqualified cognitive and imaginative powers, and full factual and nomological information about his physical and pshychological constitution, capacities, circumstances, history, and so on.' [17] A has then become A+, an idealised version of A with 'complete and vivid knowledge of himself and his environment, and whose instrumental rationality is in no way defective'. [18] A+ is to advise A about what he would want A to want. A+ can be seen as A's 'ideal advisor'. One of Rosati's lines of criticism of this account questions whether a *person* can be suitably informed in the relevant way. Suppose that this ideal advisor is to advise A on which of all the lives that are open to him is best. The advisor would, on Rosati's view, have to have adequate information and knowledge to get a sense for how all the relevant lives feel from the inside, with each life having its own feel and perspective, while retaining a knowledge of the life and circumstances of A. A+ would then survey all the relevant lives to see which would be best for A. Rosati rightly notes that such an idealised version of the person would have to have 'capacities of reason, memory, and imagination far surpassing those' the person actually has. [19] In fact she suggests that these capacities are such that we could not, without violating the laws of psychology and physiology, fully inform a person. [20] Put another way, the ideal adviser would not be a human being at all, given the limitations on human capacities. This problem is surely not adequately addressed by suggesting that the ideally informed person does not need to

[16] I am grateful to James Griffin for pointing this out to me.

[17] Peter Railton, 'Moral Realism', *The Philosophical Review*, XCV, No. 2 (April 1986), 173.

[18] Ibid., 174.

[19] Connie Rosati, 'Persons, Perspectives and Full Information Accounts of the Good', *Ethics*, 105, No. 2 (January 1995), 310.

[20] Ibid., 315.

experience all the lives which are open for choice, but merely propositional knowledge that is relevant to these lives. [21] Acquiring all the relevant knowledge would sometimes be beyond human capacities.

How do informed desire accounts deal with the adaptation problem? There are at least two possibilities here. The first is articulated by James Griffin. He suggests that:

> Our desires are shaped by our expectations, which are shaped by our circumstances. Any injustice in the last infects the first. There is no denying that some accounts of well-being will, therefore, distort moral thought in this way. Actual-desire accounts will. A moral theory should not use as its base persons' actual expectations. It has to get behind them to what are in some sense legitimate expectations ... It does not matter if some persons have modest expectations; their informed desires include what they would want if they raised their sights,... [22]

On this view, the desires of people who have adapted in the light of their straitened circumstances, which lead to diminished expectations, are not 'informed'. It is not surprising that Griffin takes this line. For him informed desires are simply those formed with an appreciation of the nature of their objects. If adaptation poses a genuine problem for actual desire views, on Griffin's account, it must be because adaptation can undermine a person's appreciation of the nature of the objects of desire. The adaptation problem does not, thus, cause a problem for the informed desire account. At a purely *formal* level, this seems to be a solution to the adaptation problem.

Richard Arneson takes a rather different approach to informed desire accounts in the context of adaptation. He contrasts an ideal advisor version of the informed desire account with an 'objective-list theory' which—on Derek Parfit's definition—is a theory according to which 'certain things are good or bad for us, whether or not we want the good things, or want to avoid the bad things'. [23] Arneson considers two examples, one involving someone with very

---

[21]   Richard Arneson suggests this response, in Richard Arneson, 'Human Flourishing Versus Desire Satisfaction', *Human Flourishing* E.F. Frankel, F. D. Miller, Jr., J. Paul (ed.) (Cambridge: Cambridge University Press, 1999), 129–130.

[22]   *Well-Being*, 47.

[23]   Derek Parfit, *Reasons and Persons* (Oxford, Oxford University Press, 1984), 493.

demanding ambitions, and another involving lack of ambition. It is the latter case which is relevant to the adaptation problem. Arneson writes that:

> Someone in unfortunate circumstances forms quite limited and unambitious desires that are reasonable given the bleak conditions she faces. Being blind, I don't have ambitions that require eyesight; being impoverished, I don't form ambitions that require wealth to have a reasonable prospect of success; being unintelligent I don't form ambitions that would strain my limited brain power; and lacking social connections, I don't form ambitions that can be achieved only with the help of powerful allies. Judged against the baseline of my original grim life circumstances, I am reasonably lucky and most of my important desires are fulfilled over the course of my life. These desires are not ill-chosen and would be endorsed and affirmed by the fully informed and rational ideal advisor whose advice determines what is prudentially valuable according to full-information accounts of the good. In these circumstances it seems that I succeed in leading a good, choiceworthy life according to informed-desire fulfilment, but not by a plausible application of an objective-list theory. [24]

This reading of adaptation and informed desire is clearly quite different from Griffin's. For Arneson, this example suggests that there is a case for rejecting informed desire views in favour of an objective-list theory. His understanding of the informed desire account is based on an interpretation of the views of Richard Brandt and Peter Railton. Since the desires of the unfortunate person in this example are restricted precisely because of his information about the world, his limited capacities and what one can reasonably achieve in the light of that information, making the information more vivid, or increasing one's powers of reasoning will not make the adaptation problem any less serious.

Arneson admits that Griffin's view is not an informed desire account of the sort he is concerned with. He thinks that the view Griffin 'ends up defending is complex, and not unambiguously a full information account.' [25] One reason for this is, no doubt, that Griffin's account is relatively close to an objective-list theory. Indeed, Griffin states that the informed desire account 'has to set the standards for a desire being "informed" in a place not too

[24] 'Human Flourishing Versus Desire Satisfaction', 133.
[25] Ibid., 126.

distant from an objective-list account'. [26] Nonetheless, Griffin's view links the components of well-being with desire (albeit in a complex way) and this distinguishes it from an 'objective-list theory'. While Griffin's informed desire view seems to deal with the adaptation problem at a formal level, the 'technical sense' of 'informed desire' that he proposes sets very tough standards for a desire to be 'informed'. It is because versions of the informed desire account tend to set such tough standards that they do not leave much space for human limitations. Griffin's later work may be seen as even closer to an objective list theory, and I return to it in section 3.

2. Authentic Happiness, Autonomy and Sour Grapes

In his *Welfare, Happiness and Ethics* Wayne Sumner rejects the desire account. Instead he suggests that welfare 'consists in authentic happiness, the happiness of an informed and autonomous subject'. [27] 'Happiness' here refers to a positive evaluation of the conditions of one's life, 'a judgement that, at least on balance, it measures up favourably to your standards and expectations'. [28] The information requirement used in this account relates to the 'relevance' of such information, which in turn relates to 'whether it would make a difference to a subject's affective response to her life, given her priorities'. [29] Sumner thinks that if someone's endorsement of her life is factually uninformed, or misinformed, 'that gives us one reason for doubting its authority'. [30] While this information requirement is perhaps less demanding than those adopted in some informed desire views, it clearly does some of the same work.

Sumner argues that an information requirement cannot adequately deal with the adaptation problem. He takes the issue very seriously, because according to his account the evaluation of one's life relates to one's 'standards and expectations'. If these standards and expectations have been seriously affected by disadvantage, that must distort the metric of happiness. He writes

[26] Ibid., 34.
[27] L.W. Sumner, *Welfare, Happiness and Ethics* (Oxford: Clarendon Press, 1996), 172.
[28] Ibid.,145.
[29] Ibid.,160.
[30] Ibid.,161.

that: 'the requirement that endorsement be empirically informed will not suffice to exclude ... social influences on the standards by which people judge how well their lives are going; the problem here is rooted not in the adequacy of people's factual information but in the malleability of their personal values'. [31]

Sumner's discussion of the adaptation problem focusses almost entirely on a passage from Amartya Sen's *On Ethics and Economics*, where Sen expresses worries about the metric of 'utility' when this is understood in terms of desire-satisfaction or happiness. He writes:

> A person who has had a life of misfortune, with very limited opportunities, and rather little hope, may be more easily reconciled to deprivations than others reared in more fortunate and affluent circumstances. The metric of happiness may, therefore, distort the extent of deprivation, in a specific and biased way. The hopeless beggar, the precarious landless labourer, the dominated housewife, the hardened unemployed or the overexhausted coolie may all take pleasures in small mercies, and manage to suppress intense suffering for the necessity of continued survival, but it would be ethically deeply mistaken to attach a correspondingly small value to the loss of their well-being because of this survival strategy. [32]

Sumner's response to this problem involves supposing that we do not take at face value the life satisfaction reported by the hopeless beggar, the dominated housewife, etc. because their 'standards for self-assessment have been artificially lowered or distorted by processes of indoctrination or exploitation'. [33] He thinks that the common feature of these cases is that the relevant people lack *autonomy*. In responding to this problem, Sumner suggests that happiness or life satisfaction should only count as authentic if it is autonomous. In considering how to incorporate what is, in effect, an 'autonomy requirement' he follows John Christman in suggesting that one significant factor determining whether or not a value is autonomous relates to the manner in which it was formed.

[31] Ibid.,162.

[32] Amartya K. Sen, *On Ethics and Economics* (Oxford: Blackwell, 1987), 45–6. For a discussion of Sen's examples see Miriam Teschl and Flavio Comim 'Adaptive Preferences and Capabilities', Paper presented at a conference on Capability and Happiness, St. Edmund's College, Cambridge, March 2004.

[33] *Welfare, Happiness and Ethics*, 166.

Looking at the process of forming values is not, however, adequate on its own. We need also to be able to distinguish 'normal' processes of socialization from those that are 'manipulative'. Following this line of thought, Sumner ends up articulating the following autonomy requirement for socialization processes: 'an autonomy-preserving socialization process will be one which does not erode the individual's capacity for critical assessment of his values, including the values promoted by the process itself.' [34] While his account is developed in defence of a happiness view of welfare, it is easy to see how this response to the adaptation problem could be applied to desire accounts. One would have to exclude those desires that are formed as a result of socialisation processes which erode the capacity for critical assessment of values or objects of desire, including values or objects of desire promoted by the process.

Sumner's response works well for cases of adaptation where there is clearly a form of indoctrination or some other social process at work. It may be particularly useful when one is concerned with a socialisation process or a social institution which encourages women to be submissive. It is less obviously pertinent to the attitudes of the overworked coolie, the precarious landless labourer or the hardened unemployed. In these cases, the relevant attitudes may not necessarily be part of a socialisation process. Rather they can—as Sen suggests—be part of a survival strategy that the relevant people have themselves adopted in the light of their life circumstances. Those circumstances need not emerge through a process of indoctrination or socialisation. [35] They may just be the result of bad luck. Resignation to such circumstances may, in some cases, help to avoid anxiety. However, even if, by avoiding anxiety, the hardened unemployed remains relatively satisfied with his life, one might suspect that his well-being is quite a bit lower than would be suggested by an autonomous and informed self-assessment. For this reason, I suggest that Sumner's attempt to address the adaptation problem does not adequately deal with the cases that Sen mentions.

Sumner's discussion is in some ways related to, while also different from, Jon Elster's classic discussion of 'adaptive preferences'. Like Sumner, Elster suggests that the key problem is lack of autonomy. However, Elster individuates the notion of

[34]   Ibid., 170.
[35]   Indeed, the case of the hardened unemployed may be better understood in terms of 'social exclusion' rather than socialization.

adaptive preference very sharply, so that it is exclusively related to the phenomenon of 'sour grapes'. This phenomenon is exemplified by La Fontaine's tale: the fox who, dying of hunger, cannot reach some ripe grapes finds them to be too green and fit only for boors ('goujats'). [36] Elster sets about distinguishing it from a variety of related phenomena, including certain forms of manipulation and indoctrination. [37] Here Elster argues that in the phenomenon of adaptive preferences even if '[i]t is good for the rulers that the subjects are resigned to their situation, ... what brings about the resignation—if we are dealing with sour grapes—is that it is good for the subject.' [38] He also distinguishes the case of adaptive preferences from the case of 'character planning' where someone intentionally shapes her desires. It is crucial to the case of adaptive preferences, as he defines it, that the process which leads to them works 'behind the backs' of those who adapt.

The scope of Elster's notion of 'adaptive preferences', as regards the range of examples it covers, is quite different from that of the adaptation problem. Clearly a woman who responds to her living conditions by adopting commonly held beliefs and desires consistent with her having a subordinate role in the household would exemplify the 'adaptation problem'. However, if her change of beliefs and desires was a form of manipulation or indoctrination which benefits men in society, that would not necessarily classify as a case of adaptive preferences on Elster's account. On the other hand, one might adapt one's preferences—in Elster's sense—even if one were not living a particularly blighted life. If John's love for a beautiful woman is not requited, he might cease to see her as beautiful. While this would not be an example of the adaptation problem, it would certainly be a case of 'adaptive preferences' in Elster's terms.

Nonetheless, Elster's attempt at defining an autonomy require-ment is relevant here. His 'condition on the autonomy of preferences' states—very roughly—that preference reversals ought not to occur if the feasible set that a person faces changes. [39] Whatever its merits, this condition, formulated as it is to home in on the 'sour grapes' problem, does not cover the range of cases which Sen discusses where a person becomes reconciled to

  [36] Ibid., 109.
  [37] Ibid., 115–7.
  [38] Ibid., 116.
  [39] Ibid., 131.

deprivation. So, as with Sumner's autonomy requirement, Elster's condition does not cover the range of examples where the adaptation problem arises.

It is worth noting that Elster also distinguishes his examples of adaptive preferences from cases where preferences are formed through some form of 'learning'. One's preferences may be shaped by past experiences. Having lived in cities for most of one's life, one might prefer to live in cities rather than the country. An experience of living in the country might, of course, change one's preferences. Elster—following John Stuart Mill's well-known discussion of 'competent judges'[40] —thinks that '[o]ne should attach more weight to the preferences of someone who knows both sides of the question than to [those of] someone who has at most experienced one of the alternatives.' [41] He adds that '[t]hese informed preferences are, of course, those of the individual concerned, not of some superior body. They are informed in the sense of being grounded in experience, not in the sense of being grounded in the meta-preferences of the individual.' [42] This notion of informed preference may avoid some difficulties with standard full information accounts. It could, on Elster's view, be implemented through a policy which gave people the opportunity to try out new alternatives. [43] While this is an interesting suggestion, it is unlikely to help in the cases of the hardened unemployed and the dominated housewife. Their predicament—as Sen explained it—involved a lack of opportunities. They may be aware that there are alternatives (which they may indeed have experienced in the past), but see these as ones they cannot, for lack of opportunity, pursue in their current predicament. They may, thus, be informed in Elster's sense, but resigned nonetheless. So this notion of informed preference does not deal with the adaptation problem.

Finally, Johan Brännmark has also suggested a 'narrative autonomy' requirement which might deal with the problem of adaptation in developing his 'holistic' approach to well-being. [44] Brännmark's notion of narrative autonomy involves a person leading 'a life of her own'. It sees her as occupying the positions of

[40]   John Stuart Mill, *Utilitarianism, On Liberty, Essay on Bentham* (ed.) M. Warnock, (Glasgow: William Collins Sons & Co.), 261.
[41]   Ibid.,113.
[42]   Ibid., 113.
[43]   Ibid., 114.
[44]   Johan Brännmark, 'Leading a Life of One's Own: On Well-Being and Narrative Autonomy,' this volume.

both 'protagonist' and 'author' in relation to the contents of her life. On this account the position of a person as 'protagonist' might be undermined by adaptation. In the case of the hardened unemployed, Brännmark suggests that this might occur because his preferences may involve 'too much of a surrender' to his situation.[45] Similarly, in the case of servants who have internalised the norms of their society so that they are happy to play the role of 'supporting characters' in a narrative, Brännmark suggests that 'they would not be the protagonists of their own lives in a sufficiently substantial sense'.[46] Does Brännmark's formulation of the autonomy requirement cover the cases of adaptation that Sen mentions? I am not convinced that it does. When the hardened unemployed and the precarious landless labourer suppress their suffering, this is, on Sen's account, a survival strategy. To this degree, it may not necessarily involve 'too much of a surrender' to their situation. It may rather be the best way of addressing and coping with it. If that is the case, they may well remain 'protagonists' in the way they see the contents of their lives. If the survival strategy succeeds, and their lives improve, they may later recall, or recount, how they coped in less fortunate times. So I suggest that there is at present no form of autonomy requirement which adequately deals with the adaptation problem.

3. Prudential Value List Views

In *Well-Being*, James Griffin's account is formulated as an informed desire account. Even in this formulation, as we saw, the mere fact that a desire is fulfilled is of no real significance. Unsurprisingly even in *Well-Being* Griffin hesitates about whether to describe his account as a desire account. [47] In his later book *Value Judgement*, Griffin suggests in discussing the 'taste model'—which sees something as valued because it is desired—that the mere fact that informed or rational desire accounts retain the word 'desire' does not show that much if any of the 'taste model' survives in such accounts. [48] In most standard desire accounts, by contrast, this model is central. Such accounts include the 'informed preference' account in John Harsanyi's later writings. In this part of

[45]   'Leading a Life of One's Own,' 77.
[46]   Ibid., 78.
[47]   *Well-Being*, 34.
[48]   *Value Judgement*, 23.

his work, Harsanyi argues that the objects of informed preferences are prudential values. [49] However, what makes these objects intrinsically valuable is that they are objects of 'basic desires'. [50]

By contrast, Griffin paints a complex picture of the relationship between desire and value, which is very critical of the 'taste model'. [51] He thinks that we need an account of prudential values—an account of those things that make a distinctively human life go better. Griffin's list of such values has remained remarkably constant over the years. It includes: the components of a characteristically human existence (freedom from great anxiety and pain, basic capabilities, autonomy, liberty and minimum material provision); understanding; accomplishment—the sort of achievement that gives a life point and weight; deep personal relations; and enjoyment. [52] Inasmuch as Griffin's discussion of well-being in his later work is not best characterised as a desire account, I describe it here as a 'prudential value list view.'

Griffin's later work is attentive to the nature of human capacities and the limits of information. Much of what he says about the good life focusses on prudential values and deliberation about such values. Since deliberation about prudential values must be concerned with what makes a *distinctively* human life better, it must of necessity take account of the fact that we are not omniscient beings or endowed with perfect powers of calculation. Indeed, in *Value Judgement* Griffin sees prudential values as relating to two aspects of human nature—the biological and the rational or intentional aspect. [53] His discussion of prudential deliberation is clearly related to his earlier work and he suggests that we can sensibly claim that prudential judgements can be correct. Underlying his account of the correctness of such judgements is a view of sensitivity to prudential values, and a picture of what would constitute failure of such sensitivity. [54] While he admits that such

[49] John C. Harsanyi, 'Utilities, Preferences and Substantive Goods', *Social Choice and Welfare* 14, (1997), 129–145. For a comparison of Harsanyi's and Griffin's positions see my, 'Griffin, Harsanyi and Others at the Fuzzy Borderline Between Economics and Philosophy', *Telos*, X, No. 1, (2001), 99–119.

[50] 'Utilities, Preferences and Substantive Goods,' 141.

[51] See particularly James P. Griffin, 'Against the Taste Model', *Interpersonal Comparisons of Well-Being*, J. Elster and J. Roemer (ed) (Cambridge: Cambridge University Press), 45–69.

[52] *Value Judgement*, 29–30.

[53] Ibid., 53–4.

[54] Ibid., 57–9.

'sensitivity is complex in its workings and fairly rich in its connections', he thinks that 'we can say a fair amount about what is needed to make it work well.' [55] On his view one needs 'a lot of knowledge of the familiar, undisputed factual sort about the world. One has to have sufficient capacities to know how enjoyment, say, figures in a human life.' [56] This is not, I suggest, too demanding. I have also argued elsewhere, that individuating prudential values does not require the 'full information' invoked in some informed desire accounts. [57] Sharing some such values—like the avoidance of great anxiety—is a necessary requirement for our mutual intelligibility as human beings, and one does not need much information to recognise and individuate them. Articulating other values—like accomplishment or significant personal relations—which might seem more complex, requires basic capacities involved in language mastery which is a characteristically human competence. [58]

Griffin also sees the relevance of human capacities and information in the context of inter-personal comparisons of well-being. He suggests that quite apart from a profile of prudential values, we need knowledge of human nature and information about particular persons to make such comparisons. [59] Much the same would presumably be necessary for intra-personal comparisons—comparisons of various different lives a person might lead. Given limitations on our knowledge and information, such comparisons may well be out of reach. This is part of the reason that Rosati and David Sobel attacked 'full information' accounts of well-being [60]- since most of their examples are about which of a set of lives is best. Nonetheless, on Griffin's view, the information requirements of comparisons may also not be as demanding as suggested by the informed desire accounts that Rosati and Sobel discuss. One may not need to have a

[55] Ibid., 58.
[56] Ibid., 58.
[57] See my 'The Concept of Well-Being', 69–70.
[58] Indeed, if an informed desire account only requires sufficient information to individuate such values (which are seen as the objects of informed desires), it would not ask much of human capacities. Yet, as we have seen, informed desire accounts often go beyond merely listing such values, and involve comparisons between, and information about, various lives a person might lead.
[59] 'Against the Taste Model', 65.
[60] See Rosati's 'Persons, Perspectives and Full Information Accounts of the Good', and David Sobel, 'Full Information Accounts of Well-Being,' *Ethics* 104, (July 1995), 784–810.

phenomenogical feel for each of the lives being compared. In the context of a comparison between a life of accomplishment and one of short-term pleasures, he writes that:

> It does not take great feats of imagination or especially finely textured comprehension to know what short-term pleasures are nor what it takes to carry off something major in one's life. Nor does the comparison turn much on the 'phenomenological' feels or fine textures ... There are considerable epistemological problems involved, but they may not be of the imagination-defeating kind presented by fine textures. [61]

Griffin here recognises 'considerable epistemological problems' which would rule out some comparisons.

Does his more recent work address the adaptation problem? Griffin does not discuss this issue in his more recent writings. Nonetheless, his later view is close to an objective-list theory—inasmuch as there is not much reference to desire[62]—and Arneson's discussion of the adaptation problem suggests that a prudential value list view would deal better with adaptation. Certainly, the fact that someone has fulfilled his or her desires—after adaptation—while having realised few, if any, prudential values would not mean that that person's life is judged as going particularly well in terms of a prudential value list view. The actual analysis of the range of cases Sen mentions—i.e. of what makes the exhausted coolie, the dominated housewife or the hardened unemployed person particularly badly off—would differ from case to case. The lack of autonomy which Sumner takes to be the unifying characteristic of these cases may be one reason why, on a prudential list view, these lives may not be going well. However, lack of enjoyment or accomplishment or adequate rest or hope may also be cited in a prudential value list view which involves a longer list of such values. [63]

Since prudential deliberation is at the heart of Griffin's view, it is worth asking whether the kinds of adaptation that Sen mentions can somehow distort such deliberation. This is relevant to Griffin's

---

[61] 'Against the Taste Model', 66.

[62] Griffin's account is nonetheless not best seen as an objective-list theory because he rejects standard versions of the objective/subjective dualism in this context. See *Well-Being,* 33 and *Value Judgement,* 35–6.

[63] I develop a longer list of prudential values—which includes a basic amount of rest and hope or aspiration in my 'The Concept of Well-Being', 67.

account at a number of levels. First consider his discussion of his list of prudential values. He is not worried by the possibility that people might disagree with *his* list and he thinks that '[w]e all, with experience, build up such a profile of the components of a valuable life, including their relative importance'.[64] My suspicion is that the examples that are typically used in articulating the adaptation problem do not undermine people's ability to define a list of prudential values. In some of these examples, the relevant person may have decided to *avoid great anxiety* by only going for those forms of *enjoyment* or *accomplishment* that are within her reach. That would not mean that she cannot see *accomplishment* or *enjoyment* or *freedom from anxiety*, as prudential values. In fact, the decision to avoid anxiety and to aim for certain limited forms of accomplishment and enjoyment shows that prudential deliberation is operating perfectly well. The constraints we face and a recognition, or estimation, of our limitations inevitably come into play in prudential deliberation and the formation of our life plans. Equally, suppose that someone values autonomy but is frustrated because she only has a limited amount of it, but learns to live with it. Here both the restriction on her autonomy and the frustration it brings can enter into the reckoning when her lifetime well-being is judged in terms of prudential values. She does not necessarily, however, cease to value autonomy. Furthermore, while someone who has adapted may come to value specific realisations of prudential values—which reflect diminished ambition—rather than others, this would be reflected in lists of the specific realisations of values ('value-tokens')—such as specific forms of enjoyment or accomplishment—which different people might list. It would not change the list of general values—i.e. of 'value-types'—each person puts forward. So adaptation of these forms need not lead to alterations in the list of prudential values a person articulates.

The more serious problem for a prudential value list view would arise if, through adaptation to straitened circumstances, someone's capacity for prudential deliberation is more seriously impaired. In its most extreme form, such as complete despair, it might be argued that such impairment might involve not being able to see anything at all as making a life go better. In less extreme forms, it may involve someone only endorsing a limited set of values—such as freedom from great anxiety and pain—while not deliberating on, or endorsing, other values, for lack of time or the ability to articulate or pursue them. Or, to take a more complicated case, a dominated

---

[64] *Value Judgement*, 30.

housewife may conclude that only a small subset of values—such as security, the avoidance of pain and enjoyment—make a woman's life better, while conceding that other values—such as accomplishment—make a man's life go better. In another case, it may be that one is not able to make much progress in prudential deliberation because, for example, one is not able to see beyond the limited achievements that are within one's reach and has not thought about achievements which would fulfil a human life. The exhausted coolie might see 'achievement' as a value and regard his completing his work each day in this light, while not progressing to the point of thinking about what more refined form of achievement might fulfil his life.

I find these lines of argument implausible for a number of reasons. Firstly, take the exhausted coolie. His work may not, in itself, involve the kind of achievement that gives a life point and weight. However, supporting his family through his work may be an accomplishment (in Griffin's sense) for him, given the conditions he finds himself in. Next, consider the case of the dominated housewife who adapts to injustice and concludes that only a small subset of values (such as the avoidance of pain and enjoyment) further women's lives whereas a fuller set of values (including autonomy and accomplishment) is appropriate for men. My feeling is that this description of adaptation in the face of gender inequality is flawed. It seems more plausible that even when women adapt, they may endorse a full list of values, including values like accomplishment. Adaptation is more likely to involve women only seeing certain sorts of accomplishment—such as those consistent with their role in society—as realisable. So women may endorse the same range of value-types, while being resigned to the idea that only certain value-tokens are feasible in their own lives. The same general argument can be made for other values such as autonomy.

We gain further insight from studies which engage with, and attempt to listen to, the poor or disadvantaged (including poor women). These typically show that the poor or disadvantaged can be very articulate about their living conditions. Indeed, some studies suggest that they endorse many of the items listed by philosophers.[65] The important point to take from these studies in

---

[65] See Susan Moller Okin, 'Poverty, Well-Being and Gender: Who Counts, Who's Heard?' *Philosophy and Public Affairs*, 31, No. 3, (2003), 33–59; Sabina Alkire, *Valuing Freedoms: Amartya Sen's Capability Approach and Poverty Reduction* (Oxford: Oxford University Press, 2000);

the present context is not that they support one list or the other, or that they suggest items which are sometimes not listed in standard accounts of well-being. [66] Those observations may be relevant to the application, or refinement, of various approaches to well-being. Rather the key point to note is that these studies suggest that the relatively disadvantaged are capable of sophisticated deliberation about what makes a life go well. So we can, I suggest, conclude that adaptation may not pose as serious a problem for prudential value list views as it might for some desire accounts. In particular, prudential value list views can help to elucidate the nature of the adaptation problem—by invoking the constituents of well-being which are missing in, or available in, the lives of people living in straitened conditions—in a way that a purely formal requirement on desires does not.

4. Capability Views and Informed Desire

It was, at least in part, the adaptation problem which led Amartya Sen to reject some accounts of well-being or 'utility'—understood in terms of desire-satisfaction, happiness and choice—and to develop his own 'capability approach'. Martha Nussbaum has also developed a version of this approach. On Sen's account 'capability' is an important 'space' for the evaluation of the quality of life, egalitarian justice and development. A person's capability relates to the range of lives—constituted by valuable 'beings' and 'doings' or 'functionings'—from which she can choose one. [67] On this view, the good life is thought of as made up of valuable functionings. Sen gives no complete or definitive list of such functionings— mentioning a variety of them, such as avoiding starvation, achieving self-respect, appearing in public without shame, and participating in the life of the community. He also distinguishes

---

David A. Clark, *Visions of Development* (Cheltenham, Edward Elgar, 2002); and Deepa Narayan *et al*, *Voices of the Poor* (Washington: World Bank, 2000).

[66] See David Clark's *Visions of Development* and Susan Moller Okin's 'Poverty, Well-Being and Gender: Who Counts, Who's Heard?' for arguments with this flavour.

[67] See Amartya K. Sen, 'Capability and Well-Being,' *The Quality of Life*, M. Nussbaum and A.K. Sen (eds.) (Oxford: Oxford University Press, 1993), 31.

'basic' capabilities—which relate to the ability to achieve certain crucially important functionings (such as being nourished) up to minimally adequate levels, from other capabilities. [68] Sen has a number of reasons for not endorsing any particular list. He suggests that different lists will be appropriate in different contexts and also that people with different values or 'evaluative procedures' may arrive at different lists, which are compatible with his general approach. [69] His relatively modest hope is that people with different values and evaluative procedures will accept the importance of capability as a space for the evaluation of the quality of life.

By way of contrast, Martha Nussbaum has developed a very specific list of capabilities over the years. Her work on capability initially emerged out of a reading of Aristotle's *The Politics*, [70] where she noted some important links between Aristotle's and Sen's views. Her subsequent work on capability can be seen as involving two distinct phases. The first phase—constituted by a range of papers in the early 1990s—developed her neo-Aristotelian view, and articulated a list of capabilities. [71] In the second phase, notably in her more recent books, *Sex and Social Justice* and *Women and Human Development*, Nussbaum's neo-Aristotelianism has been more 'self-effacing' and she has suggested that her list of capabilities might be the object of an overlapping consensus amongst people with different conceptions of the good life. [72] In these later versions her capability approach is seen as shaping political principles which are the basis of constitutional guarantees in all nations. [73]

[68]   'Capability and Well-Being,' 40–1.
[69]   See 'Capability and Well-Being,' 46–49; and Amartya K. Sen, *Development as Freedom* (Oxford: Oxford University Press), 86. For a discussion of this aspect of Sen's work see my 'Development, Common Foes and Shared Values', *Review of Political Economy,* 14, No. 4, 463–480.
[70]   Martha C. Nussbaum, 'Nature, Function and Capability: Aristotle on Political Distribution', *Oxford Studies in Ancient Philosophy*, 6 Supplementary Vol., (1988), 145–184.
[71]   The relevant contributions include Martha C. Nussbaum, 'Aristotelian Social Democracy', *Liberalism and the Good,* B. Douglass, G. Mara and H. Richardson (eds.) (London: Routledge, 1990), 203–252; and 'Human Functioning and Social Justice. In Defence of Aristotelian Essentialism', *Political Theory*, 20, (1992) 202–246.
[72]   Martha C. Nussbaum, *Sex and Social Justice* (Oxford: Oxford University Press, 1999) and *Women and Human Development* (Cambridge: Cambridge University Press, 2000).
[73]   *Women and Human Development,* 35.

Both Sen and Nussbaum refer to Marx's notion of the 'rich human being' and the 'rich human need' and have been concerned with a characteristically human existence. As regards human limitations, Sen's writings on capability indirectly refer to his version of the 'maximization' view of rationality, [74] which allows for limitations in our calculative abilities, as well as imperfect information and potential problems in making comparisons. To this degree, his capability approach can be developed in such a way as to address human limitations. As for Nussbaum, her neo-Aristotelian approach—which was crucial in the initial articulation of her list of capabilities—relies on the contrast between human and non-human beings. [75] She also rejects that part of Aristotle's *Nicomachean Ethics* which sees the good life in terms of a godlike life of contemplation. [76] Her neo-Aristotelian account is for human beings, not for beings with capacities beyond ours.

As regards the adaptation problem, Nussbaum has argued that Sen's failure to give a substantive account of capabilities means that some people's lists might reflect evaluative judgements which are 'distorted' by adaptation in the same way that desires can be. [77] Wayne Sumner has also argued that inasmuch as Sen's approach is 'subjective'—because people can affirm their own lists of valuable capabilities—he runs into the adaptation problem. [78] In responding to Nussbaum's criticism, Sen worries that providing a fully specified list of capabilities or functioning involves a danger of *over-specifying* the capability approach. [79] There are ways of 'completing' or further specifying that approach, which need not take a neo-Aristotelian route, and Sen wants to allow for these. Nonetheless, Sen has also typically argued that there are some 'elementary' functionings—such as avoiding starvation—which will be agreed on by people with different conceptions of a good life, while others—such as 'achieving self-respect'—are more 'complex'

[74] See Amartya K. Sen, *Rationality and Freedom* (Oxford: Oxford University Press, 2002).

[75] See, in particular, Martha C. Nussbaum, 'Aristotle on Human Nature and the Foundation of Ethics', *World, Mind and Ethics: Essays on the Ethical Philosophy of Bernard Williams* J.E.J. Altham and R. Harrison (eds.), (Cambridge: Cambridge University Press, 1995), 86–131.

[76] See Martha C. Nussbaum, *The Fragility of Goodness* (Cambridge: Cambridge University Press, 1986), 373–78.

[77] 'Nature, Function and Capability: Aristotle on Political Distribution,' 176.

[78] *Welfare, Happiness and Ethics*, 66–7 and 163–4.

[79] 'Capability and Well-Being', 45–6.

and may prove to be more controversial, even if they are still quite widely shared. [80] I have argued elsewhere that Sen's distinction between elementary and complex functionings can be developed in such a way as to find a middle way between Sen's 'under-specificity' and Nussbaum's 'over-specificity'. [81] In particular, the items on the list might be individuated at a very general level so that they relate to general values—such as significant personal relationships or knowledge—rather than functionings which consti-tute specific realisations of these values—i.e. to the specific relationships and instances of knowledge that are considered valuable. If the process of adaptation has the effect of lowering people's aspirations that could certainly influence a list which was made up of specific valuable capabilities such as the ability to go skiing or the ability to prove an important theorem or the ability to eat lentils and rice. It may have little or no effect on a list which related to general values so that it included items such as the abilities to nourish oneself, enjoy oneself and to have significant personal relations. [82]

In her recent work on the capability approach, Martha Nussbaum has gone much further in discussing adaptive prefer-ences and 'rational' and 'informed' desire views. Her insightful reading of these views and of Jon Elster's discussion of 'adaptive preferences' suggests that the various ways in which desire theorists tend to modify their accounts to allow for problems relating to irrationality and lack of information are themselves informed or suffused by an underlying set of human interests or 'substantive' values (or goods). [83] Since such values are what desire accounts are supposed to provide (rather than presuppose) this is, on her view, a problem for such accounts. The capability approach, in her hands, goes directly to such values. On her view, furthermore, the capability approach allows us to distinguish—in a way that other approaches (including Elster's) do not—those forms of adaptation which ought to concern us from those which are quite benign. She suggests that, sometimes, taking a realistic view of, and adapting to, the circumstances in which one finds oneself, is positively good. [84]

[80]   'Capability and Well-Being', 31.
[81]   I develop this argument in my 'Development, Common Foes and Shared Values', *Review of Political Economy,* 14, No. 4, (2002), 468.
[82]   Sabina Alkire develops such a list influenced by John Finnis' work in her *Valuing Freedoms: Sen's Capability Approach and Poverty Reduction.*
[83]   *Women and Human Development*, 119–148.
[84]   Ibid., 138.

It is, on her view, only when adaptation arises from a failure to have or to realise certain capabilities that we need to be especially concerned. Indeed, she thinks that Sen's discussions—exemplified in the passage from *On Ethics and Economics* quoted earlier—are helpful precisely because they focus on cases involving the adaptation of desires or attitudes in the face of significant shortfalls in capabilities or opportunities. [85]

While making these arguments in favour of the capability approach, Nussbaum also suggests that her capability approach should give some role to desire. She distinguishes two extreme responses to the possibility of adaptation. One reaction, which she terms 'Platonism' supposes that 'the fact that people desire or prefer something is basically not relevant, given our knowledge of how unreliable desires and preferences are as a guide to what is really just and good'. [86] The other reaction—which she terms 'subjective welfarism'—'holds that all existing preferences are on a par for political purposes, and that social choice should be based on some sort of aggregation of them all'. [87] Nussbaum rejects both positions. On her view, desire is important for at least two reasons. For anyone arguing in favour of political principles based on a capability list, she thinks that unless the items on the list are, or come to be, objects of desire or want, it is hard to justify such a list. Furthermore, without a connection between people's desires and the items on a list, any principles or institutions based on the capability list are unlikely to be stable.

At this point Nussbaum takes some consolation in the convergence between informed desire accounts and substantive good views, [88] since it suggests a route to justification and stability. She suggests that:

> When people are respected as equals, and free from intimidation, and able to learn about the world, and secure against desperate wants, their judgements about the core of a political conception are likely to be more reliable than judgements formed under the

---

[85]   Ibid., 139.
[86]   Ibid., 116–7.
[87]   Ibid., 117.
[88]   Her discussion focusses on Thomas Scanlon's 'Value, Desire and the Quality of Life', *The Quality of Life* M.C. Nussbaum and A.K. Sen (eds.) (Oxford: Oxford University Press, 1993), 185–200.

pressure of ignorance and fear and desperate need.) Informed desire plays a large role in finding a good substantive list, for epistemic reasons. [89]

In the context of her attempt to develop a brand of international feminism, she suggests that serious problems would arise if we could show that 'women who have experienced the full range of the central capabilities choose, with full information and without intimidation (and so forth), to deny these capabilities, politically to all women.' [90] Here Nussbaum's reference to 'full information' echoes Brandt, Railton and others. Unlike Brandt, Railton and others, however, she is not making the claim that informed desires are the basis of value. Rather she is setting up a procedure to test the list of capabilities. She thinks that—in the context of her version of feminism—a list of capabilities is most likely to be stable and justifiable if those women who are not ignorant, harassed etc. have desires that are not inconsistent with political principles based on the list.

Nussbaum's use of the term 'full information' in this context is unfortunate since it suggests that her position might be criticised for the same reasons that 'informed' and 'rational' desire accounts are criticised. Nonetheless, it is clear that Nussbaum is concerned about ignorance which can be remedied by an amount of information which falls well short of 'full information' as this is understood in some informed desire views. Indeed, she treats the desires of various women she meets as being informed and considers alterations to her list in the light of discussions with them. [91] However, Nussbaum may need to go further in addressing the question of just what sorts of informed desires would do the work she needs, since she reminds us that 'to consult all actual desires, including the corrupt and mistaken, when we justify the list of basic entitlements and opportunities itself would put the political conception, and the liberties of citizens, on much too fragile a foundation.' [92] This is particularly so because her discussion of this issue oscillates between a sense that some desires cannot be undermined, especially for a long period of time, by cultural influences, and a continued recognition of the importance of the adaptation problem. So she writes that:

[89] Ibid., 152.
[90] Ibid., 153.
[91] Ibid., 157–8.
[92] Ibid., 160.

Well-Being, Adaptation and Human Limitations

Desire for food, for mobility, for security, for health and for the use of reason—these seem to be relatively permanent features of our makeup as humans, which culture can blunt, but cannot altogether remove. It is for this reason that regimes that fail to deliver health, or basic security, or liberty, are unstable. My stability argument relies on this view of the personality, as not thoroughly the creation of power. Of course, we still have to recognize that there is considerable space for social deformation of desire: it is for this reason that we rely, primarily, on an independently justified list of substantive goods. [93]

These worries about deformation lead her to insist, in a recent reply to Susan Okin, that, even as regards informed desire conceptions 'the relationship we should have to these conceptions is edgy and complex.' [94]

In spite of her ambivalence about the role of desire, Nussbaum clearly thinks that promoting items on the list of capabilities will itself help ensure that people have 'more adequately informed desires'[95] and contribute to a convergence between informed desires and a list of substantive goods or capabilities. Until people have reached the point where their desires take this form, it is perhaps best, on her view, to rely on an independently justified list. Following a discussion of a Rabindranath Tagore story she concludes that:

> In relation to stability, the problem of adaptive selves suggests that in the first generation we cannot expect the same convergence between the informed-desire account and a substantive good account that we might expect over generations. Powerful people simply will not yield power happily, and in the first generation moral education cannot possibly alter deeply enough people's perceptions of the equality of citizens. [96]

Clearly, Nussbaum thinks that, in some contexts, moral education will only lead to a convergence between desires and substantive values over the long term. My feeling is that all Nussbaum needs are desires that are 'adequately informed' through a particular sort of education. Her reference to 'moral education' is likely to worry some of her readers. Is such education merely a way of changing

[93] Ibid., 155–6.
[94] Martha C. Nussbaum, 'On Hearing Women's Voices: A Reply to Susan Okin,' *Philosophy and Public Affairs*, 32, No. 2, (2004), 193–205.
[95] Ibid., 161.
[96] Ibid., 165.

people's values from one sort—say traditional values of some sort—to another—say liberal values which are compatible with international feminism? When she talks of 'moral education' I doubt very much that Nussbaum has in mind anything akin to a form of indoctrination which can undermine people's capacity for critical assessment. That would run contrary to the entire thrust of her approach. However, such education presumably will sometimes involve raising people's consciousness and allow them to consider alternatives they may not have previously considered. [97] Another relevant issue here relates to the fact that education and upbringing can often directly affect capabilities. Mill wrote of the women of his time that a 'hothouse and stove cultivation has always been carried on of some of the capabilities of their nature, for the benefits and pleasure of their masters.' [98] Nussbaum may need to address this possibility in relation to education and upbringing.

5. Conclusions

While desire accounts initially seem plausible, their strongest versions—which involve informed desires—set tough standards for a desire to classify as informed. If these standards are set high enough (as they are in Griffin's version of the informed desire account), that may deal with the adaptation problem at a formal level. However, these standards are sometimes set so high that informed desires seem to be beyond human beings, given their limitations. Sumner, Elster and Brännmark diagnose the adaptation problem in such a way that it signals a lack of autonomy. They all define an autonomy requirement to address it. However, the proposed autonomy requirements do not address all the forms that the adaptation problem can take. Accounts which look to the distinctive nature of human beings—notably prudential value list views and capability views—deal better with both human limitations and the adaptation problem. I have argued that adaptation need not pose serious problems for such accounts.

[97] Nussbaum inevitably discusses 'consciousness-raising' in this context, though her discussion is restricted to the experiences of Indian women in self-help groups. See ibid., 161–2.

[98] John Stuart Mill, *The Subjection of Women*, S.M. Okin (ed.), (Indianapolis/Cambridge: Hackett, 1988), 22. On a related issue see my 'A Weakness of the Capability Approach with Respect to Gender Justice', *Journal of International Development*, 9 (March-April 1997) 251–263.

However, to the degree that Martha Nussbaum's more recent version of the capability approach does invoke informed desires in relation to stability and justification, she needs to elaborate further on the kind of education that would lead to a convergence between informed desire and substantive good accounts.

Consequentialism and Preference Formation in Economics and Game Theory

DANIEL M. HAUSMAN[1]

When students first study expected utility, they are inclined to interpret it as a theory that explains preferences for lotteries in terms of preferences for outcomes. Knowing U($100) and U($0), the agent can calculate that the utility of a gamble of $100 on a fair coin coming up heads is U($100)/2 + U($0)/2. Utilities are indices representing preferences, so in calculating the utility of the gamble, one is apparently giving a causal explanation for the agent's preference for the gamble.

This interpretation of expected utility theory is questionable. It takes expected utility theory to be a theory concerning how agents form preferences over lotteries. But expected utilities only *represent* preferences; they do not *determine* them. Though it might be possible and useful to use expected utility theory to guide one's preferences in tricky situations,[2] expected utilities could not be assigned to outcomes in the first place unless agents already had preferences over an infinite set of lotteries.

Rather than regarding expected utility theory as a theory of preference formation, most decision theorists and economists would maintain that one should regard it merely as representing preferences that satisfy its axioms. To the extent that one regards these axioms as requirements of rationality or as reasonable idealizations, expected utility theory places justified constraints on sets of preferences. For example, suppose that for some agent, who cares only about money, the utility of a $100 bet on a fair coin landing heads were not U($100)/2 + U($0)/2. In that case, the agent must violate one of the axioms of expected utility theory. If the

[1] I am indebted to James Andreoni, Françoise Forges, Joshua Hausman, Pablo Mitnik, Larry Samuelson, William Sandholm, Elliott Sober and especially Philippe Mongin for useful conversations and comments concerning this paper.
[2] For example, when faced with Allais' problem, in which many people – including even Leonard Savage – are tempted to violate the independence axiom, calculation can save one from making mistakes.

axioms are either idealizations or conditions on rationality, then either one of the idealizations leads to error, or the agent is irrational. To conform his or her utilities to expected utility theory, the agent must change some preference. But there is no reason to change the expected utility of the bet rather than to change the expected utility of one of the prizes.

The orthodox view is that economics has nothing to say about where preferences come from, or how agents should modify their preferences if they violate the axioms of expected utility. Economists favor a division of labor, whereby economics concerns itself with agents whose preferences are complete and already conform to the axioms of expected utility theory and leaves questions about how agents came to have those preferences and about what therapy should be applied to agents whose preferences, do not satisfy the axioms for psychologists or sociologists to resolve. For example, in the case of standard consumer choice theory, economists suppose that consumers have a complete preference ordering over the commodity space. In deciding how to spend their incomes, consumers calculate how much different bundles of commodities cost so as to identify the set of affordable commodity bundles that best satisfy their preferences.

Yet this textbook case shows that the orthodox view that preferences are already given cannot be the whole story. It misses a complication that arises even in the case of consumer choice theory and which is, as we shall see, more intricate in expected utility theory and in game theory. Although consumer choice theory takes preferences *over the space of commodities* as given, it does not take as given preferences over alternative *actions*—that is, purchases of commodity bundles. On the contrary, the point of consumer choice theory is to predict how consumers' preferences among alternative purchases *depend on* preferences among commodities, incomes and prices and thereby to derive generalizations concerning demand. If preferences over purchases were already given, all that would be left for economists to say is that consumers purchase whatever they prefer to purchase. From the dramatic decrease in the price of DVD players in 2002 and 2003, economists could have predicted a surge in purchases of DVD players and DVDs. In predicting this change in behavior, they were also predicting a change in preferences among alternative ways consumers might spend their money. They were implicitly making claims about how consumer preferences over expenditures are formed.

Consumer choice theory is an instance of an explanatory strategy which I shall call 'consequentialism.' By 'consequentialism', I do not mean the ethical view that actions and policies should be evaluated in terms of the goodness of their consequences. I mean instead that an agent's choices and preferences among *actions* causally depend exclusively on (a) constraints, (b) the agent's beliefs about the consequences of the alternative actions the agent is aware of, and (c) the agent's evaluation of these consequences. Consequentialism denies that agent's preferences among actions are governed by principles that are not concerned with the consequences of the actions. The asymmetrical treatment of preferences among commodities versus preferences among purchases in consumer choice theory is an instance of consequentialism. I do not believe that consequentialism is a plausible general view of means-end reasoning (see Dewey 1922), but it may be a perfectly reasonable first approximation with respect to consumer choice.

This sense of consequentialism is closely related to Peter Hammond's notion (1988a, 1988b), but it is not the same. One difference is that the context in which I shall discuss consequentialism is broader than the decision trees he discusses. A more important difference is that I shall take consequentialism to impose a structure on predictive and explanatory theories of choice: choices (or preferences among the objects of choice themselves), depend on a causally prior evaluation of the expected outcomes of choices. Although Hammond may have explanatory and predictive interests,[3] he is mainly concerned with consequentialism as a rationality condition. As we will see below, there are ways to hold on to consequentialism as a rationality condition while conceding its inaccuracy as an account of what explains preferences.

Although the theory of consumer choice includes a consequentialist theory of preference formation, it does not include any account of the determinants of preferences *among commodities*. Consequentialist views take preferences over the consequences of alternative actions as given. To preserve the division of labor, whereby questions about how people's tastes are formed and changed are kept out of economics proper, consequentialist economists typically insist (though usually implicitly) on a strict asymmetry between preferences among actions (purchases) and preferences among commodities. The latter are givens. Together with prices and incomes, they determine preferences among

---

[3] 'The norm β is *consequentialist* if it is defined at all decision nodes ... and specifies consequentially equivalent behaviour in any pair of consequentially equivalent decision trees. Thus does behaviour become explicable merely by its consequences' (1988a, p. 508).

purchases. There is no reverse dependence of preferences among commodities on preferences among purchases and no hint of an economic theory of the determinants of preferences among commodities.

A consequentialist view of consumer choice is a sensible first approximation, and it permits economists to regard the theory of preference formation implicit in consumer choice theory as only a minor qualification to the view that economics takes preferences as givens. Preferences among purchases are at most causal intermediaries between consumption choices and the real determinants of those choices, which are incomes, prices, and preferences among commodities. Indeed, those who are attracted to revealed preference theory might maintain that preferences among purchases are not distinct from consumption choices and are thus not even intermediaries.

Although it is sensible to pay little attention to the fact that consumer choice theory includes an account of preference formation, on the grounds that preferences among purchases are at most intermediaries, a theoretical point remains: *If economists want to say more about choice among some set of alternative actions than that people choose a preferred action, they need to say something substantial about what influences preferences over the alternatives among which people choose.* Furthermore, insofar as they are committed to consequentialism, which relies on an asymmetry between preferences among consequences, which are given, and preferences among actions, which are to be explained by preferences among consequences, economists concede something to the naive student who sees utility theory as accounting for some preferences in terms of others.

In circumstances of uncertainly, consequentialism takes preferences among actions to depend on *beliefs* about their consequences as well as an evaluation of the consequences, which may of course depend on further beliefs. For example, the announcement that Vioxx significantly increases the risk of strokes and heart attacks changed many people's preferences between taking Vioxx and taking aspirin by changing their beliefs about the consequences of taking one pill or the other. Rather than the modest view that utilities and subjective probabilities only *represent* the agent's preferences, most people—including most economists—would regard an arthritic agent's preferences among the alternative anti-inflammatory and pain medications as *causally determined by* her underlying preferences (concerning stomach upset, heart attacks, strokes, and joint pain and flexibility) and by her beliefs about the consequences of taking alternative medicines. And that seems to bring us back to the naive view that expected utility theory shows how preferences among uncertain prospects depend (or ought to depend) on subjective probabilities and preferences among the prospect's outcomes. One cannot consistently maintain that utility theory merely represents an agent's preferences while also endorsing the consequentialist view that an agent's preferences among actions causally depend on his or her preferences among their possible outcomes and the subjective probabilities of those outcomes.

This conflict arises vividly in applications of game theory. Game theory can be regarded as a theory of preference formation, since, in apparent conformity with consequentialism, it derives preferences among strategies from beliefs and preferences among outcomes. Consider the following simple game form, with the first number in each pair representing the monetary result for Player I and the second the result for Player II:

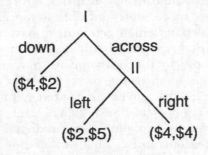

Figure 1

Player I can either play down, in which case she gets $4 and Player II gets $2, or Player I can play across, in which case Player II gets to play left or right. If Player II plays left, he gets $5 and Player I gets $2. If Player II plays right, both receive $4. All of this is common knowledge.

In order to go to work on this strategic interaction, game theorists need to know not just the *game form* or *game 'protocol'* (Weibull 2004), but the *game*—that is, they need to know the player's preferences over the results. If Players I and II are both altruists, they are playing a very different game than if they care only about the monetary results for themselves. Game theory requires that preferences over outcomes be given.

115

Daniel M. Hausman

Suppose that the preferences of players I and II over the outcomes depend exclusively on their own monetary returns. In that case, the game form shown in figure 1 constitutes the game shown in figure 2:

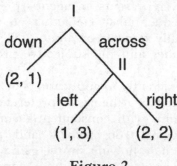

Figure 2

The numbers here are (ordinal) utilities, with larger numbers for alternatives that are more preferred. These numbers are supposed to be givens, concerning which economists have nothing to say. If Player II gets to play, he prefers moving left to right, *because* he prefers that outcome to the outcome of playing right. Player I knows this and consequently she prefers to play down rather than across. These preferences over alternative choices at particular nodes or information sets, and hence the preferences over alternative strategies are explained and predicted from the player's preferences over the outcomes. This explanation is consequentialist.

There are two crucial points. First, preferences over outcomes must be given to define the game. Second, the preferences of the players over individual moves or strategies must not be given, or else there would be nothing for the game theorist to do. *Game theorists have both an object to study and a task to carry out only if players' preferences over outcomes are given and players' strategy choices (or preferences over strategies) remain to be determined.* Game theory looks as if it were a consequentialist theory of the formation of preferences among strategies on the basis of given preferences among outcomes.

Whereas the asymmetry in the case of consumer choice theory between preferences among commodities and preferences among consumption purchases seems justifiable, the asymmetry between preferences among outcomes and preferences among strategies is

116

sometimes unsustainable. One reason for this is that the language of preferences over 'outcomes' is misleading. The numbers at the terminal nodes represent the preferences of the players for what Sen calls 'comprehensive outcomes'—that is, having followed that particular path through this particular extensive form as well as achieving its result. The preference indices attached to the terminal nodes need not match the preferences the players would have for the history-less state of affairs that obtains at the end of the game, which Sen calls 'culmination outcomes' (1997, p. 745). For example, the second player in an ultimatum game might reject Player I's proposed $8/$2 split of $10, while the same person might accept that division if it were generated by a chance mechanism (Blount 1995). The culmination outcomes—that is, the monetary results—are just the same, but the comprehensive outcomes are different. Games are defined by preferences over comprehensive outcomes rather than preferences over culmination outcomes. The (1, 3) at the end of the path (across, left) in Figure 2 expresses how the players evaluate *everything* about I playing across and II playing left, including, but not limited to, the monetary results. By 'outcome,' I shall mean 'comprehensive outcome.' When speaking of culmination outcomes, I shall talk of 'physical results,' 'monetary results,' or simply 'results.' I shall take 'payoffs' to be preferences over comprehensive outcomes. These complications do not arise in the case of the theory of consumer choice, where preferences over the space of commodities are independent of any facts about which commodity bundles are affordable. This fact about the payoffs in game theory casts doubt on whether game theory is in fact a consequentialist theory.

An alternative way of making the same point is to insist that the outcomes of the strategic interaction shown in figure 1 are incompletely specified. The outcome that results if Player I plays across and Player II plays left is not a pair of dollar payments. The outcome for both Player I and for Player II consists of the state of affairs where in this interaction Player I plays across, Player II plays left, Player I receives $2, and Player II receives $5. To define the game, one needs to know the preferences of the players over such fully specified outcomes.

The distinction between culmination and comprehensive outcomes—between (in my terminology) physical results and outcomes—is important, because people may have reasons for preferring paths through game trees, including their own strategies, that do not derive from preferences among the results. Player I might, for example, be much more interested in having Player II choose than she is in winning a few dollars more or less. This is a case of what Sen calls 'chooser dependence' (1997, pp. 747–51), and he describes perfectly ordinary circumstances where, for reasons of courtesy, one avoids choosing the piece of fruit or the comfortable chair one would prefer if one did not have to choose it. Regardless of the reasons, even if this is a game of perfect information in which Player I knows for sure that Player II will in fact play left, Player I may choose to play across because of her interest in Player II's choosing.

Although inconsistent with consequentialism (as a schema for explanation or prediction), the fact that the strategy choice does not derive from the payoffs is not a problem for game theory. Game theorists can sensibly maintain that if Player I has an overriding desire that Player II choose, then the individuals are not playing the game shown in figure 2.[4] The utilities in the game shown in figure 2 are not consistent with the players' preferences over comprehensive outcomes. Since Player I prefers to play across, even if she knows that Player II will play left, the game theorist must assign a larger utility for Player I to the comprehensive outcome of (across, left) than to the outcome of (down, left) or (down, right). Rather than playing the game shown in figure 2, the players are playing the game shown in figure 3:

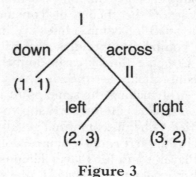

Figure 3

In order to apply game theory to interactions among people, economists must decipher people's preferences. To do this, they

---

[4] Similar comments apply if Player II prefers to play right in order to reward Player I's apparent trust and benevolence. Notice that it matters how Player II explains Player I's 'across' move. If Player II thinks that Player I plays across out of an anthropological interest, Player II may be less likely to play right than if Player II believes that Player I is taking a risk and trusting Player II to be nice.

must rely on generalizations about what people's preferences depend on. These generalizations constitute a tacit theory of preference formation. Its sole general principle is that individuals prefer a ('comprehensive') *outcome* x to another outcome y to exactly the same extent that they prefer the *physical result* (the 'culmination outcome') x^* that x involves to the result y^* that y involves. Call this generalization 'the default principle'. It is a defeasible presumption. In the interactions I shall be discussing, the results are all monetary, and the default principle can be restated as the claim that players' preferences over outcomes depend exclusively on the money the players receive.

Economists often rely on the stronger generalization that a player's preferences depend exclusively on the physical results *for that player*. This assumption of results-only self-interest entails the default principle. But the default principle is weaker. It says only that a player's preferences depend on the physical results for all the players, not that a player's preferences depend exclusively on his or her *own* results. The default principle leaves open the possibility of 'pure' altruism, though it rules out as motivations reciprocal altruism, trustworthiness, or what Sen calls 'chooser dependence' or 'menu dependence.' One reason why economists prefer to describe non-self-interested preferences as altruistic is that in that way they can continue to uphold the default principle and a consequentialist explanatory strategy.

The default principle can lead one astray, because a player's preferences can depend on features of the game form apart from the results. If a particular strategy involves betraying a trust, a player may reject it for that reason. Some people in the position of Player II might, for example, see the little interaction depicted in figure 1 this way and decide to play right in response to Player I playing across. Maintaining the default principle would mistakenly imply that (unless irrational) Player II aims at less money for himself, or more money for Player I, or a larger total amount of money. Since this implication is mistaken, the default principle must be rejected. Economists need to recognize that whether achieving a result involves betraying a trust is a relevant feature of the (comprehensive) *outcome* and adjust the utilities they assign accordingly. In this way they can continue to endorse consequentialism as a rationality condition, though not as an explanatory theory.

The default principle has the virtue of making the notion of the consequences of choices in games perfectly clear: the consequences are the results. But, as we have seen, preferences over outcomes need not coincide with preferences over results. There is nothing

Daniel M. Hausman

irrational about Player II preferring $5 for himself and $2 for someone else to $4 for each in a simple choice, while at the same time preferring to play right in the interaction depicted in figure 1 in response to Player I playing down. Unless game theorists were able to distinguish preferences over (comprehensive) outcomes of a particular strategic interaction from preferences over the results, their theory would give false predictions and bad advice. So economists must recognize that the default principle may lead them astray. When the default principle breaks down, consequentialism may not be a tenable explanatory strategy—though by adjusting the payoffs (the preferences of the players over the comprehensive outcomes), economists can continue to endorse it as a principle of rationality.

The default principle is a fragment of an unacknowledged theory of preference formation that economists need in order to define what games people are playing and hence to be able to apply game theory. This unacknowledged theory is essential to the application of game theory, but it is not regarded as a part of game theory itself. There are no other general principles in this unacknowledged theory, though there have been proposals for ways to modify the default principle to take account of non-result features of games that influence preferences over outcomes. Matthew Rabin's proposal for allowing reciprocation to influence utilities is one example (1993). Neither the default principle nor modifications of it are a part of what currently constitutes game theory itself. Game theory takes over only *after* preferences over comprehensive outcomes are specified. Game theory, narrowly construed, is just one part of a theory of strategic interactions, which also needs an account of what determines preferences among comprehensive outcomes. Such a theory is a part of economics, but not a formal or explicitly conceptualized part.

In modeling the game form of figure 1 as the game of figure 3 in the circumstances where Player I wants Player II to have to choose, economists recognize that the players have reasons to prefer certain strategies that do not derive from their results. Player I prefers the strategy (across) to the strategy (down), *despite* believing that Player II will play left and preferring the result pair ($4, $2) to ($2, $5). The size of the monetary results is still relevant because Player I's desire that Player II act would presumably not justify a limitless monetary sacrifice. But since the monetary costs of playing across are small, what motivates Player I to play across is, intuitively, a feature of the *play*, rather than of the result, even though it can be modeled as a part of the (comprehensive) outcome.

120

Consequentialism and Preference Formation

In other words, when the default assumption fails, game theory is consequentialist only in form. Having specified the game, as in figure 3, the game theorist can get to work and determine which strategies are rationally defensible. The game theorist can point out that the strategy 'across' dominates the strategy 'down' for Player I, and the strategy 'left' dominates 'right' for Player II. So there is a unique Nash equilibrium strategy pair, which is derived, in apparent conformity to consequentialism, from preferences over (comprehensive) outcomes. Though Player I prefers the result pair ($4, $2) to ($2, $5), her preference for the outcomes is not as the default assumption would predict. Instead it reflects her desire that Player II choose.

Notice that the (trivial) analysis above of the game shown in figure 3 is entirely orthodox. But in a case such as this one, game theory is doing very little work. Knowing Player I's preference for playing across, the game theorist uses an unacknowledged theory of preference formation to adjust the utilities attached to the outcomes so that when it is time to put game theory to work, it implies that Player I plays across. The game theorist derives the strategy choices from preferences over outcomes, but this turns reality on its head. Player I's choice is already determined by her desire that Player II have to move. Fortunately this fact can be embedded into the preferences over the comprehensive outcomes so that consequentialism as a principle of rationality is safe. But in this case the preferences over outcomes are not causally prior to preferences over strategies. These payoffs are given or prior only in the sense that game theory says nothing about the process of assigning them or what they depend on.

The dependence of payoffs on preferences among strategies I have explored in this case is causal rather than epistemic. The reason why preferences over payoffs do not explain preferences over strategies is not that preferences over payoffs cannot be known independently of preferences over strategies. The epistemic difficulties involved in learning the preferences of players—since one cannot read them off from a player's preferences over the results—are considerable, but they derive from the more fundamental causal complexities. The epistemic difficulties of learning people's preferences and modeling interactions as games, which may be serious or minor, reflect the failure of consequentialism— the non-epistemic fact that preferences among outcomes sometimes depend on features of game forms apart from their results.

When the default assumption holds, the structure of the explanations, predictions, and advice game theory offers is relatively unproblematic, as are the possibilities of applying game theory. Since there are significant domains where the default assumption holds, game theory clearly has important applications. But there are also many interactions where the default assumption does not hold, and game theory is of little use with respect to these interactions, unless economists or others can figure out how to model these interactions as games.

At the same time, recognizing that preferences over outcomes do not depend exclusively on preferences over results and that the task of modeling an interaction as a game is itself a subtle task helps to mitigate some apparently implausible implications of game theory. Consider the strategic situation, whose normal form is depicted in figure 4:

		Player II	
		left	right
Player I	top	$400, $400	$0, $450
	bottom	$0, $50	$50, $50

Figure 4

The default assumption coupled with the assumption that people typically show little concern with the results for others and (to make things specific) that their utilities are roughly linear in their own monetary results, permits one to model the interaction depicted in figure 4 as the game shown in figure 5:

		Player II	
		left	right
Player I	top	8, 8	0, 9
	bottom	0, 1	1, 1

Figure 5

Now that the game has been specified, the game theorist can go to work. In the game shown in figure 5, 'right' is a weakly dominant strategy for Player II. Player I knows this, and her best response to 'right' is 'bottom.' So the strategy pair (bottom, right) is the unique Nash equilibrium. The outcome is Pareto inefficient, and if Player II were able to move first or otherwise commit himself to playing left, the result would be superior for both players. But in the simultaneous-play game shown in figure 5, right is the better strategy for Player II, and, knowing this, bottom is the better strategy for Player I.

This conclusion strikes many people as unreasonable. Sensible people ought to be able to achieve the ($400,$400) outcome, and indeed in laboratory experiments involving similar games, subjects do in fact often achieve superior outcomes. In my view, intuitive uneasiness with the conclusion the game theorist draws does not reveal any fault in the game theory, narrowly conceived. Rational individuals playing precisely the game shown in figure 5 will play the Nash equilibrium strategy pair. I suggest instead that our uneasiness raises questions about whether real individuals, who are largely but not exclusively self-interested and who face the strategic situation shown in figure 4 are in fact playing the game shown in figure 5.

In particular, consider the possibility that the default assumption fails. Faced with a choice between the results—that is, the two monetary pairs ($400,$400) and ($0,$450)—Player II would choose the second. Faced with the choice between the pairs ($0,$50) and ($50,$50), Player II is indifferent, or as a non-malevolent sort has a very mild preference for the latter. But neither of these choices are the choices that Player II faces in the game form of figure 4. In this strategic interaction, Player II faces a choice between strategies, whose comprehensive outcomes bear the marks of this interaction.

Although Player II prefers the results for him of (top, right)—$450—to the results of (top, left)—$400—the difference is merely $50, while the difference for him between (top, left) and either (bottom, left) or (bottom, right) is $350. While recognizing that the *results* of (top, right) are better than the results of (top, left), Player II might come to feel that (top, left) is just as good an *outcome* as (top, right). Nothing prevents Player II from *in fact* being (or becoming) indifferent between the outcome of (top, left) and the outcome of (top, right) or even preferring the outcome of (top, left) to the outcome of (top, right). The fact that he *generally* prefers more money to less and *generally* cares little about the results for others does not determine what his preferences among the outcomes of *this* game must be. People are not in the grip of their preferences. Their preferences express their evaluations rather than determining them.

Of course, what really matters to Player II is what Player I does, and barring telepathy, Player II's thought that the outcome of (top, left) would be just as good as the outcome of (top, right) isn't going to affect what Player I does. If Player I is confident that Player II will choose to play right, then she will play bottom. (If Player I has studied too much game theory—as the subject is typically taught—the situation may be hopeless.) What influences Player I's choice are her beliefs, not what Player II actually does. But if the above train of thought is reasonable, then Player I can replicate it and come to suspect that Player II might not in fact prefer the comprehensive outcome of (top, right) to the comprehensive outcome of (top, left). Alternatively, Player I might suspect Player II of the following line of thought. 'Player I will focus on the results and will believe that I am going to play right. So she will play bottom. Her supposition that I am greedy and untrustworthy is insulting. So I should play left. That way I cost her $50 and all the regrets and self-recriminations that will come from her recognition that she could have had $400 if she'd been more trusting. If she plays bottom, playing left doesn't cost me a cent, and if I'm wrong about her and she plays top, I'll be happy as a clam with the result.' In either of these ways, Player I may conclude that there is a real possibility that Player II will play left. So the strategic interaction depicted in figure 4 might instead be modeled as either the game shown in figure 6 or as the game shown in figure 7:

		Player II	
		left	right
Player I	top	8, 8	0, 8
	bottom	0, 1	1, 1

Figure 6

		Player II	
		left	right
Player I	top	8, 8	0, 8
	bottom	0, 2	1, 1

Figure 7

The game depicted in figure 6 has two pure-strategy Nash equilibria rather than just one, and (top, left) is one rationally justifiable outcome. In figure 7, left is a dominant strategy for Player II, and (top, left) is the unique Nash equilibrium.

Consequentialism and Preference Formation

Let me repeat that I am not questioning the standard analysis of the games depicted in figures 5, 6, or 7. The game theory here is orthodox. The question instead concerns *which game people are playing*—that is, how to model strategic situations with monetary outcomes as games, when one knows (i) preferences over monetary results, (ii) reasons players may have apart from monetary results for preferring one strategy over another, and (iii) second-order preferences players may have for their preferences over outcomes and strategies (like the preference Player II might have not to prefer the outcome of (top, right) to the outcome of (top, left)).

Real strategic interactions are usually more accurately, though less informatively, modeled as games of incomplete information than as games of complete information, since real people usually do not know for sure what the preferences of the other players are. When facing the game form shown in figure 4, some people in the role of Player II will be influenced by the fact that for a sacrifice of only $50, the outcome can be $400 for both rather than nothing for the other player. Some will be influenced by the dominance reasoning, and the default assumption will hold. Some will decide that the difference between $400 and $450 is small enough that they can regard it as negligible. Some will want to punish Player I, if she plays bottom. Someone in the role of Player I, who presumably most prefers the (top, left) outcome will need to make some guesses about the preferences of Player II. Since all it takes is a subjective probability that Player II will play left of greater than 1/9 for the expected monetary return to Player I from playing top to be larger than the expected return of playing bottom, one would expect people often to achieve the ($400,$400) outcome. If this is correct then the strategic situation in figure 4 is not well modeled as the game shown in figure 5. Unlike the analysis of the game depicted in figure 5, which has an unequivocal conclusion and which, when taken as capturing the interaction depicted in figure 4, seems counterintuitive, the analysis of the strategic interaction depicted in figure 4 allows for multiple possibilities and encompasses our intuitions in its recognition that the interaction might be modeled as the games in figures 6 or 7 or as a game of incomplete information, rather than as the game in figure 5. The multiple epistemic possibilities reflect the non-epistemic complexity of the factors that determine the preferences of the players.

Sometimes preferences over outcomes are so heavily dependent on features of the strategic interaction and in such a complicated

Daniel M. Hausman

way, that the players can scarcely be said to be playing a *game* at all. Consider, for example, the centipede-like interaction depicted in figure 8:

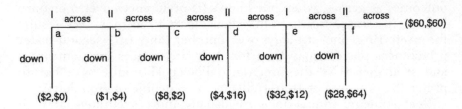

Figure 8: A Six-Legged Centipede Strategic Interaction

If people's preferences over results depend exclusively on their own monetary return (which implies the default principle) and the preferences and game form are common knowledge, then one has a centipede game, as in Figure 9, in which Player II prefers playing down to playing across at node f, and each player prefers to play down at each node if the other player is going to play down at the next node:

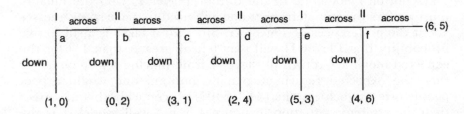

Figure 9: A Six-Legged Centipede

In a centipede game such as the one shown in figure 9, backwards induction shows that the only Nash equilibrium strategy pair involves both players playing down at every node. So the game ends at the first move.

It seems *stupid* to play down on the first move of the strategic interaction, and in experiments involving strategic situations like those depicted in figure 8, very few people play down on the first move (McKelvey and Palfrey 1992, p. 804). If Player I plays across at nodes a, c, and e, and Player II plays down at f, Player I winds up with $28, rather than the $32 she would have had if she had played down at node e, but she'd still be enormously better off than if she had played as the game theorist recommends. There are also well known difficulties making sense of the counterfactual reasoning implicit in the backwards induction argument.

I suggest that the paradoxes attached to the backward induction argument concerning centipede interactions may reflect (among other things) problems in supposing that there could be a well-defined game here in advance of players' decisions concerning which strategy to play. Unless the default principle holds, it is unlikely that there are any utilities attached to comprehensive outcomes until *after* the players decide whether to play across or down at each of the nodes.[5] In order for Player II to face a choice at node f, Player I must first play across at nodes a, c, and e, and Player II must first play across at nodes b and d. Though it is possible to consider the counterfactual supposition that Player II in the centipede *game* shown in figure 9 faces a choice at node f (perhaps because of a series of 'trembles,' whereby the players played across despite preferring to play down, it seems more plausible to conclude that if the players in the strategic interaction depicted in figure 8 reach node f, then they are not playing a centipede game. Though in advance of the interaction, each may prefer more money to less and have little concern with the monetary results for the other, if Player I plays across at node a, that will set off a chain of consequences that will influence the players' beliefs or their preferences over the comprehensive outcomes.

To figure out what the game might be and what to do, players need to envision how the interaction might go. There is no well-developed theory of 'envisioning' play in a strategic interaction. Indeed, unlike standard game theoretic reasoning, envisioning cannot be fully rigorous, because the game is not yet given. In envisioning the play, the players are constructing their preferences over the comprehensive outcomes and hence constructing the game itself. Unless the default assumption holds, this task is largely unavoidable, and in practice it cannot be passed on to some other discipline. Assigning preferences to outcomes of games has, I believe, as much claim to be a subject of economic investigation as the task of predicting strategy choices once preferences over outcomes are given.

[5] McKelvey and Palfrey 1992 show how complicated things can be if one maintains the default assumption, but permits a few of the players to be altruists and the other players to be uncertain whether their opponents are altruists. They do not address the problems that arise if one rejects the default assumption.

Daniel M. Hausman

Many interactions are much less motivationally complicated than centipede interactions, and efforts to construct preferences (and hence to model interactions as games) by theorists and players are not always so inconclusive and ambiguous. Furthermore, there are certainly circumstances in which the default assumption holds (at least to a high degree of approximation). When the default assumption holds, then preferences over outcomes are causally prior to preferences over strategies, and game theory provides an account of strategy choice that is consequentialist in both form and reality. But when the default assumption does not hold, preferences over outcomes have to be constructed before game theory can take over and treat them as exogenous—and thereby provide the appearance of a consequentialist determination of strategy choices.

The accepted view that economics has nothing to say about preference formation and should have nothing to say about it is misleading both with respect to circumstances in which the default assumption holds and preferences over outcomes are truly given and with respect to circumstances in which the default assumption does not hold and preferences over outcomes have to be constructed from non-result features of strategic situations over which individuals have preferences. When the default assumption holds, game theory and, *a fortiori*, expected utility theory are theories that explain preferences over gambles or over strategies in terms of given preferences over their results. When the default assumption does not hold, then the conventional view of expected utility theory as merely representing preferences may seem more justified, but at the same time, there is another activity (for which there is no explicit theory) that derives preferences over comprehensive outcomes from the many different reasons people have for preferring strategies, actions, and results.

In either case, in order to provide a non-trivial model that predicts choices or offers advice on choices, economists must show what the preferences for those choices depend on and thus must provide a theory of the formation of those preferences. Consequentialism provides one structure within which economists accomplish this task. But when consequentialism fails—when the default assumption does not hold—then game theory and expected utility theory merely represent preferences and beliefs, and they may readily fail to provide a non-trivial account of choice. With respect to parts of economics, such as the theory of consumer choice, this observation is of little interest, since the preferences of interest—that is the preferences over the commodity space—can be taken as exogenous, and consequentialism is relatively unproblematic. But this observation is not trivial with respect to game theory, because in addition to the game-theoretic account of the determination of preferences over strategies by preferences over outcomes and other features of games, there is an unavoidable, though less explicit task of determining what people's preferences over the outcomes of games depend on. Though the only account of preference formation that shows up explicitly within game theory is the account of preferences over strategies implicit in the determination of optimal strategies, applying game theory requires that preferences over outcomes be given, and to figure out what those preferences are requires understanding how they depend on features of games. That understanding is a task for economists. Game theory is only one important part of the theory of strategic interactions.

References

Blount, Sally. 1995. 'When Social Outcomes Aren't Fair: The Effect of Causal Attributions on Preferences,' *Organizational Behavior and Human Decision Processes* 63: 131–44.

Dewey, John. 1922. *Human Nature and Conduct*. Rpt. Carbondale: Southern Illinois University Press, 1998.

Hammond, Peter. 1988a. 'Consequentialism and the Independence Axiom.' In B. Munier, ed. *Risk, Decision and Rationality*. Dordrecht: Reidel, pp. 503–16.

Hammond, Peter. 1988b. 'Consequentialist Foundations for Expected Utility.' *Theory and Decision* 25: 25–78.

McKelvey, Richard and Thomas Palfrey. 1992. 'An Experimental Study of the Centipede Game.' *Econometrica* 60: 803–36.

Sen, Amartya. 1997. 'Maximization and the Act of Choice.' *Econometrica* 65: 745–79.

Weibull, Jörgen. 2004. 'Testing Game Theory,' in Steffen Huck, ed. *Advances in Understanding Strategic Behaviour, Game Theory, Experiments, and Bounded Rationality: Essays in Honor of Werner Güth*. London: Macmillan, pp. 85–104.

Preference, Deliberation and Satisfaction

PHILIP PETTIT

In his famous lecture on 'The Concept of Preference' Amartya Sen (1982) opened up the topic of preference and preference-satisfaction to critical, philosophical debate. He pointed out that preference in the sense in which choice reveals one's preference need not be preference in the sense in which people are personally better off for having their preferences satisfied. And on the basis of that observation he built a powerful critique of some common assumptions in welfare economics.

I endorse Sen's observation and critique and I think that, suitably recast, they can be nicely situated within a broader picture of preference and deliberation that Michael Smith and I developed elsewhere (Pettit and Smith 1990). This paper is an attempt to do just that, sketching an overall picture of the nature of preference, the nature of deliberation, and the way they interact around the idea of preference-satisfaction.

But the paper is not just an attempt to keep the books on these topics; there is also a bottom line. That line is that preference-satisfaction should not normally figure as a deliberative concern. When individuals deliberate about what they ought individually to do, they should not normally focus on what will bring them most preference-satisfaction. And when authorities or commentators deliberate about what good government ought to try to do for its people, they should not normally search for what will maximize the overall preference-satisfaction of people in the community.

The paper is in three sections. The first sketches an overall view of preference, arguing—contrary to Sen, as it happens—that there is one concept of preference, not many.[1] The second outlines the view of deliberation that derives from my joint work with Michael Smith. And the third looks at how preference and deliberation interact and at the place of the idea of preference-satisfaction in this interaction.

---

[1] Here and in other aspects of that discussion I have been influenced by hearing a presentation of Dan Hausman's at a conference in St Gallen, May 2004.

Philip Pettit

1. Preference

The first thing to say about the notion of preference is that unlike that of desire, preference is always a preference for one thing rather than another; it always involves a ranking of alternatives. Thus it makes no sense to ask someone whether they prefer X; the only sensible question will be whether they prefer X to Y, X to Z, or whatever. Preference, as we can put it, is inherently comparative.

This introduces straight away a complexity that is often ignored in economics, though it has recently attracted attention among philosophers (Hurley 1989; Broome 1991; Pettit 1991). This is that before we can tell what someone prefers amongst various alternatives, we have to be clear about what exactly those alternatives are. In particular, we have to be clear about how they are individuated, and whether two superficially similar alternatives that appear in difference choice contexts really remain the same option.

Consider in this connection a case where over time you are offered three choices, in each of which another person will get what you leave over. First you are offered a large apple or an orange. Next you are offered an orange or a small apple. And finally you are offered a large apple or a small apple. And suppose that you display a preference for the large apple over the orange, the orange over the small apple, and—surprisingly—the small apple over the large. Does that mean that your preferences are cyclical and, intuitively, irrational? Not necessarily: not if the alternative of taking a large apple and leaving an orange for the other person is a different alternative from taking a large apple and leaving a small apple. And of course those are intuitively different options. The one is perfectly polite, the other downright rude.

In what follows, I shall abstract from the issue of how the alternatives between which people have preferences are to be characterized and individuated. I shall assume that that does not make for a serious difficulty. I have argued elsewhere for a particular resolution of the difficulty but I shall not build particularly on that account (Pettit 1991). So on now to the main topic.

There are three broadly different ways in which we might conceptualize preference, assuming that there is one single concept of preference involved in the way we talk in everyday life and in the manner in which economists conduct their discussions. These different analyses correspond with broader styles of analysis that have been important over the last fifty years or so in the philosophy of mind. The first is a behavioral account of preference, the second a dispositional account and the third a functional one.

The behavioral notion

The behavioral account is associated broadly with the approach described in economics as the revealed-preference theory—see Samuelson (1938) and Little (1950)—though I am not convinced that all revealed-preference theorists would have endorsed it; some, I think, may have aligned themselves with what I go on to describe as the dispositional analysis instead. According to the behavioral account, there is no content to saying that someone prefers one alternative to another over and beyond the claim that he or she chooses that alternative rather than the other. A preference for an alternative is nothing other than what is actually revealed in the choice of the alternative.

This is an extraordinary theory. It means that short of being revealed in choice, there is no preference for anything, so that we cannot say that someone is led to make this or that choice as a result of their preferences and we cannot even say that someone's preference is frustrated by not being able to make a corresponding choice. Equally, we cannot say that people have preferences over matters between which they are unable to choose, whether for the contingent reason that they are not offered the choice or for the deeper reason that the alternatives in question—say, between the world being as it is and the world being dramatically different in some way—are never going to be presented as matters of choice to anyone.

Revealed-preference theory may have lent itself to elegant axiomatization and mathematical development, then, but it looks philosophically very strange. It appears to deny the reality of preference in the accepted sense, rather than giving an account of what that reality involves. In my view it is nothing short of an eliminativist or error theory of preference.

The dispositional notion

The most obvious alternative to the strict behavioral approach retains the tight connection between preference and choice. According to this account, to say that someone prefers one alternative to another is to say that they are disposed, should they be given a choice between those alternatives, to choose the first rather than the second. What does that disposition consist in? The natural way to think of it will be as a categorical state of the agent, or as something grounded in such a categorical state. Thinking of it this way, we can say that when a person chooses the preferred alternative, then the choice is causally explained by the presence of that state within them.[2]

The dispositional analysis gets over the more obvious difficulties with the behavioral. It makes sense of the idea that people are caused to make their choices by the preferences they hold, as it does of the idea that people can have a preference frustrated. And it equally makes sense of the idea that people might have a preference between alternatives that will never be available as matters of choice. I can prefer a perfectly just world, for example, to the world as it is, for were I to be given a choice between those alternatives—impossibly, as it happens—then I would choose the world that is just.[3]

The functional notion

The dispositional account, however, looks to be less general than it ought intuitively to be. It focuses on the connection between preference and choice and makes that connection into something definitional or constitutive; nothing is to count as a preference for X over Y unless it disposes the agent to choose X over Y. But there are connections that we firmly expect a preference to have with other attitudes, and not just with choice, and there is good reason to treat these also as constitutive of preference.

---

[2]   The alternative would be to represent the preference as a bare disposition, which would bring the account back in line with revealed-preference theory. For on the bare-disposition account, there need be no categorical difference between two agents who differ in a choice-disposition and so in some preference.

[3]   Can the account make sense of what it might mean to say that I prefer one alternative to another, when the alternatives cannot logically be presented as matters of choice: one might be the alternative of taking a small apple rather than an orange and the other the alternative of taking a small apple rather than a large apple? This issue is raised in (Broome 1991). For an attractive response see (Dreier 1996). His line is that we can have preferences over options, where we abstract from properties that would make the options incomparable.

Preference, Deliberation and Satisfaction

The most obvious example of other such connections are the connections between preferences themselves. Suppose that I prefer X to Y, that I am indifferent between Z and not-Z, and that I am offered a choice between having X-and-Z or Y-and-not-Z. Will I prefer X-and-Z over the alternative offered? I must certainly be expected to do so, unless some special, perturbing factors get in the way. Absent those factors—absent temporary insanity or blindness or passion or whatever—a failure to hold by that derived preference would raise a serious question as to whether I really prefer X to Y, or am really indifferent about whether Z or not-Z.

Or consider the sort of connection that holds between preferences and beliefs. Suppose that I am presented with two alternatives, A and B. And imagine that, while the alternatives otherwise leave me indifferent, I believe that A has some desirable property that B lacks; it does not matter how exactly we analyse the notion of desirability or, for that matter, the notion of believing that a feature is desirable. Will I be expected to prefer A to B? Of course I will. Did I not form that preference then, absent some special obtruding factors, it would seem that I cannot be otherwise indifferent between A and B or that I do not really think that A has a desirable property that B lacks.

These observations suggest that we should conceptualise preference so that the connections between a preference and other states are given the same definitional prominence that is given, under the dispositional account, to the connection between a preference and choice. After all, the failure of those connections, like the failure of the connection with choice, would raise a question as to whether there is a preference present at all.

These observations, if we go with them, take us toward a functional analysis of preference. According to such an analysis, to say that someone prefers one alternative to another is to say that they are in a state such that, in the absence of perturbing conditions, that state will dispose them to choose the first rather than the second, and will connect in such and such a manner with other preferences and other states of mind. Preferences, roughly speaking, are not just any sorts of dispositions to choice; they are dispositions that are collaterally sensitive to a variety of other states.

Philip Pettit

How exactly will a preference have to connect with other states? Without going into detail, it is worth observing that decision theory can give us a lead on this question.[4]

There are certain intuitive connections that are important to the notion of preference—connections like those that link them with judgments of desirability, for example—that are not registered in decision theory (Pettit 1991). But the theory does map a range of connections of a kind that certainly are relevant, suggesting that for a given state in the agent to count as a preference, and as a preference with a specific content, it must relate to other states in a certain pattern, at least in the absence of perturbing factors. Thus it stipulates that for one state to be a preference for X over Y, and for another state to count as indifference between Z and not-Z, the states must connect in such a way that they give rise to a preference for X-and-Z over Y-and-not-Z. Decision theory consists in a set of axioms that dictate a range of such functional connections that *bona fide* preferences must satisfy.

The connections marked in decision theory include connections to preferences, not just over particular alternatives, simple or compound, but preferences over probabilistic gambles involving those alternatives: preferences over gambles assigning such and such a probability to one alternative, and such and such a probability to another. It turns out that by doing this, it makes it possible for each alternative over which an agent registers relevant preferences to construct an index of how relatively intensely the agent prefers that alternative; the scale whereby those intensities are determined is known as the agent's utility function (Ramsey 1990). The degree of preference that is thereby determined for an alternative can be represented as corresponding to the person's desire for that option; it will attach to each alternative within the agent's preference-ordering and can be attached without mention of any explicit alternative.

I have argued that we ought to conceptualize preference so that any state that is to count as a state of preferring one alternative to another should connect in certain ways, at least in the absence of

---

[4] There is one important complexity to note. This is that a full functional analysis will need to provide an analysis, simultaneously, of what is involved in someone's having each of the preferences they display, not just a single one, and perhaps each of the other connected attitudes as well. It will have to be holistic in the sense of conforming to the familiar Ramsey-Carnap-Lewis framework for functional analysis (Lewis 1983, Essay 6). Decision theory might be recruited to this holistic task.

perturbing factors, with choice, with other preferences, with beliefs of various sorts, and so on. Decision theory gives us a good lead on the connections that anything deserving the name of 'preference' should be expected to satisfy, though not a lead on all plausible connections; I mentioned as an example the connection to judgments of desirability. I do not mean to go further into positive detail about the connections that are important to preferences but there are three negative remarks that I should certainly make. They are independently intuitive and they combine to provide a workably specific notion of preference.

The three remarks are that preferences in general should not be expected to have the connections associated with matters of taste, feeling and self-interest. As a rule,

- they are not disconnected attitudes like tastes;
- they do not have any phenomenal or felt quality; and
- they do not spring from self-interested desires.

These remarks are important because there are models under which preferences are nothing but tastes, preferences are conscious, qualitative phenomena, or preferences are invariably self-interested.

To hold that preferences are tastes is to suggest that they are brute states in which one finds oneself, as one finds oneself with a taste for dark beer or bright clothes or the smell of garlic. In particular, it is to suggest that they are exogenous to decision-making and are not themselves up for adjudication or revision. There is no debating about tastes; *de gustibus non disputandum*. There is no debating about tastes and, as the other cliché has it, no accounting for tastes. But what is true of tastes in these regards is certainly not true of preferences in the functional sense in play here. Preferences in general are susceptible to deliberative connections with a variety of factors—more on this in the next section—and do not have the insulated, unmoveable character of tastes.

One reason why people might think that preferences are like tastes is that they think of preferences, more specifically still, as phenomena with their own qualitative feel. They are taken to be the sorts of conscious inclinations that we describe as yens and hankerings, urges and impulses, cravings and passions and itches. All of these attitudes have a phenomenal quality in the sense that there is something it is like to have them. And because they represent such a salient if not common aspect of decision-making, they are easily taken as the basis for a model of preferences. But any such model would be quite misleading. Understood in the functional sense, it is quite clear that most preferences—most collaterally sensitive dispositions to choice—do not have a phenomenal side.

The final remark I want to make about preferences is that as there is no reason to take them as tastes or as itches, there is no reason to think that they necessarily connect—as of course tastes and itches might be thought to connect—with the self-interest of the agent. I may have a preference defined over any alternatives, no matter how disconnected from my sense of my own welfare. I may even have a preference for one alternative rather than another, when that alternative promises to do worse by my personal welfare than the other. There is no incoherence, and every plausibility, in the idea of my instantiating and acting on such a detached ranking of options.

This completes my discussion of the notion of preference itself. It is time now to turn to the second topic of deliberation. With that topic covered, we will be able to turn to the interaction between preference and deliberation and to look at its significance for the role of preference-satisfaction.

2. Deliberation

Folk psychology and decision theory

The fundamental tenet of our common sense psychology of human agents is that agency involves acting to realize various goals in a way that is sensible in light of the apparent facts: that is, in a way that adjusts to the facts, as one construes the facts (Jackson and Pettit 1990). Agents seek goals, construe facts, and choose an action that will achieve their goals—or will maximize the chance of their goal being achieved—if the facts answer to how they are construed. For short, people act so as to promote their goals according to their construal of the facts.

This common sense view—this folk psychology—can be just as well expressed in the language of preference, which is exactly what decision theory does. The output of decision-making under this variant is the formation of a preference ordering over the options available in a choice; this then leads directly to choice and action. The inputs are the agent's background preferences over the possibilities that action might affect—the agent's degrees of preference for those scenarios—together with the agent's degrees of confidence or probability that this or that scenario will be realized in the event of this or that action being taken. The agent's goals are the scenarios that attract relatively high degrees of preference and the agent's degrees of probability represent his or her construal of the facts.

Putting the two schemas together, the view shared between folk psychology and decision theory goes, roughly, like this.

- To seek certain goals is to be in corresponding goal-seeking states, described in common sense as desires; these are represented in decision theory by relatively high degrees of preference or utility.
- To construe facts is to be in corresponding fact-construing states, described in common sense as beliefs; these are represented in decision theory by degrees of probability or confidence.
- To seek certain goals according to how one construes the facts is to be caused to act—not by accident but 'in the right way' (Davidson 1980)—by the presence of the relevant complex of belief and desire, probability and preference.
- More particularly, it is to be caused to act so that the agent's desires are promoted according to the agent's beliefs—so that the agent's expected utility is maximized, with the option that attracts the highest degree of preference being selected.

Given the concordance between talk of seeking goals and construing facts, and talk of preferences and probabilities, we can speak indifferently in either idiom. When it comes to situating deliberation in human decision-making, the folk-psychological idiom of goals and facts is easier to work with and this is how I shall mainly write in this section. The issue of how to place deliberation in relation to preference is just the issue of how to place it within the folk-psychological schema of goal-seeking, fact-construing agency: of an agency of belief and desire.

Introducing deliberation

The first thing to notice in approaching the topic of deliberation from this angle is that folk psychology, understood as the affirmation of the goal-seeking, fact-construing nature of agency, may apply in the absence of anything we would naturally describe as deliberation. This comes out in the fact that by most accounts, though not by all (Davidson 1980), the psychology is true of non-human as well as human animals.

Philip Pettit

The idea is that many non-human animals are tuned by evolutionary and experiential pressures so that in appropriate circumstances they will act for the realization of certain goals and, in particular, will act in a manner that makes sense under the way they take the facts to be: under the representations of the environment—the more or less reliable representations—that their perceptions and memories evoke. Such animals will instantiate goal-seeking and fact-construing states and those states will interact in such a way as to produce suitable behaviour. They will be rational agents in the sense of conforming to folk psychology and decision theory. Or that will be so, at any rate, in the absence of intuitively perturbing influences, and within intuitively feasible limits: for short, in normal conditions.

But if folk psychology is as likely to be true of various non-human animals as it is of creatures like us, there is still a yawning divide between how we and they manage to conform to this psychology. We do not just possess beliefs and desires in the manner of non-humans, and act as those states require. We can give linguistic expression to the contents of many of those states—we can articulate the goals sought and the facts assumed. We can form beliefs about those goals we pursue or might pursue and those facts believe or might believe; beliefs, for example, to the effect that certain forms of consistency or coherence or mutual support do or do not obtain amongst them. And we can ask questions about those properties and relations of goals and facts, with the beliefs we form in response to that interrogation serving as checks on the overall pattern of attitudes that is going to unfold within us (Pettit 1993, Ch 2; McGeer and Pettit 2002).

The exercise whereby we impose such checks on our overall attitudes is easily illustrated. Suppose I find myself prompted by perception to take it to be the case that p, where I already take it to be the case that r. While my psychology may serve me well in this process, it may also fail; it may lead me to believe that p, where 'p' is inconsistent with 'r'. But imagine that in the course of forming the perceptual belief I simultaneously ask myself what I should believe at the higher-order level about the candidate fact that p and the other candidate facts I already believe. If I do that then I will put myself in a position, assuming my psychology is working well, to notice that 'p' and 'r' are inconsistent, and so my belief-forming process will be forced to satisfy the extra check of being squared with this higher-order belief—a crucial one, as it turns out—before settling down.[5]

In this example, I find a higher-order truth—that 'p' and 'r' are inconsistent—which is relevant to my fact-construing processes and imposes a further constraint on where they lead. But the higher-order truth recognised in the example could equally have had an impact on my goal-seeking processes; it would presumably have inhibited the simultaneous attempt, for example, to make it the case both that p and that r.

With these points made, I can introduce what I mean by the activity of 'deliberation' or 'reasoning' or 'ratiocination'. Deliberation is the enterprise of seeking out higher-order truths—truths about consistency, support and the like—with an implicit or explicit view to imposing further checks on one's fact-construing and goal-seeking processes. Not only do we human beings show ourselves to be rational agents, as we seek goals, construe facts, and perform actions in an appropriate fashion. We also often deliberate about what goals we should seek, about how we should construe the facts in the light of which we seek them, and about how therefore we should go about that pursuit: about what opportunities we should exploit, what means we should adopt, and so on. We do this when we try to ensure that we will form beliefs in suitably constraining higher-order truths about the properties and relations of candidate goals and candidate facts.

The fact that we human beings reason or deliberate in this sense means that not only can we be moved by goal-seeking and fact-construing states—by the belief that p or the desire that q—in the manner of unreasoning, if rational, animals. We can also reflect on the fact, as we believe it to be, that p, asking if this is indeed something we should believe. And we can reflect on the goal we seek, that q, asking if this is indeed something that we should pursue. We will interrogate the fact believed in the light of other facts that we believe, or other facts that perceptions and the like incline us to believe, or other facts that we are in a position to inform ourselves about; a pressing question, for example, will be whether or not it is consistent with them. We may interrogate the goal on a similar basis, since the facts we believe determine what it

---

[5] I abstract here from the crucial question of how we come to form concepts like truth and consistency and the like and how we come to be able to form the sophisticated beliefs mentioned in the text. For a little on this see McGeer and Pettit (2002).

makes sense for us to pursue. Or we may interrogate it in the light of other goals that also appeal to us; in this case, as in the case of belief, a pressing question will be whether or not it is consistent with such rival aims.

Nor is this all. Apart from drawing on deliberation to interrogate the facts we take to be the case, and the goals we seek, we can ask after what actions or other responses we ought to adopt in virtue of those facts and goals. Not only can we ask after whether they give us a reliable position at which to stand; we can ask after where they would lead us, whether in espousing further facts or goals, or in resorting to action. We may be rationally led in the manner of non-human animals, for example, to perform a given action as a result of taking the facts to be thus and so and treating such and such as a goal. But we can also reason or deliberate our way to that action—we can reinforce our rational inclination with a deliberative endorsement—by arguing that the facts, as we take them to be, are thus and so, the goals such and such, and that this makes one or another option the course of action to take; it provides support for that response.

One final comment. Drawing on deliberation in full explicit mode, as this account suggests, involves asking after certain higher-order matters. But I may be subject to deliberative control even in cases where I do not explicitly deliberate in this sense. Suppose that without explicit deliberation I tend generally to go where such deliberation would lead me and that if I do not—if my habits take me in intuitively the wrong direction—then the 'red lights' generally go on and I am triggered to activate deliberative pilot. Under such a regime, deliberation will 'virtually' control the evolution of my beliefs and desires; it will ride herd on the process, being there as a factor that intervenes only on a need-to-act basis.[6]

The truth-serving, value-serving structure of deliberation

So much by way of introducing deliberation. But what exact form does deliberation take? What are the premises invoked when I deliberate my way to some novel conclusion, whether a conclusion that I should believe such and such, desire so and so, or choose this or that action?

Suppose that my holding by a certain belief, say that p, makes it rational to form a further response: for example, to hold by an

---

[6] See Pettit (2001), Ch.2.

entailed belief that r or, given suitable goals, to perform a certain action, A. And now imagine that I am reflecting on whether there is a reason why I should hold that r or perform A. Should I think 'I believe that p; so therefore I should hold that r, or perform A'? Reflection suggests not; or it suggests at least that I should not confine myself to this project (Broome 2004). There will always be a question as to whether I should believe that p. And if it is not the case that I should believe that p, then there may not be any reason to believe that r or to perform A. It may be that I am mistaken or unjustified in believing that p, for example. It may even be that the belief that p is lodged unmoveably within me, despite all the evidence I register against it (Dennett 1979); it may represent a sort of pathology.

How should I deliberate and think, then, if I am to raise the question as to whether there is a reason to believe what 'p' entails or to act as it suggests I should act? Clearly, I should ask whether p; and if I remain convinced on that score I should reason: 'p; so therefore I should believe that r; p, so therefore I should do A'. It will be the fact that p, as I take it to be, that provides a reason for holding by the further belief, or taking the relevant action, not the fact that I believe that p. And this formulation makes that feature salient. An alternative that would do equally well, of course, is: 'It is true that p; so I should believe that r. It is true that p; so I should perform A'. For the fact that it is true that p means, not that I believe it, but that I should believe it; and in this way it serves in the same role as the fact that p. Weaker alternatives that would also serve appropriately, though not with the same force, are 'probably p, so ...' or 'it is probably true that p; so ...'. But this is not the place to get into such detail.

The question that arises now with desire is whether things go in parallel there to how they go with belief. Suppose that my holding by a certain desire, say that q, makes it rational for me, given the beliefs I hold, to form a further desire or perform a certain action: say, to desire that s or to perform B. And now imagine that I am reflecting on whether there is reason why I should hold by that extra desire or perform that particular action. Should I think 'I desire that q; so therefore I should desire that s. I desire that q; so therefore I should perform B'? Or will that leave me without the fullest ratiocinative endorsement available? Will it leave me with the thought: 'Fine, but should I desire that q; fine, but does this really give me a reason for desiring that s or for performing B?'

I think it is clear that the formula offered will leave me with that question. For as we allow that our beliefs may be false or ill-founded, and that we may not strictly have a reason for responding as they require, so we all allow that our desires may not be well-formed and that equally we may not always have a reason for responding as they require. Some desires we naturally regard as pathological, others as the products of a weak will, others as due to a lack of imagination or memory, and so on; pathologies of desire are a lot more commonplace than pathologies of belief. This being so, we cannot think that the proper ratiocinative endorsement for acting on a given desire should simply start from the existence of that desire, putting it into the foreground of deliberation, as if it were something sacred and beyond question.

What form will the ratiocinative endorsement of desire take? It cannot parallel the example with belief that goes 'p; and so ...'. But it can parallel the variant that invokes the truth that p, or the likelihood that it is true that p. As the truth of something means that I should believe it—that I have a reason for believing it—so the property of a goal that we ascribe when we say it is 'desirable' or 'good' or 'appropriate' or 'valuable' means that I should desire it, that I have at least a defeasible reason for desiring it. Assuming that there is some property deserving to be named by such a term, we can say that in deliberating our way to action we have to take our start, not from the fact that we desire certain goals, but from the fact that, as we see things, those goals are desirable or good or valuable or whatever. This line fits with our ordinary practice and with the long tradition of thinking that the major premise in a practical syllogism should not mention the fact that some state of affairs is desired but rather the fact that it is worthy of being desired (Anscombe 1957).

The picture of deliberation emerging from these considerations is that it is a truth-serving and value-serving enterprise. Deliberation tries to track the true and the valuable, not the believed and the desired, in looking at whether a novel response is well supported. And this is the case whether the response is the formation of a new belief or desire—or indeed a novel intention or policy or the like—or the performance of an action.

So far as the model depicts deliberation as truth-serving, it fits with received wisdom and will raise few questions. But won't it be more controversial in depicting deliberation as value-serving? Won't it be more controversial, in particular, when it assumes that there is a property of goals that deserves the name of 'desirability' or whatever? Truth, it may be said, is a relatively uncontested reality—at least outside of some postsmodernist circles—but desirability or value is inherently questionable.

The comment to make in response to this worry is that what makes a goal worthy to be desired may be held to consist in any of a variety of features but that almost every philosophical view will countenance some features that play this role; it will acknowledge that there are some value-making properties. That a goal counts as desirable, or at least desirable for me, may be held to require one or more of the following properties, for example:

- it is something I can bring about;
- it coheres with other things I want to bring about;
- it isn't the sort of goal that, once achieved, will seem like nothing (Milgram 1997);
- its attraction doesn't depend on any false beliefs, any failures of reason, any temporary derangements of sentiment, and the like (Smith 1994);
- my pursuit of the goal can be justified to others, serving to further common ends (Pettit 1997), or to further a sectional end that others can endorse (Scanlon 1998).

A complexity with desire

The model of deliberation introduced so far abstracts from a complexity with desire that is important to mention in concluding this discussion of deliberation. While all desires are goal-seeking states, capable of being characterized by their functional role, some desires also have a phenomenal aspect; there is something it is like to have them. Or at least that is a natural way to characterize certain examples. I am thinking of desires like the craving for a cigarette, the yearning for a drink, the ache of loneliness. With such desires we are not just conscious of the states of affairs that they make attractive to us; we are conscious of the states of feeling or inclination in which they themselves consist or by which they are attended. Those states have the presence of a disturbing itch, so that it makes perfect sense to think of endorsing a certain response—going for a smoke, getting something to drink, arranging to meet some friends—on the grounds, at least in part, that this will relieve that itch; this will restore equilibrium.

What one thinks desirable in such a case will not be the state of affairs considered in itself—the smoke or the drink or even the social gathering—or at least not exclusively that state of affairs. What one thinks desirable, at least in part, will be that state of affairs considered as a means of relieving the phenomenal desire—as a means of ensuring that the craving or yearning or ache has gone, with the pleasure associated with getting rid of it in that way as distinct from getting rid of it by resort to therapy, or treatment, or drugs. The existence of phenomenal as distinct from merely functional desires marks a genuine disanalogy between the case of belief and desire, between fact-construing and goal-seeking states. The disanalogy reveals that there are two sorts of desires. With one, the goal is simply the desired state of affairs in itself; with the other, it is, at least in part, the desired state of affairs in its role as a means of relieving the desire.

The fact that there are two sorts of desire, phenomenal and non-phenomenal, does not undermine the value-serving model of deliberation. According to that model, the reasoned endorsement of a response which a desire makes it rational to form should not invoke the existence of the state of desire but rather the desirability of the objective desired. And the mere existence of a phenomenal desire will not provide a warrant for acting so as to satisfy it. If such action is to be warranted, then it must be the case, not just that I have the desire, but that it is desirable that the desired state of affairs be realized and the desire be thereby relieved. The fact that I have a craving for a smoke will not provide a warrant for smoking except so far as it is desirable, if indeed it is, that the craving be relieved in the distinctive manner of satiated fulfilment.

But though the existence of phenomenal as well as merely functional desires does not undermine the value-serving model of deliberation sketched in this section, it does force us to be careful. It shows that we have to be alert to whether the goal-seeking state on the basis of which someone acts is phenomenal or non-phenomenal in thinking about what form their deliberation will take. This point will prove to be important to the discussion in the next section.[7]

3. Preference meets deliberation

We come finally to the question of how preference and deliberation interact in decision-making and, in particular, of what role the idea

[7] Many of the points made here about phenomenal desire apply more generally to desires such that the agent may wish to be rid of them, whether or not they have a phenomenal aspect: say, unconscious impulses or obsessions. Like phenomenal desires, these will be such that it will only make sense to act on them in the event that they continue to be present; see the next section.

of preference-satisfaction plays. I will conduct the discussion by looking in turn at three questions. First, what do I target in deliberative decision-making? Second, what makes the target or targets desirable for me? And third, what are the implications for the role of preference-satisfaction?

What do I target?

Asked what I target in deliberative decision-making, I might well answer: the satisfaction of my preferences. This would fit perfectly with everything that we have seen so far. But the various points made in the last section suggest that I should go on immediately to explain exactly what I mean and to guard against some obvious misunderstandings.

What needs to be said in particular is that the satisfaction of preferences may refer either to the realization of those states of affairs that fulfill the preferences or to the relief of the preferences, as we might call it: the removal of the preferences from one's psychology by means of fulfilling them. It is perfectly reasonable to think in the case of phenomenal desires that not only do agents seek to fulfill their preferences, they seek also to be relieved of the phenomenal itch that those preferences constitute—and of course to enjoy the pleasure associated with the relief process.

So what do I target in deliberative decision-making? In the normal, functional case, it should be clear that what I target is the fulfillment of my preferences: the realization of those states of affairs that attract sufficient intensities of preference—sufficient desires—to count for me as goals. In the case of phenomenal desires, however, I may have a double target: the fulfillment of my preferences in the sense just explained plus the relief that fulfillment will bring. Conceivably, however, I might be indifferent to the relief and seek only the fulfillment. Or I might be indifferent to the fulfillment and seek only the relief.[8]

---

[8] I might also just want to get rid of the desire, whether with or without the pleasure associated with relief. In this latter case I would presumably be happy to have the preference or desire removed by therapy or treatment or drugs, rather than by fulfillment; indeed, for reasons to do with long-term prospects, I might even prefer this mode of removal.

Philip Pettit

What makes my target or targets desirable for me?

So much for what I target in deliberative decision-making. But what now makes my target or targets desirable for me? What is it about the fulfillment of my preferences, or the relief of my preferences, that is likely to appeal to me when I am drawn to them? What are the desirability characteristics—the cherished features—that I am liable to register in those goals (Anscombe 1957)?

The main claim I want to make about the desirability characteristic of preference-fulfilment in the normal, functional case is that it is not necessarily egocentric. Perhaps I have to think of what I set out to achieve in ego-relative terms as fulfilling my preference. But the feature that will make the sought-after state of affairs attractive or desirable for me is not necessarily or generally that ego-relative sort of property. It will be for other reasons, and not because the action promises to fulfill my preferences, that I will find it desireable.

Were it important to me that some future state of affairs that I prefer to have realized will serve to fulfill my preference then, plausibly, I will only want to have it realized in the future so long as my preference itself continues into the future (Parfit 1984). But there is nothing even slightly unusual about taking steps for the fulfillment of a normal, functional preference in full awareness that by the time fulfillment comes the preference will have disappeared. I may now act on a preference for committing a fortune I will eventually inherit to the poor, well aware that by the time that I inherit the money the anxieties of age will have taken over and I will no longer have the preference on which I acted earlier. Again, I may now act on a preference for publishing a paper, conscious on the basis of past experience that by the time it appears I will have lost the preference for having it in print. These phenomena would make no sense if what was supposed to make giving away my fortune or publishing my article desirable was the fact that it would fulfill a concurrent preference.[9]

The lesson, I think, is clear. In seeking the fulfillment of a preference, the desirability characteristic of the fulfilling state of

---

[9] At least these phenomena would not make sense, assuming that the supposed desirability characteristic was that realizing the preferred state of affairs in each case would fulfill a contemporary or concurrent preference. It remains possible in principle that I might be focused on this desirability characteristic instead: that when the preferred scenario comes to be

affairs need not be ego-relative and the preference need not be egocentric. I may find that state of affairs desirable for egocentric reasons, of course, such as that it will further my prospects in life. But again I may find it desirable for a variety of other more altruistic or neutral considerations too: that it will help you or some others in this or that manner, that it will make for greater justice in the world, that it will increase the sum of sentient happiness, or whatever.

So much by way of commentary on the regular case of functional desire. But it is worth remarking that there is a contrast here with phenomenal desire. Suppose that I want something, not just because of the inherent appeal of the preference-fulfilling state of affairs—the inherent appeal, if there is any, in scratching or smoking or whatever—but because of the appeal of that action as a way of relieving me of a phenomenal desire: assuaging the itch, satiating the yearning for nicotine. In such a case I will be preferring the state of affairs sought for a characteristically ego-relative property and the preference will be to that extent egocentric. Thus it may make little or no sense for me to arrange to have the preference satisfied at a later time, if I believe that at that later time the preference will already have disappeared. To believe this will be to believe that the fulfilment of the preference—the fulfilment in the future of what will be by then a past preference—cannot have the desirability characteristic of relieving a phenomenal state.

We have seen that while I may be said to pursue the satisfaction of my preferences in deliberative decision-making, this is ambiguous between saying that I pursue fulfillment of the preferences and saying that I pursue relief from the preferences. We have seen that only fulfilment is relevant with normal, functional preferences but that relief is relevant—on its own or alongside fulfilment—with preferences of a phenomenal kind. And we have seen, finally, that whereas preference-fulfillment may be desirable for non-egocentric or egocentric reasons, there is something essentially egocentric about the desirability of preference-relief.

---

realized it will serve at that time to fulfill retrospectively the preference that I now have for its realization. This possibility is so bizarre, however, that we need not delay over it.

Philip Pettit

What are the implications for the role of preference-satisfaction?

There are two implications for the role of preference-satisfaction supported by these lines of argument. The first is that it is potentially misleading to frame one's practical decision-making in terms of satisfying one's preferences. And the second is that it would be a serious mistake for policy-makers to think that increasing people's preference-satisfaction is a sensible goal.

To frame one's decision-making in terms of preference-satisfaction would be to deliberate, implicitly or explicitly, along these lines: I have preferences such that the best way of satisfying them is to perform an action, A; it is desirable to satisfy my preferences; so I should perform action A. But this mode of reasoning suggests that what makes the satisfaction of my preferences desirable is not the character of the preference-fulfilling scenario in itself, or least not entirely that. What is also crucial, so the implicature goes, is the fact that the scenario has the ego-relative property of fulfilling my preferences.

This will not generally be an implicature I should endorse. It will be sound in the case where the preferences are phenomenal in nature and their fulfillment is desirable in part for the relief it will bring. But it will not generally carry. Consider the case, for example, where I am persuaded of the value of helping to ameliorate third world poverty by making a financial contribution. What is likely to make that contribution desirable by my lights? It just might be that doing so will relieve a guilt-related preference for making a contribution. But in the more regular sort of case the contribution will be desirable by my lights for reasons unrelated to any such egocentric return. That might appear, for example, in the fact that I am happy to precommit some future earnings to the cause of third world poverty, even as I foresee that I will later come to have different, more self-serving preferences and feel no guilt whatsoever.[10]

Were I always to frame my practical reasoning in terms of preference-satisfaction then there might be a danger of losing the distinction between seeking preference-fulfilment and seeking preference-relief. It might begin to seem that acting on one's preferences always means acting for a sort of personal advantage and that egocentricity is built into the very logic of human

[10] It is just possible in this case of course that I now precommit to contribute in the future because of the relief from guilt that doing this gives me now.

150

decision-making. I think it is very important to resist this mistake, if only to guard against a sort of global demoralization about our species.

The mistake is not always avoided, particularly among the economically minded theorists who make the notion of preference-satisfaction central in their accounts of agency. Consider this remark, for example, from Anthony Downs (1957, 37), a classic exponent of the rational choice approach to politics. 'There can be no simple identification of acting for one's greatest benefit with selfishness in the narrow sense because self-denying charity is often a great source of benefits to oneself. Thus our model leaves room for altruism in spite of its basic reliance upon the self-interest axiom'. Downs's idea is not that it pays to be charitable—he is not a homespun philosopher—but that acting for charity, presumably because it is a case of acting for the satisfaction of one's own charitable preferences, will inevitably have a self-interested aspect. He suggests that self-interest will be present as much in altruism, then, as in 'selfishness in the narrow sense'.

So much for the first implication of our considerations, that it is potentially misleading to frame one's practical decision-making in terms of satisfying one's preferences. The second implication is that it would be a serious mistake for policy-makers to think that increasing people's preference-satisfaction is a sensible goal.

The point here is one that Amartya Sen (Sen 1982; Sen 2002) is famous for having emphasized and it fits nicely with our picture of preference and deliberation. Suppose that people were as inescapably egocentric as they would be were every form of practical deliberation directed towards the relief as distinct from the fulfilment of preference. In that case they could each be represented as seeking their own advantage—the satisfaction of their own preferences, as in the relief that that provides. And now consider under that supposition how people in government might reasonably think about the point of the policies they are to introduce. It would make perfect sense for them to act—assuming that their own egocentric concern allows them to act—for achieving the best overall satisfaction of people's individual preferences. If individuals are supposed to be concerned only with their own welfare—the satisfaction, as in the relief, of their own preferences—then it must seem reasonable to think that an agency that acts in their name as a group should be concerned with looking for an arrangement in which their individual preferences are equally satisfied, or in which the net balance of preference-satisfaction is maximized, or something of the kind.

151

Philip Pettit

This, however, will look like an absurd policy-goal once it is recognized that, as we have been arguing, people are often quite non-egocentric in acting on their preferences. Suppose that some people act out of egocentric preferences, and others out of more or less altruistic preferences: say, preferences for the welfare of others, including others of an egocentric bent. Then a government that sought to equalize or maximize preference-satisfaction in the society would be double-counting the egoists. They would be looking after them on two counts: both as objects of their own concern and as objects of concern to the more altruistic.

The point here, like the point of the first implication, is hard to miss once it is spelled out but easy to miss in the absence of some emphasis. I hope that situating the two points within an overall view of what deliberation and preference are and of how they work together will help to make them absolutely inescapable. They are platitudinous in character but they represent platitudes that economic theorizing and policy-making has sometimes proved capable of overlooking.[11]

References

Anscombe, G. E. M. (1957). *Intention*. Oxford, Blackwell.
Broome, J. (1991). *Weighing Goods*. Oxford, Blackwell.
Broome, J. (2004). Reasons. *Essays in Honour of Joseph Raz*. J. Wallace, M. Smith, S. Scheffler and P. Pettit. Oxford, Oxford University Press.
Davidson, D. (1980). *Essays on Actions and Events*. Oxford, Oxford University Press.
Dennett, D. (1979). *Brainstorms*. Brighton, Harvester Press.
Downs, A. (1957). *An Economic Theory of Democracy*. New York, Harper.
Dreier, J. (1996). 'Rational Preference: Decision Theory as a Theory of Practical Rationality.' *Theory and Decision* **40**: 249–76.
Hurley, S. (1989). *Natural Reasons*. New York, Oxford University Press.
Jackson, F. and P. Pettit (1990). 'In Defence of Folk Psychology.' *Philosophical Studies* **57**: 7–30; reprinted in F.Jackson, P.Pettit and M.Smith, 2004, *Mind, Morality and Explanation*, Oxford, Oxford University Press.
Lewis, D. (1983). *Philosophical Papers Vol 1*. Oxford, Oxford University Press.

[11] I am very grateful for the many helpful comments I received when the paper was presented at the Royal Institute of Philosophy Conference in Cambridge, July, 2004, and when it was discussed in a seminar I taught with Adam Elga in Princeton, Fall 2004. Jeremy Butterfield provided a particularly useful set of comments and I am in his debt.

Little, I. M. D. (1950). *A Critique of Welfare Economics*. Oxford, Oxford University Press.

McGeer, V. and P. Pettit (2002). 'The Self-regulating Mind.' *Language and Communication* 22: 281–99.

Milgram, E. (1997). *Practical Induction*. Cambridge, Mass., Harvard University Press.

Parfit, D. (1984). *Reasons and Persons*. Oxford, Oxford University Press.

Pettit, P. (1991). Decision Theory and Folk Psychology. *Essays in the foundations of Decision Theory*. M. Bacharach and S. Hurley. Oxford, Blackwell; reprinted in P.Pettit 2002 *Rules, Reasons, and Norms*, Oxford, Oxford University Press.

Pettit, P. (1993). *The Common Mind: An Essay on Psychology, Society and Politics,* paperback edition 1996, New York, Oxford University Press.

Pettit, P. (1997). A Consequentialist Perspective on Ethics. *Three Methods of Ethics: A Debate*. M. Baron, M. Slote and P. Pettit. Oxford, Blackwell.

Pettit, P. and M. Smith (1990). 'Backgrounding Desire.' *Philosophical Review* 99: 565–92; reprinted in F.Jackson, P.Pettit and M.Smith, 2004, *Mind, Morality and Explanation*, Oxford, Oxford University Press.

Pettit, P. (2001). A Theory of Freedom, Polity, 2001.

Ramsey, F. P. (1990). *Philosophical Papers*. Cambridge, Cambridge University Press.

Samuelson, P. (1938). 'A Note on the Pure Theory of Consumers' Behavior.' *Economica* **N.S. 5**: 61–71.

Scanlon, T. M. (1998). *What We Owe To Each Other*. Cambridge, Mass., Harvard University Press.

Sen, A. (1982). *Choice, Welfare and Measurement*. Oxford, Blackwell.

Sen, A. (2002). *Rationality and Freedom*. Cambridge, Mass., Harvard University Press.

Smith, M. (1994). *The Moral Problem*. Oxford, Blackwell.

Content-Related and Attitude-Related Reasons for Preferences

CHRISTIAN PILLER

In the first section of this paper I draw, on a purely conceptual level, a distinction between two kinds of reasons: content-related and attitude-related reasons. The established view is that, in the case of the attitude of believing something, there are no attitude-related reasons. I look at some arguments intended to establish this claim in the second section with an eye to whether these argument could be generalized to cover the case of preferences as well. In the third section I argue against such generalizations and present a case in favour of accepting attitude-related reasons for preferences. In the fourth section I present an objection to which I react in the fifth section where I try to strengthen my case for attitude-related reasons for preferences. Finally, I discuss and reject criticisms raised by two opponents of the view defended here.

I The Distinction

Think of any attitude we might have towards some proposition p, which, because we have some attitude towards it, I call the content of this attitude. It might be an epistemic attitude like belief or doubt, an attitude like desiring or intending, or an emotional attitude like anger or gratefulness. For all these attitudes we can have reasons that speak in favour of or against adopting them. On a conceptual level we can distinguish between two kinds of reasons. Content-related reasons are such that, if we are aware of them, they show us p, the content of an attitude, in a certain light. They point to some feature of p, which makes a certain attitude towards p the appropriate one to have. Attitude-related reasons, by contrast, are such that, if we are aware of them, they show us our having a certain attitude towards p in a certain light. They point to some feature of our having this attitude that makes it the appropriate one to have. Thus, reasons for adopting a certain attitude might be

155

grounded in two different ways: either by their relation to some feature of the content of an attitude or by their relation to some feature of the attitude itself.

The following examples show that we can handle this distinction well enough. Take the attitude of believing first. The propositional content of my belief that p might be entailed by other things I believe with good reason. This feature of the proposition that p, namely being entailed by what I reasonably believe, makes it the case that I have good reason to believe that p. Because we are talking about a feature of the proposition that p, the reason mentioned is a content-related reason. In contrast, believing that p might be beneficial in some way. This, if there are such things, would be an attitude-related reason for believing that p, as being beneficial is a property of believing that p. Similarly with emotions: being incapable of doing something most other people can do might well be a reason for me to be ashamed of myself. I am ashamed of myself because I have the property of being incapable of doing something others can do easily. My reason for feeling shame is content-related. If my being ashamed, in fact, prevents me from doing what others can do easily, then I have an attitude-related reason against feeling ashamed. My attitude of feeling ashamed has the property of preventing me from doing something the doing of which is important to me. Similarly for preferences: I might prefer apples to oranges on grounds of how apples and oranges taste. If so, this would be a content-related reason for this preference. Preferring home-grown products might be an aspect of being supportive of one's local community. If to support one's local community is a desirable feature, then, as I am not living in a country where oranges grow easily, I would have an attitude-related reason for preferring apples to oranges, as it is my preference for apples over oranges that has this desirable feature.

The distinction between content-related and attitude-related reasons has been explained by the distinction between features of an attitude's content and features of the attitude itself. This might not look like a solid enough foundation for the following reason. Instead of saying that the attitude A with content C has a feature F, we could almost equivalently say that C is such that the attitude A towards it is or would be F. For example: To call one's confidence in one's own abilities useful is almost the same as saying that one's abilities are such that belief in them is or would be useful. Thus, features of attitudes, which, according to our initial suggestion, provide attitude-related reasons, can, it seems, simply be re-described as features of the content of these attitudes and would then provide content-related reasons. The same argument also works the other way around. What looks like a content-related reason, namely that some content C has feature F, can be re-described as an attitude-related reason, namely as A being such that its being related to C would make it an A that relates to something that is F. According to this objection, it is simply arbitrary whether we pick out some feature as a feature of an attitude A or as a feature of its content C.[1]

Does the idea that we can describe the same situation— something's having some feature—with varying grammatical subjects really undermine the suggested distinction between two different kinds of reasons? On the one hand we have what looks like a purely grammatical point; on the other hand we have examples that indicate an ability to draw a plausible distinction. It certainly would come as a surprise if it turned out that there couldn't be this ability to distinguish, which we are confident to have.

The objection points to a *possibility* of re-describing features. We can understand what, intuitively, is a feature of an attitude as a feature of the attitude's content, but we also *need not do so*. We can understand what, intuitively, is a content's feature as a feature of a thus directed attitude, but, again, *we need not*. This is all that is needed to answer the objection. Features of the content of an attitude, I said, provide content-related reasons. What this amounts to is that we *can* describe the features of this content without mentioning our attitude towards it. This provides us with a real contrast to attitude-related reasons. If we *cannot* describe the content's feature without referring to the attitude we have towards this very content, then we are dealing with an attitude-related reason. Consider the following example: the usefulness of one's belief in one's own abilities would, intuitively, be an attitude-related reason for this belief. One might well say that one's abilities are such that belief in them would be useful. But even if, grammatically, one describes the reason-giving feature as an aspect of the belief's content, one nevertheless cannot refer to it as a

---

[1] This objection is presented and defended in Rabinowicz&Ronnow-Rasmusson 2004, 404–410. Their concern, however, is not the denial of attitude-reasons—in fact they are sympathetic to the idea that there are such reasons—but to exclude attitude-related reasons in a deontic analysis of value.

feature of the content without mentioning the attitude one has towards it. This makes it an attitude-related reason for believing in one's abilities.[2]

Note that facts concerning people's attitudes, including my own, can be content-related reasons for attitudes. Only if the reason for an attitude cannot be described without mentioning this very attitude, do we have an attitude-related reason for this attitude. Liking him because he likes my liking of football is for me a content-related reason for liking him: From my perspective it shows him to be appreciative of others having appropriate interests and as such specifies a feature of him, which I take to be a reason. The feature which is a reason, his liking of people interested in football, can be described without mentioning the attitude it is a reason for, which is my liking him. If, however, I would like him because he would like my liking of him, then, assuming that I have good reason to please him, I would have an attitude-related reason for liking him. The feature which gives me reason to like him, namely his liking of my liking him, cannot be described without referring to what the feature is a reason for, i.e. without referring to my liking him.

Another worry about the concept of an attitude-related reason runs as follows: Attitude-related reasons, we have learnt, make essential reference to a feature of the attitude. Think about the following feature: Believing that p might be such that it has the weight of reasons on its side. This is certainly a feature that we can only identify with reference to the very attitude of believing that p. Nevertheless it seems wrong to call it an attitude-related reason. Similarly, any principle concerning reasons for belief will have to mention the belief or the kind of belief for which reasons are specified. It would, however, completely undermine our distinction if all principles of reasons could only ever specify attitude-related reasons.

Let me answer this worry: The fact that the evidence at hand best supports a belief is not an attitude-related reason because it is not a reason at all. It rather is a statement about reasons and about where their force lies. Similarly, a statement that specifies that something is a reason for something else is not itself a reason but a statement about a reason. What is the reason for believing that there is a fire? It is the smoke or the fact that I notice the smoke.

---

[2]   My account of the distinction between content-related and attitude-related reasons is similar to the more complicated account offered by Olson (2004).

The fact that noticing the smoke is a reason to believe there is a fire—this whole epistemological fact—is not itself a reason to believe that there is a fire. As we can obviously refer to what is the reason, namely my noticing the smoke, without having to refer to what it is a reason for, noticing the smoke is a content-related reason for believing that there is a fire.[3]

One last remark on the distinction between attitude-related and content-related reasons: A reason is always a reason for something. If we vary what the reason is a reason for, then what was an attitude-related reason for something can become a content-related reason for something else. The usefulness of my believing that p is, if it is a reason for believing at all, an attitude-related reason for believing that p. Suppose we can intend to believe that p. If so, the usefulness of the belief that p would be a feature of what the intention is about and, thus, it would be a content-related reason for intending to believe that p. If, however, it would be a waste of time to intend to believe that p, then this feature of this intention would be an attitude-related reason against intending to believe that p, which in turn could be a content-related reason for wanting not to intend to believe that p.

The distinction between content-related and attitude-related reason is supposed to be completely general. It applies to all attitudes for which there could be reasons and, furthermore, it is supposed not to exclude any substantive view about what is a reason for what. Having clarified the concept of an attitude-related reason, we can now turn to the more interesting question: Are there such reasons?

II Attitude-Related Reasons for Beliefs

Most people think there would be something odd about accepting attitude related reasons for beliefs. The fact that it would be beneficial for me to believe something, in general, does not, it seems, bear on the question whether my belief is held rationally or on whether it is justifiable. Only facts that somehow bear on its

[3] The feature that is indicted by a content-related reason for adopting some attitude will, of course, vary depending on which attitude it is. In the case of preferences we can think of it as comparative desirability, a notion that itself will vary depending on which substantive theory of desirability one adheres to. In the case of beliefs the notion of comparative likelihood can play a similar role.

truth, i.e. facts that primarily have to do with the content of the belief, can play a justificatory role. What explains this common resistance to accepting attitude-related reasons for beliefs?

A salient fact about beliefs is that often we are unable to adopt a belief by simply deciding to adopt it. 'Can we, by any effort of our will, or by any strength of wish that it were true, believe ourselves well and about when we are roaring with rheumatism in bed [...]?' asks William James and he answers, 'we can say such a thing [namely that we are well] but we are absolutely impotent to believe [it].' (James 1897, 5) No one disagrees with James about his example. But there are other cases. Can't I decide to close my investigation into a matter and settle on the view most plausible at the moment, and isn't this a decision to adopt a certain view of the matter? For example, can't I decide to believe the student who assures me that he was unwell (maybe roaring with rheumatism in bed) and thus grant him an extension to his deadline (cf. Harman 1997)? And can't I decide that some matter is so serious that my usual standards for sufficient evidence are too lax, and, therefore, decide not to believe anything (cf. Nozick 1993, 86f.)? Taking these cases at face value, we should set limits to when we cannot decide to believe. The limit is easily drawn: We cannot decide to believe something in the face of strong reasons to the contrary. In short, we cannot decide to believe against our reasons.[4]

How does our inability to decide to believe undermine the idea that there could be attitude-related reasons for beliefs? The answer already lies in what has been said. We agreed that we couldn't decide to believe that we are well when obviously ill. Why not? Because we cannot decide to believe something if we have strong reasons to the contrary, as belief is an attitude governed by reasons. The existence of attitude-related reasons would undermine the correctness of this explanation.

Decisions are guided by reasons that have to do with the value or desirability (however we conceive of these things) of what is brought about by these decisions. Attitude-related reasons are

---

[4]   Some authors, see for example Owens (2000, 30), have suggested that we cannot decide to believe even if the evidence is indecisive. Take a coin toss: you cannot simply decide to believe it will come up heads. I agree that we cannot do that. But I'd say that this is just an instance of the above drawn limit to decisions to believe. In case of a coin toss it would be against reason to do anything but withhold one's judgment. To withhold one's judgment need not indicate lack of evidence but might, in fact, be best supported by one's evidence. See, for example, Keynes 1921, 'The Weight of Arguments', 71–91.

usually of this very kind, they mention desirable or useful features of attitudes. If there were attitude-related reasons for believing something, then our inability to decide to believe that we are well, when ill, could not be explained by the fact that we cannot decide to believe against reason. After all, the attitude-related reasons for believing to be well could be quite strong. If there were strong enough attitude-related reason for believing oneself to be well, it would not be against reason to hold this belief. Thus, we would have lost our explanation of our inability to decide to believe in this case. This inability, however, needs an explanation. Regardless of how strong we imagine these attitude-related reasons to be, it will still hold that we cannot acquire the beneficial belief simply by decision. Thus, assuming that the correct explanation of the inability to decide to believe, when present, has to do with the fact that belief is governed by reasons, there cannot be attitude-related reasons for beliefs. Their existence would undermine the correct explanation of an obvious fact. For future reference I call this 'the undermining argument'.

There might be deeper reaching explanations of why there are no attitude-related reasons for beliefs. Believing, it is often said, is an attitude that has truth as its constitutive aim. David Velleman, for example, presents such a position as follows: 'We believe a proposition when we regard it as true for the sake of thereby getting the truth right with respect to that proposition: to believe something is to accept it with the aim of doing so only if it really is true.' (Velleman 1996, 183) It is the aim of getting things right, which distinguishes believing from other attitudes like assuming. The fact that it would be nice to have a certain belief need not be indicative of its truth. Thus, when we are trying to come up with a belief about a subject matter, considerations of value, insofar as value isn't truth-related, don't count. These considerations don't count because if they did, we would not be anymore in the business of coming up with a belief.

Velleman allows that someone might not be interested in getting things right; one might just be indifferent to truth (and interested in believing that p regardless of whether p is true or not) or one might want, for some reason, to believe what is wrong, whatever it is. Thus, it need not be the agent who aims at getting things right. But what things besides agents have aims? One aspect of Velleman's view is that attitudes or mechanisms which produce such attitudes have their own aims.

Here, however, I am not really concerned with the details of Velleman's argument. I use it as a contrast to the previous argument. In both arguments a feature of beliefs, namely that we can't believe against reason in the first argument and that belief aims at truth in Velleman's argument, is employed to argue against attitude-related reasons for beliefs. The first argument, however, is set on a more general level; it mentions reasons but not truth. Thus, it seems to invite us to draw a more general lesson. We can't just believe at will, because belief is guided by reasons. Similarly, we can't just desire at will, because desire is also guided by reason, and we can't just intend to do something at will, because intentions are also guided by reasons. The first argument, it seems, is generalisable to all attitudes. If so, it would support a denial of attitude-related reasons for all attitudes. David Owens endorses such a generalization in the following passage: 'I have already established that beliefs are not subject to the will because a belief could not be justified simply by reference to the desirable consequences of having the belief. Something similar is true of practical decisions: what makes a decision rational is not the advantages of the decision itself but those of the action decided upon' (Owens 2000, 81).

Let me try to support for a moment such a generalization. Attitude-related reasons look odd because they might threaten a certain form of realism about reasons. By realism I mean that there are conditions of appropriateness and/or correctness for all attitudes, which are independent of how the fulfilment of these conditions affects us. A belief is justified if what I believe is well supported by my evidence. Whether I like believing what I believe or not is irrelevant for a belief's normative status. The same holds, according to realism thus understood, for all attitudes for which there can be reasons. We can give conditions of appropriateness and/or correctness and our liking of the resulting attitudes should, again, not change their normative status. For example, my preference for A over B is correct if and only if A is indeed better than B (however we understand betterness; we could well understand it in the subjective terms of decision theory). My intention to φ is appropriate if and only if φ-ing is the best option (again, however, we understand bestness). And similarly for emotions: 'It is irrational [or inappropriate],' Allan Gibbard writes, 'say, to be angry at the messenger who brings bad tidings, but rational to be angry at the miscreant who deliberately wrongs one.' (Gibbard 1990, 36) Whether my anger at either one of them is useful or harmful does not affect the conditions of appropriateness indicated by this example.

One more piece has to be added to fully describe what could well be called the Standard View, according to which there are no attitude-related reasons. A defender of attitude-related reasons might have argued as follows: harmfulness is often a reason against doing something. Why, if some attitude is harmful, should it not be a reason against holding this attitude? The Standard View accepts the normative force of harmfulness but relocates it. It is not a reason against holding the harmful attitude; it rather is a reason for trying to prevent holding the harmful attitude.

It first looked like a normative conflict, when the content-related reasons speak in favour of some attitude, but the harmfulness of holding this attitude speaks against it. According to the Standard View it is not a case of conflict after all. There are only content-related reasons for attitudes. What looked like attitude-related reasons are in fact reasons for something else, namely for trying to bring it about or to prevent holding some attitude. On this view it might well be rational to do something the expected result of which is an irrational attitude. The rationality of our attempts to bring an attitude about is simply irrelevant to the rationality of the attitude itself. Believing or wanting and bringing it about that one believes or wants something are two separate things, governed by different groups of reasons.[5]

In this section I considered why attitude-related reasons for beliefs look odd. My central concern, however, is whether there are attitude-related reasons for preferences, and three points have emerged that bear on this issue. First, we can try to generalize the idea that we cannot simply decide to believe because belief is governed by reasons. Preferences are governed by reasons as well. If, for that reason, we can't simply decide what to prefer, we might have an analogous argument against attitude-related reasons for preferences. Secondly, a realist understanding of the conditions of appropriateness and/or correctness of attitudes might extend to preferences. A preference, we might want to say, is fitting if and only if it is a preference for what actually is better. Whether we like having this preference might well be irrelevant for such an assessment. Thirdly, the distinction between reasons for believing something and reasons for trying to bring it about that one believes something can be applied, with the same plausibility, to preferences. Thus, the normative force of the considerations that a

---

[5] I call this the Standard View as almost everyone accepts it. To mention only those who play more than one role in this paper, see the cited work of Broome, Gibbard, Nozick, Owens, and Parfit.

defender of attitude-related reasons for preferences will appeal to, for example that having a preference is useful, can be accepted by the Standard View, but its relocation to the realm of attempts to influence one's preference structure renders the acceptance of attitude-related reasons for preferences spurious.

III Attitude-Related Reason for Preferences

Think of the following three choice situations.[6] In all of them your host offers you one of two fruits: you choose first and he takes the remaining one. If the choice is between a big apple and an orange, you take the big apple. Apples and oranges are pretty much on a par for you, apples just having a small advantage. If the choice is between an orange and a small apple, you take the orange. The small loss in quality of enjoyment is outweighed by the larger quantity of enjoyment the orange offers you. When the choice is between a big and a small apple, you take the small apple. Why? You don't want to leave the host with what you can reasonably expect to be his less preferred option. Doing so would be impolite. As you don't know (and are not expected to know) whether your host prefers oranges to apples, you can in those situations choose the fruit you like best. If the choice is between apples, however, you leave the fruit you expect your host to like more, and thereby choose the fruit you like less.

What does this example teach us? When we think about what to choose, we should not only think about the features of what we choose but also of the features of our so choosing. Tasting nice is a feature of what we choose; being polite is a feature of our choosing.

If it is legitimate to apply the distinction between content-related and attitude-related reasons to choice, then the apple example shows us that there are attitude-related reasons for choices. Politeness is a feature of choices, not of apples. Even if we can say that the apple is such that choosing it is polite, we have to refer to our choosing it when we describe this property of the apple, which, in accordance with our discussion in section 1, makes it an attitude-related reason for choosing the small apple.

Accepting attitude-related reasons for choices does not encounter the following problem which we would have to face if we accepted attitude-related reasons for beliefs. In the case of belief, when

[6] The example which follows is a popular variant of a case discussed in Sen (1977, p. 328).

attitude-related reason and content related reasons pull in different directions, we would have no clue how to weigh degrees of evidential support against something like the potential harmfulness of believing something. But in the case of choices such a weighing of different kinds of reasons poses no special difficulties. It is very much like weighing reasons of one and the same kind. In our example the attitude-related reason of politeness trumps the content-related reason which points to a difference in enjoyment. However, if we strengthened the content-related reasons we might get a different result. If the meal had been rather insubstantial and the small apple on offer was really very small, the balance might shift. It would also shift if the small apple had been treated with some chemical agent you but not your host are allergic to.

When I discussed the question why we are not inclined to accept attitude-related reasons for beliefs, three considerations emerged which one could try to use against the claim that preferences allow for attitude-related reasons. But when we try to undermine the force of the example above we realize that none of them works. The first argument doesn't get off the ground, in contrast to the case of belief, we can decide which apple to choose. According to the second argument, the acceptance of attitude-related reasons would threaten a realist understanding of them. The correctness condition for choice suggested above told us that a choice is correct if and only if what is chosen is best. A polite person, however, chooses what is worse, and, it seems, correctly so. Thus, this correctness condition needs to be changed in the light of our example: Choosing some G is correct if and only if the choosing of G is best. Such a principle is meant to make room for both content-related and attitude-related reasons. They are what determine whether our choosing is correct. Whether this new correctness conditions is satisfied or not is sufficiently independent of our attitudes towards the correct choice as these attitudes already partially determine which choice satisfies the condition. Thus, attitude-related reasons pose no threat to realism about reasons. What about the idea that we separate the domains to which content-related and attitude-related reasons apply? It would be absurd to apply this idea to the case at hand, as we would have to choose the big apple but we would also have to try to bring it about that we choose the small apple. To act politely, on this view, would only be possible if we succeeded in making ourselves choose irrationally. Not even rude people will accept this view.

So far I have talked about choices. Can we simply retell the above example in terms of preferences?[7] Just thinking about the fruit on offer, I would prefer the big apple. But when thinking about what to prefer I have to think not only about features of the object of my preference but also about features of my preferring. Politeness goes deeper than choice: A truly polite person doesn't have to grind her teeth when doing what is polite. The polite person, on the strength of her attitude-related reasons, does indeed *prefer* the small apple. She does so because preferring the small apple has an attractive feature: to prefer the small apple is to be polite.

If this picture is correct, one must wonder how attitude-related reasons for preferences could ever have been in dispute. Politeness is just one minor virtue, but what we find there seems to be an important aspect of any virtue. Kindness, for example, may demand something that, in a way, inconveniences oneself. But if one really is a kind person, one does what is kind wholeheartedly. After all, the inconvenience relates only to what one chooses or prefers and will be outweighed by the features of so choosing or preferring. In general, we care not only about what we get, we also care about who we are. Who we are is revealed in the choices we make and in the preferences, which usually are thus expressed. If it matters to us who we are, it matters to us which preferences we have. And if it matters to us which preferences to have, the door has been opened for attitude-related reasons.

What role does this defence of attitude-related reasons for preferences assign to second-order desires? Preferring the small apple has a desirable feature. It also has an undesirable feature, as it is a preference for what is worse. But as politeness is more important for one than the difference in the amount of enjoyment, one will overall want to have a preference for preferring the small

[7]   Some philosophers hold that the rationality of choices is directly determined by the rationality of the preferences that are expressed by these choices: 'Whether a voluntary action is rational, then, is a matter of the rationality of preferences and intentions' (Gibbard1990, 39); see also Scanlon 1998, 21. Once we allow for attitude-related reasons, however, the relation between rational preferences and rational choices is less straightforward. A preference for doing something might have desirable features that aren't accountable for purely in terms of what such a preference is a preference for. Thus, I won't make use of the general principle endorsed by Gibbard and Scanlon. For the case in question, though, I will argue that taking the small apple is indeed rational for the polite person because in her circumstances she correctly prefers the small apple.

apple. In a case like this, however, this second-order preference plays no important normative role. A rational agent is someone who will correctly respond to the force of her reasons. Thus, a rational agent will prefer the small apple on the strength of her attitude-related reasons for this preference. The second-order desire is simply an endorsement of a preference, which is the right one to have for independent reasons. Consequently, conflicts between second-order desires and first-order desires will raise the suspicion that a thus conflicted agent has not fully aligned his preferences with his reasons. Suppose I prefer the big apple, and prefer to prefer the small apple. There are two ways of describing this case. First, somewhat childishly, I cannot resist the promise of greater enjoyment. Thus, I prefer the big apple. But on reflection, I think that politeness should carry more weight. Thus, I prefer to prefer the small apple. My judgment that politeness is more important is obviously a criticism of my first-order preference. I don't prefer as, in my own view, I have most reason to prefer. Secondly, I can't free myself from the influence of conventional rules, though I doubt their normative significance. Thus, I do prefer to prefer the small apple. But, somehow, fortunately, this preference remains motivationally idle. I prefer the big apple in spite of my opposed second-order preference. I think that politeness in this context is of negligible importance and so my second-order preference is not as, in my view, it ought to be.

In the apple case and in cases relevantly similar, second-order desires don't play an independent normative role. Conflicts between second-order and first-order desires in such cases are indicative of a failure of having all one's preferences aligned with one's reasons. In other cases however—and I will introduce them later on—second-order preferences do play a significant normative role. This happens when first-order preferences leave matters underdetermined.

My defence of attitude-related reasons for preferences bears strong similarities to a view prominent in Amartya Sen's work. A crucial thought in this respect is the following: 'Rather than expressing moral views in terms of one ordering of outcomes, it may be necessary to express them through a ranking of the possible orderings of outcomes' (Sen 1974, 62).[8] In terms of our example, this would imply that the importance of politeness is captured by

[8] Above quote is not an isolated occurrence in Sen's work, as he has endorsed the importance of meta-rankings throughout his work; see Sen (2002, 18).

my preference for preferring the small apple, i.e. I rank the ranking which has the small apple on top higher than the alternative ranking. I regard this second-order preference as an endorsement of the result of having correctly weighed attitude-related and content-related reasons. Thus, I agree with Sen's claim that meta-rankings add needed explanatory power to preference theory, I only add a further explanation: these second–order preferences reflect the force of attitude-related reasons.

Here is another example, in which we meet attitude-related reasons:[9] One player has a dominant strategy. Playing it would secure him a small advantage over playing the other strategy. If he does so, the other player, however, will have no chance to receive a comparably good outcome. Many people play the dominated strategy. I suggest they do so because the payoff of the game is not the only relevant consideration. Interacting in a way that leaves one's partner with considerably less than he could have had had one made a small sacrifice, is being greedy or being nasty. But people commonly want to be nice. To prefer the dominated strategy is to be nice and, thus, to be the kind of person one usually wants to be. This explanation does not primarily appeal to a feeling of sympathy with the opponent: it is not that the amount the player receives is valued less by him if the other player fails to achieve a good result. Thus the effect should be preserved in conditions of increasing anonymity. If one values being nice, and thus takes attitude-related reasons into account, sympathy is not needed to influence the way one behaves.

Such an account fits well with Sen's distinction between sympathy and what he calls 'commitment': 'Sympathy is, in some ways, an easier concept to analyse than commitment. When a person's sense of well-being is psychologically dependent on someone else's welfare, it is a case of sympathy; other things given, the awareness of the increase in the welfare of the other person then makes this person directly better off [...]. On the other hand, commitment does involve, in a very real sense, counterpreferential choice, destroying the crucial assumption that a chosen alternative must be better than (or at least as good as) the others for the person choosing it [...]. Commitment is, of course, closely connected with one's morals' (Sen 1977, the three quotes come from 327, 328, 329). Sen's aim in this article is to broaden the framework of economic analysis. He wants to make room for commitments. In my view, he

---

[9] It is discussed in detail in Daniel Hausman's contribution to this volume.

thereby endorses attitude-related reasons. Is there a sense in which acting on one's commitments is 'counterpreferential'? One acts against preferences one had, if one would have only thought about content-related reasons. This is not an odd counterfactual, as thinking about issues in isolation from their social dimension might well be a natural step in the process of deliberation. Thus, the acceptance of attitude-related reasons offers both an account of the nature of commitments and a justification of including them in the analysis of rational behaviour.

IV An Opposed Analysis

The example by which I tried to illustrate the force of attitude-related reasons moves from polite choices to polite preferences. We choose the small apple, because we prefer it, and we prefer it because preferring it is to be polite. An opposed analysis of polite behaviour—an analysis that does not introduce attitude-related reasons—is, however, possible.[10]

The opposed analysis starts by inviting us to specify the objects of our preferences in more detail. In the context of our example we should distinguish between two distinct preferences involving the two apples: one preference is for *taking* the small apple, the other is for *receiving* the big apple. Politeness, let us plausibly assume, comes only into play when we consider what to do, not when we consider what should happen to us. Thus, although we do not prefer to receive the small apple, we do prefer to take it. The more detailed description of the objects of preferences renders this set of preferences unproblematic. They are simply preferences for different objects and, therefore, content-related reasons alone can account for them. We can think of these objects as bundles of goods: one bundle consists of a small apple and being polite, the other bundle consists of a big apple and being rude. Our

---

[10] See Broome (1991) for general support of this strategy and Pettit (1991, 163–6) for applying it to the apple example. Although in the context of preferences Pettit figures as a prominent opponent of my defence of attitude-related reasons, it is noteworthy that in Pettit (2004), he argues for the rationality of hope on the basis of the positive features of having this attitude and, thus, allows attitude-related reasons for hoping.

preferences are determined by our evaluations of these bundles. What we prefer, and not any features of our preferring, fully explains our preferences.[11]

When I described the apple example on the level of choices, I said that the set of relevant considerations is not exhausted by features of what one chooses but that it extends to features of one's so choosing. The opposed analysis will agree that features of one's choosing are normatively significant, but in order not to admit attitude-related reasons on the level of choice, it will embrace the following argumentative move, a move familiar from expositions of consequentialism: having acted in a certain way is one of the consequences of so acting. When we choose the small apple we also choose to act politely, i.e. we also choose to make a certain (polite) choice. In general, choosing A is itself one of the things that we choose when we choose A. This self-referentiality of choice—choosing A is always also a choosing of the choosing of A—explains the success of the opposed analysis. Content-related reasons are sufficient because one's choosing something is supposed to be a part of what one chooses.[12]

[11]   In section IV I pointed to Sen's work as sympathetic to the view defended here. In his 1995 paper, he continues to develop his ideas in a new conceptual framework, distinguishing between two conceptions of consequences or outcomes: 'A person's preferences over *comprehensive* outcomes (including the choice process) have to be distinguished from the conditional preferences over *culmination* outcomes *given* the acts of choice. The responsibility associated with choice can sway our ranking of narrowly-defined outcomes (such as commodity vectors possessed), and choice functions and preference relations may be parametrically influenced by specific features of the *act* of choice (including the *identity* of the chooser, the *menu* over which the choice is being made, and the relation of the particular *act* to behavioural social norms that constrain particular social actions)' (Sen 1995, 159). Against one's initial reaction, using the outcome terminology does not imply that Sen has switched to what I have called the opposing analysis. He indeed wants to show that even polite people can be seen as maximizers. This is, however, a purely technical result. About the function R(s*) that could describe polite people as maximizers he says: 'The *as if* preference R(s*) is, of course, a devised construction and need not have any intuitive plausibility *seen as preference*. [...] The *as if* preference works well enough formally, but the sociology of the phenomenon calls for something more than formal equivalences.' (Sen 1995, 191).]

[12]   In footnote 5 I mentioned Gibbard's and Scanlon's view that the rationality of choosing some X depends on the rationality of preferring X. According to the opposing analysis, new reasons come into view once we

According to my argument of the previous section, a choice of A is explained by a preference for A. If this is correct, the agent will usually also have a preference for choosing A. This preference gives the opposed analysis its starting point, because the attitude-related reason for preferring A will usually be mirrored in an analogous feature of choosing A. Such is the case in the apple example: both preferring the apple as well as preferring to choose it manifests politeness.

The search for an undisputed case of attitude-related reason, one in which the above absorption of their force is not feasible, will thus have to follow one of two routes: either we consider preferences that are not preferences for choosing things or we consider cases in which the feature of the preference which grounds the attitude-related reason will not be mirrored in a feature of the corresponding choice. I will pursue both lines in the next section.

V More Attitude-Related Reasons for Preferences

In section III I have argued that second-order desires are not normatively significant in the apple example. In cases of indifference, however, they are normatively significant. Here is what Harry Frankfurt says about the usefulness of having final ends:

> 'Without ends, there are no means. And if no activity serves as a means, then no activity is useful. Thus, having a final end is a condition of engaging in useful activity. Now the fact that an activity is useful endows it with meaning. Suppose that we never acted in order to attain or to accomplish something which we regarded as desirable. Suppose, in other words, that we never did anything that we believed to be useful. In that case, our activity would appear to us to serve no purpose. We would find it empty and vain, for it would seem to have no point. It would be, to our minds, altogether meaningless. A life constituted entirely by activity of that sort would be, in an important sense, a meaningless life. Life cannot be meaningful in this sense, then, without final ends' (Frankfurt 1992, 84f.)

---

replace X as the objects of one's preference by choosing X. Thus, whenever there are what I call attitude-related reasons, the opposing analysis is incompatible with the view endorsed by Gibbard and Scanlon.

The reason offered for wanting something for its own sake, for having a final end, is not connected with what it is that is our final end. Thus, wanting something for its own sake is not simply a matter of getting one's wants in line with the perceived value of the states which our activities might accomplish. The reason for wanting something for its own sake is that wanting something for its own sake is useful in a fundamental sense: without such wants life couldn't be meaningful. Note the structure of Frankfurt's claim: Some attitudes have desirable features. This is a reason, an attitude-related reason, for having them.

For reasons related to those mentioned by Frankfurt, we encourage young people to engage in various activities so that they might find things that really interest them. The case that he describes, however, a case of complete indifference, of not caring about anything, is something alien to most of us. Localized indifference is a much more common phenomenon and gives rise to examples of attitude-related reasons structurally analogous to Frankfurt's case. I was born close to Graz and, for reasons unimportant here, it was always Sturm Graz and not GAK, the other local team, who had my allegiance. Supporting a team makes football more interesting. Living in England I watch English football and want to support a team, not primarily because of the 'value' of the team in football terms but because supporting a team makes football more interesting. This attitude-related reason doesn't solve my problem just on its own. (The same is obviously true in Frankfurt's case as well.) It doesn't decide which team to support. It leaves me with wanting to want some team to win. And this second-order desire is normatively significant. It sets me the task of finding a team to support. I will look for content-related reasons to prefer one team to another. Content-related reasons that by themselves, i.e. without the task set by the second-order desire would not sway me one way or the other. This project need not be successful. If allegiance to a team is very important to one, then one could have an attitude-related reason against forming any more or less arbitrary allegiances. This attitude-related reason could well outweigh the attitude-related reason tied to enjoyment.[13]

---

[13] The most common case of indifference occurs when content-related reasons are tied. I have preferences for certain cereals but no preferences for any of the packets of the same cereal. I choose one, any one, not because of what is chosen but because of the advantages of choosing. Can we retell this case in terms of preferences? Note that I don't really act randomly in such a situation. Usually I choose the one closest, i.e. I prefer

Frankfurt is certainly right in that we need to care about something. Being involved with the world is a necessary condition for leading a good life. But here as elsewhere one has to strike the right balance. There can be too much interest and too much engagement which would put a strain on our limited resources and, to mention a famous Epicurean thought, would make us vulnerable to a multitude of disappointments. Frankfurt's point and its Epicurean flipside highlight important features of preferences which are not reducible to features of their objects and, thus, introduce attitude-related reasons for preferences on which the opposed analysis is silent.

We can illustrate Frankfurt's minimal point—features of attitudes matter—in other ways. Preferences can be socially unacceptable. They can make it difficult for us to fit in and gain the respect of the people around us. One might be drawn to what others find appalling or at least sufficiently odd to withdraw from normal levels of interaction. If one is attracted by death, and the dead cat still lies in the shed so that one can study the natural processes of decomposition, one won't be invited for tea at one's neighbour's house. Not so much because of what one does, rather because of the creepy character one is. If one regrets such social exclusion, the weighing of attitude-related and content-related reasons might well make one want to change one's preferences in order to become socially more acceptable.[14]

At the end of the last section I said that there are two areas which escape the opposed analysis: it cannot be applied if a preference is not a preference for choosing something and it fails if the benefit one gains from preferring something is not matched by a benefit of choosing it. I now turn to the latter case.

---

the closest packet as choosing it is easiest. This preference arises—I want to suggest—only because I prefer to prefer something and thus, because of an attitude-related reason, which sets us the task of finding content-related reason that in other circumstances wouldn't decide the matter.

[14] In the framework presented here, this project is rational, because it is the project of aligning one's attitudes with one's (attitude-related) reasons. If these attitude-related reasons are sufficiently strong, any resistance such a project of change might meet would be a sign of irrationality. The stronger the resistance, the more we would speak of an *obsession* with death, thereby lending support to my view that conflicts between second-order and first-order preferences indicate failures of having one's attitudes in line with one's reasons.

Christian Piller

We are looking for examples in which preferences can have desirable features that cannot be described as features of choosing what the preference is a preference for. Let me start with the attempted generalization of the 'undermining argument'. Remember, we cannot choose what to believe because belief is governed by reasons. Along the same lines it is argued that we cannot simply choose to prefer something. For example: when offered a choice between a saucer of mud and a pot of gold, one cannot simply choose to prefer the saucer of mud. The suggested explanation is the same as in the belief case: such a preference would be crazy. In the belief case, however, we had a further datum: whatever the size of the reward offered, we simply cannot decide to believe to be well, when ill. Does the same hold in case of preferences?

What if we got two pots of gold, if we preferred this saucer of mud to a pot of gold? I would certainly say 'Yes, please, can I have the saucer of mud'. Would there be any reason to doubt my honesty, when I say this? I think not. In a 'normal' setting in which we choose between mud and gold it would be crazy to ask for the mud but, given the offer, it strikes me as very reasonable to do so. If I honestly and instantaneously say 'I want the mud, not the gold. Please!' then I do prefer the saucer of mud to the pot of gold. This reaction does not oppose but arises from the view that preferences are constrained by reasons. They are constraint by content-related and by attitude-related reasons.[15]

We cannot apply the opposing analysis to this example. In the apple case the desirable feature of preferring the small apple, namely to be polite, could also be understood as a feature of choosing the small apple. But the desirable feature of preferring the saucer of mud (or, indeed, of preferring to choose the saucer of mud), namely to be rewarded by two pots of gold, is not a feature of choosing the saucer of mud. If it were we simply would have a different example, one in which you choose between two bundles of goods: a saucer of mud and two pots of gold on the one hand and one pot of gold on the other. The example as told here has it that preference but not choice is rewarded.

---

[15]   Here we may understand 'preferring the saucer of mud' as 'preferring to choose the sauce of mud'. The important point remains: preferring to choose the saucer of mud will be rewarded but choosing the saucer of mud will not be rewarded. Thus, if we prefer to choose the saucer of mud, we do so on the strength of the attitude-related reasons in play.

I claim that we are able to prefer what is worse because doing so is better for us. This turns the undermining argument upside down. Whereas in the belief case attitude-related reasons would undermine what looks like the correct explanation of an inability, in the case of preferences we need attitude-related reasons to explain our ability to prefer what is worse.

According to the Standard View, the view I am arguing against here, it is one thing to prefer something and quite another thing to try to bring it about that one prefers something. In the case under discussion we should prefer the pot of gold but we should also try to bring it about that we prefer the saucer of mud. We should, in other words, try to make ourselves irrational.

Because beliefs and preferences are reason-guided, making ourselves irrational is always a complex project for rational people like us. But is it really plausible to assume, as the Standard View entails, that I could only get the two pots of gold if I consulted the hypnotist who could make me prefer the saucer of mud? Think of the Toxin Puzzle, where intending to act but not acting is rewarded. This puzzle essentially relies on the future directedness of the intention. How can I form an intention to do something tomorrow when I know now that tomorrow I won't have any reason for doing it? If we collapse the timely split between forming the intention and acting, the puzzle disappears. The attitude-related reason, however, keeps its force. My wanting to drink the toxin now has a desirable feature that is not a feature of my drinking or choosing to drink the toxin. I will get the reward as long as I want to drink it now, whether I drink it or not. Having the preference indicated by all my reasons, I would ask for the toxin and drink it. Nothing more could be asked for to give me the reward. I have no need for a hypnotist; I come to want to drink the toxin by a normal process of reasoning that respects attitude-related reasons.[16]

Why should we follow the Standard View and separate the domains to which the two kinds of reasons apply? The Standard View owes an answer to this question. A good answer would be that separation is needed because the reasons to be separated derive their normative force from different sources. This answer is defensible in the case of beliefs, because the reasons provided by the evidence and the reasons provided by the potential benefit that believing carries with it look nonnegotiable. Trying to bring about

---

[16] For the Toxin Puzzle see Kavka 1983. Some of the points made here can also be found in the last section of Piller 2001, where I specifically focus on attitude-related reasons for intentions.

a belief that is neither in your power to make true nor supported by the evidence can only be a reasonable project if the benefits outweigh the costs. How strong the epistemic reasons are against whose force we want to believe will only be relevant if this would make a difference to the costs involved. If we had the believe-that-p pill, the strength of epistemic reasons we want to counteract would be irrelevant. This incommensurability does suggest that epistemic and practical reasons have different sources and, as I said, this lends independent support to the separation of domains to which these reasons apply. The benefits from preferring something, however, are clearly commensurable with the benefits from what we prefer. In our example it is all about gold. Thus, why should we distinguish reasons for trying to bring it about that one prefers something from reasons for preferring it, if these reasons come from the same normative force?

We could argue for such a separation by distinguishing different addressees of norms of reason. I am one of the addressees: I ought to prevent my having a preference for the pot of gold. But who or what is the addressee of the norm that gold is preferred to mud? Is it the preference itself, so that it ought to exist as my preference? Isn't it much more plausible to claim that I am the addressee of all norms, be they about what to believe, what to prefer or how to act?

The Standard View leaves us with a seriously strained picture of practical reason. I ought to prefer the pot of gold to the saucer of mud and I ought to prevent myself from having this very preference. If I ought to prefer gold to mud, then, in following this norm, should I not try to bring about that I prefer gold to mud? Similarly, if I ought to bring it about that I prefer mud to gold, I ought to do so not because of any aspects of my trying but because of the normative significance of the result of my trying. The Standard View leads practical rationality to the edge of inconsistency. Think about how implausible the analogous claim in the theoretical domain would look like. Epistemic reasons make it rational to believe that p. But you are also asked to believe that not-p, i.e. to bring this about, on purely epistemic grounds. This does sound as if both the belief in p and the belief in its negation are epistemically required. I conclude that the Standard View can only be plausible if it is underpinned by a separation of normative force. Thus, it can only be applied in a case in which we are confronted with an apparent conflict between practical and epistemic reasons for believing something. It cannot introduce a useful distinction between preferring something and trying to bring it about that one prefers, because the reasons for both cases stem from the same normative force.

Let me summarize my position: The norms of practical reason apply to me. Practical normativity is not divided in itself. The acceptance of attitude-related reasons is necessary to endorse the idea of a coherent and unified notion of practical normativity.

But isn't there a price to pay? Doesn't the acceptance of attitude-related reasons threaten realism, the view that there are appropriateness conditions for preferences which are unaffected by whether we like preferences that fulfil these conditions or not? There is no reason for such a suspicion, as whatever the right substantial theory of reasons is, it will simply apply to attitude-related reasons as well. Some preferences have features that are reason-giving. It might be that preferring something is being polite or it might be useful as it promises some reward. Allowing attitude-related reasons extends the domain of reasons, but it doesn't change any of the principles of reason offered by substantial theories.

There is a further consequence. We have replaced one correctness condition for preferences—a preference is correct if and only if what is preferred is best—with another—a preference is correct if and only if so preferring is best. The original correctness condition invites the following appropriateness condition for preferences: A preference is appropriate or rational if and only if one reasonably believes that what one prefers is best. Thus, we could have a thoroughly cognitivist account of rational preferences, one in which rational preferences necessarily coincide with beliefs.[17] The same possibility still holds after we have allowed attitude-related reasons for preferences. A preference is appropriate or rational if and only if one reasonably believes that preferring in this way is best. This, I think, is a remarkable result: even if rational preferences are thus connected with beliefs, and even if there couldn't be attitude-related reasons for beliefs, there could still be attitude-related reasons for preferences. Their force is simply absorbed in the content of the belief which determines the

[17] For more details about why David Lewis's worry about this equivalence is, in my view, misguided, see Piller 2000.

rational preference. Thus, there really is no price to pay for accepting attitude-related reasons for preferences.[18]

VI Against the Critics

Finally let me speak directly to two prominent opponents of the view outlined here. Pursuing the generalization of the inability argument discussed above, Alan Gibbard writes: 'Now preferences and intentions are not themselves voluntary. In the case of preferences, that is clear enough. I might, for instance, be convinced that I will be happy if and only if I cease to want to be happy, but I cannot on that account stop wanting to be happy' (Gibbard 1991, 39).

I have a content-related reason to want to be happy—being happy is very good. I have an attitude-related reason not to want to be happy—wanting to be happy prevents me from being happy. Let me introduce the following distinction: The force of attitude-related reasons might be genuine or borrowed. I like apples for their taste. Suppose I like my liking of apples for the following reason: liking apples makes it more likely that I stick with my apple-eating habit, even when obstacles emerge, e.g. when eating apples becomes socially less acceptable. The force of this attitude-related reason, which is reflected in my liking to like apples, is derived or borrowed from the value of apples. I endorse the apple-eating habit because I like (for good reasons) eating apples. If the discovery of the superior taste and the higher health benefits of kiwis extinguishes my liking of apples, my liking of my liking of apples will go at the same time. Let me contrast this case with one in which my attitude-relate reasons for liking to eat apples does not depend on the value assigned to eating apples. I might like to like eating apples because I like to like home grown products. In this case, where the normative force of the attitude-related reason

[18] Let me add one further thought. Joseph Raz, especially in Raz (1990), has drawn our attention to what he calls 'exclusionary' reasons, i.e. reasons not to act for certain reasons. An agent's tiredness or the fact that an agent has been ordered to do something might be, on his account, such an exclusionary reason. The excluded reasons are content-related reasons. In Piller (2006) I try to show that an analysis in terms of attitude-related reasons of the phenomena on which Raz bases his exclusionary reasons is a plausible alternative to Raz's own account. If correct this would give us further examples for the role of attitude-related reasons. A view similar to my own on this matter can already be found in Jeffrey (1966).

does not depend on those qualities of apples that make me like them in the first place, the discovery of kiwis will result in a conflict that needs to be resolved: Is the increase of enjoyment experienced when eating kiwis and their higher health benefit reason enough to undermine my allegiance to the local farming community?

Having distinguished between derived and genuine force of attitude-related reasons, we can turn to Gibbard's example. I don't think it shows that we couldn't want something for attitude-related reasons, reflected in our wanting to want it. The difficulty it presents is much more specific: the reason for wanting not to want to be happy derives its normative force from happiness. Thus, one only has reason not to want to be happy anymore, as long as one wants to be happy. There is something paradoxical about engaging in a project that, if successful, would have undermined its own rationale. But this is by no means a general feature of wanting something because one wants to want it. The peculiar difficulty in the project Gibbard describes is no reason for a general denial of attitude-related reasons for preferences. How we deal with attitude-related reasons has been sufficiently illustrated by the examples I have given.

Derek Parfit writes: 'If we believe that having some desire would have good effects, what that belief makes rational is not that desire itself, but our wanting and trying to have it. Irrational desires may have good effects. Thus, if I knew that I shall be tortured tomorrow, it might be better for me if I wanted to be tortured, since I would then happily look forward to what lies ahead. But this would not make my desire rational. It is irrational to want, for its own sake, to be tortured. The good effects of such a desire might make it rational for me, if I could, to cause myself to have it. But that would be a case of rational irrationality. (Parfit, 2001, 27)

In Parfit's example he has a comparably weak attitude-related reason to want to be tortured. It would make him have a more relaxed time until tomorrow. He also has a very strong content-related reason not to want to be tortured tomorrow. Any plausible aggregation of reasons will show that Parfit's verdict is correct: It would be irrational for him to want to be tortured. This, however, by no means shows that there are no attitude-related reasons. Parfit refutes the view that there are only attitude-related reasons and no content-related reasons for preferences. This is a view, I agree, no one should hold.[19]

Bibliography

Broome, John, *Weighing Goods*, Blackwell, Oxford: 1991.

Broome, John, 'Normative Practical Reasoning', *Proceedings of the Aristotelian Society*, Suppl. Vol. 75, 2001, 175–193.

Diamond, Peter, 'Cardinal Welfare, Individualistic Ethics and Interpersonal Comparisons of Utility: Comment', *Journal of Political Economy* 75, 1976, 765–766.

Frankfurt, Harry 1992, 'On the Usefulness of Final Ends', repr. in his *Necessity, Volition, and Love*, Cambridge University press, Cambridge: 1999, 82–94.

Gibbard, Allan, *Wise Choices, Apt Feelings*, Clarendon Press, Oxford: 1990.

Harman, Gilbert 1997, 'Pragmatism and Reasons for Belief', repr. in his *Reasoning, Meaning and Mind*, Oxford University press, Oxford: 1999, 93–116.

James, William 1897, *The Will to Believe and Other Essays in Popular Philosophy*, Dover, New York: 1956.

Jeffrey, Richard, 'Preferences Among Preferences', *Journal of Philosophy* 71, 1974, 377–391.

Kavka, Gregory, 'The Toxin Puzzle', *Analysis* 43, 1983, 33–36.

Keynes, John Maynard, *A Treatise on Probability*, Macmillan, London: 1921.

Nozick, Robert, *The Nature of Rationality*, Princeton University Press, Princeton: 1993.

Olson, Jonas, 'Buck-Passing and the Wrong Kind of Reason', *Philosophical Quarterly* 54, 2004 295–300.

Owens, David, *Reason Without Freedom*, Routlegde, London: 2000.

Parfit, Derek, 'Rationality and Reasons', in: Dan Egonsson, Björn Petersson, Jonas Josefsson, Toni Ronnow-Rasmussen (Eds), *Exploring Practical Philosophy: From Action to Values*, Ashgate: 2001. 17–41.

Pettit, Philip, 'Decision Theory and Folk Psychology', in M Bacharach & S Hurley (eds), *Foundations of Decision Theory*, Blackwell, Oxford: 1991.

[19] I want to thank all the participants of the conference where this paper was first presented for many informative and enjoyable discussions. Drafts of this paper have been read by John Broome, Philip Percival, Philip Pettit, Anthony Price and Wlodek Rabinowicz and I thank them for their helpful comments.

Pettit, Philip, 'Hope and its Place in Mind', in V Braithwaite (Ed), *Annals of the American Academy of Political and Social Science*, Vol. 592, 2004, pp.152–65.

Piller, Christian, 'Doing What is Best', *Philosophical Quarterly* 50, 2000, 208–226.

Piller,Christian, 'Normative Practical Reasoning', *Proceedings of the Aristotelian Society*, Suppl. Vol. 75, 2001, 195–216.

Piller, Christian, 'Kinds of Practical Reasons: Attitude-Related Reasons and Exclusionary Reasons', forthcoming in: S Miguens, J A Pinto and C E Mauro, eds., *Actas do Encontro Nacional de Filosofia Analítica II*, Porto: Porto University, 2005

Rabinowicz, Wlodek & Ronnow-Rasmussen, Toni, 'The Strike of the Demon: On Fitting Pro-Attitudes and Value', *Ethics 114*, 2004, 391–423.

Raz, Joseph, *Practical Reason and Norms*, 2nd ed, Princeton University Press, Princeton: 1990.

Scanlon, Thomas, *What We Owe To Each Other*, Harvard University Press, Cambridge/Mass.: 1998.

Sen, Amartya, 'Choice, Orderings and Morality', in S Körner (ed), *Practical Reason*, Blackwell, Oxford: 1974, 54–67.

Sen, Amartya, 'Rational Fools: A Critique of the Behavioral Foundations of Economic Theory', *Philosophy and Public Affairs* 6, 1977, 317–344.

Sen, Amartya, 1995, 'Maximization and the Act of Choice', in his *Rationality and Freedom*, Belknap Press, Cambridge/Mass: 2002, 158–205.

Sen, Amartya, 'Introduction: Rationality and Freedom', in his *Rationality and Freedom*, Belknap Press, Cambridge/Mass: 2002, 3–64.

Velleman, David, 1996, 'The Possibility of Practical Reason', repr. in his *The Possibility of Practical Reason*, Oxford University Press, Oxford: 2000, 170–199.

Reasoning with preferences?

JOHN BROOME

1. Reasoning and requirements of rationality

Rationality requires certain things of you. It requires you not to have contradictory beliefs or intentions, not to intend something you believe to be impossible, to believe what obviously follows from something you believe, and so on. Its requirements can be expressed using schemata such as:

> *Modus ponens.* Rationality requires of N that, if N believes p and N believe that if p then q, then N believes q.

> *Necessary means.* Rationality requires of N that, if N intends that e, and if N believes that e will be so only if m is so, and if N believes m will be so only if she intends that m, then N intends that m.

> *Krasia.* Rationality requires of N that, if N believes she ought to F, and if N believes she will F only if she intends to F, then N intends to F.

('She' is to be read as a reflexive pronoun.) It may be questioned whether any of these formulae express genuine requirements of rationality. Their precise formulation may be inaccurate, at least. But these formulae are not the subject of this paper, and for the sake of argument I shall assume they are correct. In any case, they are only examples of requirements of rationality (or 'rational requirements', as I shall often say); rationality requires many things of you besides these. Notice that all of these particular requirements govern conditional statements. They have a 'wide scope', as I shall say. None governs a single belief or intention of yours.

Many people think that rationality makes requirements on your preferences, too. In order to have an example to work with, I shall concentrate on this familiar one:

> *Transitivity.* Rationality requires of N that if N prefers a to b and N prefers b to c, then N prefers a to c.

This too has a wide scope. It is particularly controversial whether or not this is a genuine requirement of rationality. But in this paper

John Broome

I shall not engage directly in controversy about it; I shall assume that *Transitivity* expresses a genuine requirement. I shall ask how, given that it is a rational requirement, you may come to satisfy it.

By what process can you come to satisfy a particular requirement of rationality? Often, you simply find yourself satisfying it. You intend to visit Venice; you believe the only way to do so is to buy a ticket (and that you will not do so unless you intend to); and you find yourself intending to buy a ticket. You satisfy *Necessary means* in this instance. You come to do so as a result of some automatic, unconscious causal process that you do not control; it just happens. Many of your preferences satisfy *Transitivity* in a similar way. Presumably there is some evolutionary explanation of why this sort of thing happens.

Possibly an ideally rational creature would find itself satisfying all the requirements of rationality this way. But mortals fail to satisfy very many of them. However, we mortals do have a way of improving our score. We can bring ourselves to satisfy some requirements by our own activity of reasoning. Reasoning is an activity—something we do—through which we can satisfy some requirements in particular instances. For example, we can come to believe a particular consequence of what we believe by thinking the matter through.

Some unconscious processes could be called unconscious reasoning. But in this paper I am interested only in conscious processes, and I shall give the name 'reasoning' to those ones only. Unconscious processes are not activities, and I am interested in reasoning as an activity.

I am assuming rationality imposes requirements on your preferences, such as *Transitivity*. No doubt you find yourself satisfying some of those requirements through unconscious processes. But when you do not, can you bring yourself to satisfy them through reasoning? Briefly: can you reason with preferences? That is the topic of this paper.

I am interested in correct reasoning only. Various mental activities of yours might accidentally lead you to satisfy a rational requirement, and various of those activities might qualify as reasoning. But a reasoning activity that systematically leads you to satisfy a rational requirement would have to be *correct* reasoning.

Why does it matter whether you can reason with preferences? It is important in itself to understand the process of reasoning, but there is another reason too. In 'Why be rational?', Niko Kolodny argues that, for any rational requirement on you, there must be a process of reasoning through which you can bring yourself to

184

satisfy that requirement. If he is right, and if it turned out that you cannot reason with preferences, it would follow that there are no rational requirements on preferences.

As it happens, I am not convinced by Kolodny's arguments, for reasons I cannot set out in this paper.[1] I remain agnostic about his conclusion. For all I know, there may be requirements of rationality that you can come to satisfy only by unconscious processes that you do not control. But even so, if it should turn out that no process of reasoning could bring you to have, say, transitive preferences, that would cast some doubt on the claim that rationality requires you to have transitive preferences. We would certainly want an explanation of how there could be this requirement on you without your being able to bring yourself to satisfy it. In this way, the question of reasoning reflects back on to the question of what rationality requires.

You certainly cannot rely on unconscious processes to get all your preferences into rational order; anyone's system of preferences is too big and complex for that. This is particularly true of preferences among uncertain prospects. The axioms of expected utility theory are supposed to express requirements of rationality for these preferences, and no one satisfies those axioms automatically.

Reasoning with preferences, and indeed reasoning in general, has not been much discussed. Many authors write about what rationality requires of your preferences and other mental states. Having stated some requirements, they leave it at that. They do not consider by what process you may come to satisfy their requirements. Why not? I think they must take it for granted that, once you know what the requirements of rationality are, you can bring yourself to satisfy them by reasoning. I think they must implicitly rely on a particular model of reasoning. They must think you can reason your way to satisfying a requirement by starting from the requirement itself as a premise. More exactly, their model starts from your believing some proposition such as the ones I have labelled *Modus ponens*, *Necessary means*, or *Transitivity*, and you reason from there. These are propositions about your mental states, so your reasoning starts from a belief about your mental states. I shall call this a 'second-order belief', and I shall call this model of reasoning the 'second-order model'. It is an all-purpose model. It can be applied to reasoning with mental states of all kinds—beliefs, intentions, preferences and so on.

[1] See my 'Wide or narrow scope?'.

John Broome

But for some mental states, reasoning cannot work as the second-order model supposes. The model does not work for beliefs, for one thing. Section 2 explains why not. Section 3 describes an alternative, first-order model of reasoning, which is more successful for beliefs. It does not depend on any second-order belief about your mental states. But it is not such an all-purpose model; it is not straightforward to extend it beyond beliefs to other mental states. I shall next consider how successfully the two models can apply to preferences. Section 4 distinguishes a broad concept of preference from our ordinary one, as I need to do. Section 5 applies the second-order model to broad preferences with moderate success. Section 6 applies the first-order model to ordinary preferences, again with moderate success. The central issue that arises in section 6 is how far ordinary preferences, can be distinguished from beliefs about betterness. It may turn out that what appears to be reasoning with ordinary preferences is really nothing other than theoretical reasoning about which alternatives are better than which. Section 7 considers whether that is so.

My main conclusion is that the second-order model of reasoning is unsuccessful for ordinary preferences, as it is for beliefs. Possibly this model may work for broad preferences. Nevertheless, we may indeed be able to reason with ordinary preferences, because the first-order model is more successful. However, I remain unsure that first-order reasoning with preferences is really distinct from theoretical reasoning about betterness.

2. Second-order theoretical reasoning

I start with theoretical reasoning—reasoning with beliefs. I shall use an example in which you come to satisfy the requirement *Modus ponens*. It is a case of simple deductive reasoning, which should be paradigmatic of theoretical reasoning.

You wake up and hear rain, so you believe it is raining. Your long experience with snow has taught you that, if it is raining, the snow will melt. However, because you are still sleepy and have not yet thought about the snow, you do not yet believe the snow will melt. So you do not satisfy *Modus ponens* in this instance. You believe it is raining; you believe that if it is raining the snow will melt, but you do not believe the snow will melt. By reasoning, you can surely bring yourself to satisfy the requirement in this instance. How will your reasoning go?

This section investigates the second-order model. I shall take a generally sceptical stance towards it. I shall argue it does not work for theoretical reasoning, nor for reasoning with ordinary preferences. Given that, I shall be generous towards this model, and make concessions to help it on its way. I shall make assumptions that support it, even when I cannot fully justify them.

The second-order model supposes that your reasoning sets out from a belief in the requirement itself. So let us suppose you do actually believe the requirement *Modus ponens* in this instance. You believe rationality requires of you that: you believe the snow will melt if you believe it is raining and you believe that if it is raining the snow will melt. Can you get by reasoning from this belief to satisfying the requirement itself, as the second-order model supposes?

One plausible pattern of reasoning offers a clue as to how you might do so. Suppose you believe you ought to do something—buy cherries, say. You might say to yourself:

> *I ought to buy cherries,*
> *So I shall buy cherries.*

I mean the second of these sentences to express an intention of yours, rather than a belief that you will buy cherries. I shall say more about the idea of saying to yourself in section 3. This is plausibly a little piece of reasoning, through which your normative belief that you ought to buy cherries brings you to form the intention of buying cherries. Normally, when you intend to do something, your intention causes you in due course to do it. So in due course you are likely to buy cherries, as a final result of your normative belief that you ought to do so.

I think that what you say to yourself here is indeed reasoning, and moreover correct reasoning. By means of reasoning on this pattern, you can bring yourself to satisfy the rational requirement *Krasia*: to intend to do what you believe you ought to do. I shall call it 'kratic reasoning'. In this paper I shall not argue that kratic reasoning is genuine, correct reasoning; I shall simply assume it is. I do so to smooth the way for the second-order model; it is one of my concessions to the model. In a moment, I shall show how the second-order model can make use of it.

As a second concession, I shall assume you can derive a strictly normative belief from your belief in the rational requirement. I have already assumed you believe rationality requires you to satisfy the condition that you believe the snow will melt if you believe it is raining and you believe that if it is raining the snow will melt. Now,

John Broome

I assume you go further and derive the belief that you ought to satisfy this condition. Questions might be asked about this step.[2] First, even though rationality requires you to satisfy this condition, does it follow that you ought to satisfy it? Suppose, for instance, very bad consequences would result from your satisfying it; ought you to satisfy it then? Second, even if it does actually follow, how can we assume you make this inference, so it is reflected in your own beliefs?

To give the second-order model a chance, I cannot avoid making this questionable assumption. If correct second-order reasoning is to bring you to satisfy some condition, you need to believe you ought to satisfy it. It is not good enough for you to believe merely that rationality requires you to satisfy it. Suppose, say, you believed rationality requires you to satisfy a condition but also believed you ought not to satisfy it. In that case, correct reasoning could not possibly lead you to satisfy it. So correct reasoning needs an ought belief, not merely a belief about a rational requirement.

I give the model an ought belief, therefore. I assume you believe you ought to believe the snow will melt if you believe it is raining and you believe that if it is raining the snow will melt. That should put you in a position to go through this piece of kratic reasoning, modelled on the cherries example:

> *I ought to believe the snow will melt if I believe it is raining and I believe that if it is raining the snow will melt*
> *So I shall believe the snow will melt if I believe it is raining and I believe that if it is raining the snow will melt*

The second sentence is supposed to express an intention. Because the content of your premise-belief has a wide scope, you end with an intention that has a wide scope. What you intend is the conditional proposition that you believe the snow will melt if you believe it is raining and you believe that if it is raining the snow will melt.

Suppose you get as far as this. What happens next? If you are to follow the precedent of cherries, this intention would normally cause you to fulfil it. But there are two difficulties standing in the way of that result.

The first is the wide scope of your intention. Kratic reasoning could take you to a more specific intention only if you started with a more specific normative belief. To get by kratic reasoning to an intention to believe the snow will melt, you would have to start

---

[2]   See my 'Does rationality give us reasons?'

from a belief that you ought to believe the snow will melt. But you cannot acquire this specific normative belief by correct reasoning from your initial belief in the broad-scope rational requirement you are under.

To see why not, notice it may not be true that you ought to believe the snow will melt. Perhaps you ought not to believe it is raining; perhaps the rain you hear is on a recording that you set as your alarm call. If you ought not to believe it is raining, it may well not be the case that you ought to believe the snow will melt. On the other hand, we are assuming it is true that rationality requires you to believe the snow will melt if you believe it is raining and you believe that if it is raining the snow will melt. You cannot by correct reasoning derive a belief that may not be true from one that is true.

So by correct kratic reasoning you cannot arrive at an intention to believe specifically that the snow will melt. But it is that specific belief the reasoning is supposed to lead you to. That is the first difficulty.

It may not be a serious one. All your intentions are indefinite to some degree, and yet you manage to fulfil many of them. If you intend to buy cherries, you could fulfil your intention by going to the greengrocer or the supermarket, in the morning or the afternoon. Somehow your intention gets narrowed to a more specific one, say to buy cherries at the supermarket, leaving home at 12.30. This narrowing can happen without your having a normative belief that you ought to buy cherries at the supermarket, leaving home at 12.30. It certainly can happen; we do not have to worry about how. I shall assume the same thing could happen in the present case. I shall assume your wide-scope intention could be narrowed to an intention to believe the snow will melt. This is rather plausible, since you do in fact believe it is raining and that if it is raining the snow will melt. I treat it as another concession to the second-order model.

But now you meet the second difficulty. This is the fatal one. Intending to believe a particular proposition is normally ineffective; it normally does not get you to believe the proposition. (Because you probably know that, you probably cannot even form an intention to believe a particular proposition. You cannot intend something and at the same time believe the intention will be ineffective.)

There are exceptions. You may be able to acquire a belief in a particular proposition by using some external means—going regularly to church or taking a belief pill, for example. If an external means is available to you of coming to believe a particular proposition, then you may be able to intend to believe this proposition, and this intention may cause you to believe it, using the means. However, the last step—using an external means such as going regularly to church or taking a belief pill—is not a mental process. It therefore cannot form part of a process of reasoning. So the second-order model of reasoning cannot work through your using an external means.

On the other hand, you cannot come to believe a proposition by intending to believe that proposition, without using an external means. You can do some things without using an external means; raising your hand is one example. Intending to raise your hand can bring you to raise your hand without using an external means. But intending to believe a proposition cannot bring you to believe that proposition without using an external means. In his 'Deciding to believe', Bernard Williams argued this a necessary feature of belief; I have been persuaded by an argument of Jonathan Bennett's that it is a contingent feature of our psychology.[3] But whether necessary or contingent, it is a truth. It prevents the second-order model of theoretical reasoning from working in the way I have been investigating.

That way was through kratic reasoning, by which a normative belief leads to an intention. Could the second-order model work more directly, without involving any intention? Could it be that believing rationality requires you to be in a particular mental state, or believing that you ought to be in a particular mental state, simply causes you to enter that state, without your forming an intention of doing so? Could this happen in a way that is sufficiently regular to count as reasoning?

T.M. Scanlon thinks it can happen for some states: those he calls 'judgement-sensitive attitudes'. These are 'attitudes that an ideally rational person would come to have whenever that person judged there to be sufficient reason for them ...'. [4] So, for instance, if you were ideally rational, you would come to have a belief whenever you judged there to be sufficient reason for you to have it or, as I prefer to say, whenever you judged you ought to have it.

I find Scanlon's view implausible. Your beliefs are not normally caused by any normative beliefs you might have about what you ought to believe. If you believe you ought to have some belief, that would not normally cause you to have the belief. Suppose you

---

[3]   'Why is belief involuntary?'
[4]   *What We Owe to Each Other*, p. 20.

believe you ought to believe you are attractive, because believing you are attractive will relax you, make you more approachable and improve your life. This would not normally cause you to believe you are attractive. Normally, our beliefs are caused by evidence, not by normative beliefs about what we ought to believe.

I agree that beliefs are judgement-sensitive in a different sense. If you were ideally rational, you would come to have a belief whenever you judged there was sufficient evidence for the content of the belief. You would come to believe you are attractive when you judge there is sufficient evidence that you are attractive. Beliefs are genuinely judgement-sensitive in this sense, but it is not Scanlon's sense. Your judgement in this case is about the content of the belief, not about the belief itself. It is a first-order belief, not a second-order one.

Judgement-sensitivity in Scanlon's sense is sensitivity to a second-order normative judgement about the belief itself. A second-order judgement of this sort often accompanies a first-order one. When you judge there is sufficient evidence for some proposition, you may well also judge you have sufficient reason to believe the proposition. But what causes you to believe the proposition, if you do, is the first-order judgement, not the second-order one. A way to test this is to look at cases where you make the second-order judgement but not the first-order one. My example of believing you are attractive is one of those. Examples like that show a second-order judgement does not normally cause you to have the belief.

In any case, even if beliefs were judgement-sensitive in Scanlon's sense, that would not directly help the second-order model of reasoning. In my example, your second-order judgement is not that you ought to have a particular belief. Instead, it has a wide scope. It is the judgement that you ought to satisfy the conditional: that you believe the snow will melt if you believe it is raining and you believe that if it is raining the snow will melt. It is particularly implausible that this judgement could cause you to enter the complex mental state described by the conditional, without kratic reasoning and without your forming an intention.

I conclude that the second-order model of reasoning fails for theoretical reasoning. It requires a sort of control over your beliefs that actually you do not have. So I come to the first-order model.

John Broome

3. First-order theoretical reasoning

I shall stick to the same paradigmatic example of theoretical reasoning. You believe it is raining, and you believe that if it is raining the snow will melt, but you do not believe the snow will melt. So you do not satisfy the requirement *Modus ponens* in this instance. But you can bring yourself to satisfy it by saying to yourself that:

> It is raining
> If it is raining the snow will melt.
> So the snow will melt.

Here, I have written down a sequence of sentences, which designate propositions. You do not necessarily say the sentences to yourself; you might reason in Swedish, say. But you do say to yourself the propositions that these sentences designate. You say to yourself that it is raining, and that if it is raining the snow will melt, and then you say that the snow will melt. I shall mention the point of the word 'so' at the end of this section.

You initially believe the first two of these propositions; in saying them to yourself you are expressing your beliefs. You do not initially believe the third. But when you say it to yourself, you express a belief in it. By the time you come to say it, your reasoning has brought you to believe it. By this time, you satisfy *Modus ponens*. That is how the first-order model of reasoning works.

The propositions you say to yourself constitute the contents of your beliefs. You can reason with beliefs only because they are states that have contents. Their content gives you something to reason about.

Saying something to yourself is an act. Sometimes no doubt, you say things to yourself out loud, but more often you do it silently. In that case, I could alternatively have said you call the proposition to mind; 'saying to yourself' is just a more graphic way of describing what you do. One thing it does is to bring the beliefs together, if you have not previously done that in your mind.

Your acts of saying to yourself are part of your reasoning but not the whole. Your reasoning is the causal process whereby some of your mental states cause you to acquire a new mental state. It includes a sequence of acts, and it is itself a complex activity. To be reasoning, the process must involve acts of saying to yourself. Some of your beliefs cause you to acquire a new belief, through some acts of this sort. The process ends when you acquire your new belief.

The acquisition of this belief is an act. Described one way, the acquisition is something you intend. When you embark on your reasoning, you intend to come to believe whatever is the conclusion that emerges from the reasoning. You intend that, if p is the proposition that emerges from the reasoning, you believe p. However, you do not intend to believe the specific proposition that emerges. In the example, you do not intend to believe the snow will melt. Coming to believe the snow will melt is an act like finding your glasses under the bed, after looking for them. You intend to find your glasses, and this makes it the case that your finding them under the bed is an act. But you do not intend to find them under the bed. I said in section 2 that you cannot come to believe a particular proposition by intending to believe that proposition. But you can acquire a belief by means of a procedure you intend.

Since reasoning is a process that takes place among mental states, acts of saying to yourself can only form a part of it when they express mental states. In the example, in saying to yourself that it is raining, you must express a belief of yours that it is raining. When you say to yourself that the snow will melt, you must express a belief of yours that the snow will melt, and so on. In the context of belief, saying to yourself is asserting to yourself. True, you could say to yourself the sequence of sentences

It is raining
If it is raining the snow will melt
So the snow will melt

even if you did not have the corresponding beliefs. (In this paper, I use italics in place of quotation marks.) But in doing that you would not be reasoning because you would not be going through a process that takes place among your beliefs.

In the course of your reasoning, you do not say to yourself any propositions about your mental states; you say to yourself the propositions that constitute the contents of your mental states. In the example, you do not say to yourself that you believe it is raining, nor that you ought to believe the snow will melt. No second-order beliefs about your mental states are involved. We may say you reason *with* your beliefs. You reason *about* the content of your beliefs.

The second-order model of reasoning was supposed to set out from a belief about your beliefs. But it was blocked because there is no route of reasoning from there to actually modifying your first-order beliefs. On the other hand, the process I am now describing directly modifies your first-order beliefs, because it works on their contents. When you conclude that the snow will melt, in doing that you are directly acquiring a new belief.

This needs emphasis. There are two aspects to theoretical reasoning. One is identifying a particular conclusion-proposition on the basis of the premise-propositions. The other is your coming to believe the conclusion-proposition. It is tempting to try and divide reasoning into two stages according to these two aspects: first picking out a new proposition, then coming to believe it. But if there were these two stages, at the end of the first stage the new proposition would be parked somewhere in your consciousness, without your having any particular attitude towards it. We would have to explain how you then come to believe it. The explanation could not go through your believing you ought to believe it, nor through your intending to believe it, because, as I said earlier, neither of these attitudes will succeed in getting you to believe it. At least, they cannot have this effect through any process that can be reasoning. In any case, this explanation would leave us with the equally difficult task of explaining how you come to have one of these attitudes.

The truth is that you believe the proposition as you identify it. We cannot split reasoning into the two stages. Theoretical reasoning is imbued with belief all the way through. As I put it just now: you are reasoning with beliefs. You do not reason and then acquire a belief.

To summarize what we have learned so far from this paradigmatic example: reasoning is a process whereby some of your mental states give rise to another mental state; the mental states involved must be ones that have contents; in reasoning you say to yourself the propositions that constitute these contents, and you reason about these contents.

This cannot be a full characterization of reasoning. Not just any mental process that has these features is reasoning. For example, suppose you believe that it is raining and that if it is raining the snow will melt. Suppose you say to yourself that it is raining and that if it is raining the snow will melt, and suppose this causes you to believe you hear trumpets. That bizarre process is probably not reasoning.

You might think that true reasoning can only be separated from bizarre processes like this by the presence of a second-order belief. In my example of genuine reasoning, you moved from believing it is raining and believing that if it is raining the snow will melt to believing the snow will melt. You might think this process is reasoning only if you have the second-order belief that rationality requires you to believe the snow will melt if you believe it is raining and you believe that if it is raining the snow will melt.

Even if this was so, it would not restore the second-order model of reasoning. The reasoning is still conducted at the first order, even if a second-order belief needs to be present in the background. But actually I think it is not so. A sophisticated reasoner may have this second-order belief, but I do not see why you need so much sophistication in order to reason. I do not see why you need to have the concept of a rational requirement, or even the concept of a belief.

It is more plausible that a different sort of background belief is needed to separate your reasoning process from others such as the bizarre one. You might need to believe that, from the proposition that it is raining and the proposition that if it is raining the snow will melt, it follows that the snow will melt. That is to say, you might need in the background, not a second-order belief about what rationality requires of your beliefs, but a belief about the inferential relations that hold among the propositions that constitute the contents of your beliefs. I do not deny that a belief such as this may be a necessary conditions for you to reason. But even if it is necessary in the background, it is not itself a part of the reasoning; it does not constitute an extra premise. That is the lesson taught us by Lewis Caroll in 'What the tortoise said to Achilles'. So the first-order model of reasoning is not affected, even if this belief is necessary in the background.

My own view is that reasoning processes are computational. This is what characterizes them as reasoning and distinguishes them from bizarre ones such as the one I described. If I am right, it adds to the ways in which reasoning is an activity, since computation is something you do. You operate on the contents of your beliefs computationally. I think that, when you say to yourself the word 'so' or its equivalent in another language, it marks your computation. Computation is too big and difficult a topic to broach in this paper. I shall allow myself the assumption that theoretical reasoning is an operation on the contents of beliefs.

My snow example is paradigmatic of theoretical reasoning, in that it is an example of deductive reasoning by *Modus ponens*. But it represents only a small fraction of theoretical reasoning, and it leaves a great deal to be explained. For one thing, reasoning often does not proceed in the linear fashion illustrated in the example. In the example, your reasoning sets out from some initial beliefs and concludes with a new belief. But theoretical reasoning often leads you to drop one or more of your initial beliefs, rather than acquire a new one.[5] Dropping a premise-belief will bring you to satisfy the requirement *Modus ponens* just as well as acquiring a conclusion-belief will. A fuller account of theoretical reasoning will need to explain how it can turn around and have this backwards effect. Besides that, there are many other patterns of theoretical reasoning to be accounted for too. But none of that is for this paper. I described theoretical reasoning only in order to illustrate the the two different models of reasoning. Now I turn to preferences.

4. Concepts of preference

I need first to distinguish two concepts of preference. This conventional definition defines a broad concept:

> *Broad preference.* N prefers a to b if and only if N is in a mental state that would typically cause N to choose a were N to have a choice between a and b only.

We call the mental state a *preference* for a over b.

This definition is broad because it allows mental states of various sorts to count as preferences. For one thing, it allows an intention to be a preference. Suppose you intend to choose biking if ever you have a choice between biking and driving only. This is a state that would typically cause you to choose biking, were you to have a choice between biking and driving only. So you prefer biking to driving according to the definition.

This definition is too broad to capture accurately our ordinary concept of a preference. Ordinarily, we make a difference between preferring one thing to another and intending to choose one thing rather than another. You might intend to choose biking—perhaps on grounds of health—though actually you prefer driving. You can intend to choose something you do not prefer, and you can prefer something you do not intend to choose. The definition does not allow for that possibility.

According to our ordinary concept, a preference is like a desire rather than like an intention. It is a sort of comparative desire. The notion of preference may even be reducible to the notion of desire: to prefer A to B may simply be to desire A more than B. What is the difference between a desire and an intention? To specify the difference analytically is a difficult and contentious matter. Both

[5] Gilbert Harman particularly emphasizes this point in *Change in View*.

desires and intentions are mental states that can be identified by their functional roles; the difficulty is to spell out what their different roles are. They are similar in that a desire to do something and an intention to do something are both dispositions to do that thing. But they are dispositions of different sorts. In so far as they cause you to do the thing, they do so in characteristically different ways. It is difficult to spell out their different roles in detail. For my purposes I do not need to. We naively have a good understanding of the difference between a desire and an intention, and I only need to remind you of it. The next two paragraphs do so.

Desires are more remote from action than intentions are. When you intend to do something, you are committed to doing it, but that is not necessarily so when you desire it. To a large extent, your intentions control your actions. Often they do so through processes of reasoning, specifically through instrumental reasoning in which you figure out appropriate means to ends that you intend.[6] On the other hand, in so far as your desires influence your actions, they generally do so through your intentions. To desire to do something is to be disposed to intend to do it. Since to intend to do it is itself to be disposed to do it, to desire to do something is also to be disposed to do that thing, but more remotely. A desire of yours is only one influence on your intentions. Other influences include other desires that may conflict with it, your beliefs about what you ought to do, whims that strike you, confusions that afflict you, and so on. Consequently, if you desire to do something, you may not intend to do it, and you may intend to do something without desiring to do it.

You can acquire an intention by making a decision. For example, you may one day decide to go to Venice, and you will then intend to go to Venice. But deciding to go to Venice does not make you desire to go to Venice. You cannot acquire a desire by making a decision, without using an external means. You may have an external means available of acquiring the desire to go to Venice; you might spend hours poring over glossy picture books, for example. If so, you can decide to acquire the desire, and then acquire the desire using the means. But you cannot acquire the desire by deciding to, without using an external means. In this respect a desire is like a belief. I said it is a contingent fact of our psychology that you cannot acquire a belief by deciding to acquire it, without using an external means. I think the same is true of a desire.

---

[6]   Michael Bratman's *Intention, Plans and Practical Reason* is a full account of the characteristic role of intentions in controlling actions.

John Broome

According to our ordinary concept, a preference is like a desire in this respect. You cannot acquire an ordinary preference by deciding to, without using an external means. In his paper in this volume, Christian Piller claims that you can decide to have a particular preference, but I disagree with him about that if he is thinking of an ordinary preference.[7] His example is this:

> What if we got two pots of gold, if we preferred this saucer of mud to a pot of gold? I would certainly say 'Yes, please, can I have the saucer of mud'... . If I honestly and instantaneously say 'I want the mud, not the gold. Please!' then I do prefer the saucer of mud to the pot of gold.

If the prize of two pots of gold is awarded for having a broad preference for the saucer of mud over a pot of gold, Piller wins it fair and square. A broad preference can be acquired by decision. In this case, Piller acquires by decision the disposition to choose the saucer of mud rather than a pot of gold. This disposition is the prize-winning broad preference.

However, if the prize is awarded for having an ordinary preference for the saucer of mud rather than a pot of gold, Piller is not entitled to it. He may say 'I want the mud, not the gold. Please!', but that utterance has to be understood as a pressing request to be given the mud. I do not suggest he is dishonest in making it. However, if he really meant to assert that he wants the saucer of mud more than a pot of gold, I am sorry to say I would not believe him. His sorry tale makes it plain that gold is all he wants; he has no desire for the mud. His decision to choose the saucer of mud does not give him an ordinary preference for the mud over a pot of gold.

You can acquire some broad preferences by making a decision, because those broad preferences are intentions. Those broad preferences are not ordinary preferences. On the other hand, all ordinary preferences are broad preferences. They satisfy the definition: an ordinary preference for *a* over *b* is a mental state that typically causes you to choose *a* over *b*. But not just any mental state with this property is an ordinary preference. Evidently more conditions need to be added to the definition of a broad preference if we are to arrive at a correct definition of an ordinary preference.

[7] I have no quarrel with Piller's conclusion that there can be attitude-based reasons for a preference, even an ordinary preference. Just because you cannot choose to have an ordinary preference, it does not follow there are no attitude-based reasons for you to have it.

In his paper in this volume, Philip Pettit argues like me that the concept of broad preference is broader that our ordinary concept. He also thinks that more conditions must be added to the definition. He mentions conditions on the mental state's collateral connections with other mental states. The axioms of decision theory illustrate the sort of conditions he has in mind. But Pettit's objection to broad preference is different from mine. If a creature's behaviour is very chaotic, we might not be able to recognize the creature as having preferences at all. So even if it was in one particular state that met the definition of a broad preference, we might not count that state as truly a preference. That is Pettit's concern, and it is a real one. But only minimal further conditions are required for this reason. If a pigeon nearly always circles to the left, we have no difficulty in attributing to it a preference for circling to the left rather than the right, even if the rest of its behaviour is fairly chaotic. Certainly, we may have preferences that are very far from satisfying the axioms of decision theory.

To define a preference in the ordinary sense, we need to add conditions of a different sort from Pettit's. They need to distinguish a preference from an intention, and they will have to do so by specifying its functional role. As I say, this is difficult to do, and I shall not try to do it here. I hope I have said enough to separate the ordinary concept of preference from the broad one, by recalling our ordinary understanding of the difference between a preference and an intention.

5. Second-order reasoning for broad preferences

The central question of this paper is whether there is an activity of reasoning by means of which you can bring yourself to satisfy requirements of rationality on preferences. Now we have two concepts of preference, this question divides into two. Can you reason with broad preferences? Can you reason with ordinary preferences? I shall start with broad ones.

The broad concept of preference is an artificial, theoretical one. Nevertheless, it seems to be the one most authors have had in mind when they consider rational requirements on preferences. The most popular defence of the requirement *Transitivity* is the money-pump argument, which is directed at broad preferences. Here is the argument, put briefly.[8] Suppose you prefer a to b and you prefer b to c, but you do not prefer a to c. For simplicity, assume that your preferences are complete, so that, since you do not prefer a to c, either you prefer c to a or you are indifferent between a and c. Suppose you initially possess c. Now a dealer offers to swap b for your c, provided you pay her some small fee for making the transaction. Since you prefer b to c, you agree if the fee is small enough. Now you possess b. Next, this dealer offers to swap a for your b, again for a small fee. If the fee is small enough, you again agree. Finally, she offers to swap c for your a, this time without a fee. Since you either prefer c to a or are indifferent between the two, you are willing to make this transaction too. If you do make it, you end up possessing c, having handed over two small fees. You are back where you started, but poorer. It seems irrational to to have preferences that allow you to be exploited in this way. That is the money-pump argument.

In this story, it is your dispositions to choose that allow you to be exploited. These dispositions constitute your broad preferences. Your ordinary preferences do not come into the argument. So the money-pump argument applies to broad preferences and not ordinary ones. It is an example of a class of arguments know as 'pragmatic arguments', which are supposed to demonstrate that rationality imposes various requirements on your preferences. All of them are aimed at broad preferences.

Because a broad preference can be an intention, you may be able to acquire a broad preference by making a decision. This opens the possibility that the second-order model of reasoning can work for broad preferences. That is, you may be able to reason your way from a belief in the requirement itself to satisfying the requirement. Since I have already set out the steps of the second-order model in the context of theoretical reasoning, I need only retrace them very quickly here. Suppose that, in the broad sense, you prefer biking to walking, and you prefer walking to driving, but you do not prefer biking to driving. You do not satisfy *Transitivity*. But suppose you believe in the requirement of transitivity itself in this instance: you believe rationality requires you to prefer biking to driving if you prefer biking to walking and walking to driving. (Perhaps you have been convinced by the money-pump argument.) Suppose indeed you have the normative belief that you ought to prefer biking to driving if you prefer biking

---

[8] Details of the argument are debated. The most convincing version of it appears in Wlodek Rabinowicz's 'Money pump with foresight'.

to walking and walking to driving. By kratic reasoning, you might be able to form the intention of preferring biking to driving if you prefer biking to walking and walking to driving. The content of this intention is a conditional proposition, but since you actually satisfy the antecedent of the conditional—you prefer biking to walking and walking to driving—you may be able to narrow the intention down to a simple intention to prefer biking to driving. If so, you now intend to have a particular preference.

At the corresponding point in my discussion of theoretical reasoning, you had arrived at the intention to believe the snow will melt. There, I said this intention is ineffective, because intending to believe something cannot normally bring you to believe it, except by using an external means. But it seems that your intention to prefer biking to driving may be effective; it may cause you to have this preference, without your using an external means.

It is an intention to have a broad preference: to be in a mental state that would typically cause you to choose biking were you to have a choice between biking and driving only. You will have this broad preference if you intend to choose biking if ever you have a choice between biking and driving only. And that state of intention seems to be one you can put yourself into simply by deciding to choose biking if ever you have a choice between biking and driving only. So it seems your intention to prefer biking to driving may cause you to prefer biking to driving, without your using an external means. The only means you require is to make a decision. This is a mental act, and it may therefore form part of a reasoning process.

That was quick. I have apparently mapped out a complete route whereby second-order reasoning could bring you to satisfy the requirement *Transitivity*, by acquiring the preference you need in order to satisfy it. However, there are several questionable steps along the route. In section 2, where I developed the second-order model of reasoning, I made questionable assumptions as concessions to the model. So I do not insist that the second-order model works for broad preferences; I simply cannot rule it out. Since broad preferences are not preferences as we ordinarily understand them, I pass quickly on to those that are.

6. First-order reasoning with ordinary preferences

For ordinary preferences, the second-order model can quickly be ruled out. You cannot acquire an ordinary preference by making a decision, without using an external means. This is one of the characteristics that distinguish an ordinary preference from other broad preferences. It follows that second-order reasoning will not work for ordinary preferences. The argument is the same as the one I gave for second-order theoretical reasoning.

What about first-order reasoning? First-order reasoning for preferences would be reasoning *with* preferences, about the contents of preferences, rather than reasoning *about* preferences. Is there such a thing? The account I gave of first-order reasoning for beliefs was special to beliefs. If we are to extend it to states other than beliefs, we shall need a separate account for each state. We need one for preferences.

There is a general difficulty in the way of understanding how you can reason with states other than beliefs, operating on their contents in the way first-order reasoning requires. Beliefs have a special feature that allows you to do this sort of reasoning. When you say to yourself that it is raining, you express your mental state of belief. You also, in a different sense, express the content of that belief. You say that it is raining, which is to express the proposition that it is raining,which is the content of your belief. So you express the belief and its content together.

First-order reasoning requires this sort of double expression. It is reasoning with mental states, and you have to express those states in order to reason with them. But as well as that, reasoning is about the contents of the mental states. You need those contents before your mind, which means you have to present them to yourself, or express them to yourself. So your expression of your states also has to express the contents of those states.

But at first sight, few mental states share with beliefs the property that you can express them and their content together. Consider a desire, for example. We normally take a desire to have a content, and most philosophers take its content to be a proposition. Suppose you want to be loved. Then according to the common view, the content of your desire is the proposition that you are loved. But suppose you expressed this content by saying 'I am loved'. Then you would not be expressing the desire. If you are expressing any mental state of yours, it would have to be a belief that you are loved. You can only express this belief if you have it, and you may or may not have it, but at any rate you are not expressing a desire to be loved. So you are not putting yourself in a position to reason with your desire to be loved.

A preference is a more complicated example. We can take a preference to be a relation between two propositions, and we can take that pair of propositions to be its content. Suppose you prefer walking to driving. We can take this as a preference for the proposition that you walk over the proposition that you drive. What could you say to yourself to express this preference? Evidently neither of the propositions that constitute its content. And to say that you prefer walking to driving does not express the preference either. At best it would be expressing the belief that you have the preference, if you happen to have that belief. Consequently, it seems you cannot reason with preferences. That is the difficulty.

The difficulty arises over reasoning with all mental states apart from beliefs. But there is a way to overcome it. We can revise our notion of the content of a mental state. Philosophers commonly assume that mental states of different types can have the same content, which they take to be a proposition. So you might have a belief that you are loved, or a desire to be loved, and either state would have as its content the proposition that you are loved. Either state has the same content, but in the two different cases you stand in a different relation to the content—a believing relation in one and a desiring relation in the other. In the complicated case of a preference, you stand in a preferring relation to a pair of propositions. That is the common view.

The alternative is to take the content of a mental state to be a proposition together with a mark of some sort, which marks the type of state it is.[9] In this way the differences in mental states can be absorbed into the contents of the states. For instance, if you believe you are loved, the content of your belief is the proposition that you are loved together with a belief mark. If you desire to be loved, the content of your desire is this proposition together with a desire mark.

How do we refer to these contents? I shall explain in a moment how we do so in English. But it will be clearer if I start with an artificial language. The language must have the resources to designate marks; I shall give the name 'markers' to the linguistic items that do this job. Let the marker for belief be 'yes' and the marker for desire be 'nice'. If you believe you are loved, you might designate the content of your belief by the artificial sentence 'I am loved—yes'. If I also believe you are loved, I have a belief with the same content as yours, but I would designate it using the second person sentence 'You are loved—yes'. If you want to be loved, you

---

[9] Examples of this idea appear in Richard Hare's *The Language of Morals* and Paul Grice's *Aspects of Reason*.

might say 'I am loved—nice'. If I want you to be loved, I have a desire with the same content as yours. I might say 'You are loved—nice'.

A preference is again more complicated. If you prefer walking to driving, the content of your state is the pair of propositions that you walk and that you drive, together with a preference mark. You might designate it by the artificial sentence 'I walk—rather—I drive'.

If you say this sentence to yourself, you are expressing the preference, and you are also expressing the content of the preference. In this way, a mark gives a preference the special feature that a belief has: expressing the content of the preference is also expressing the preference itself. So, when you express the preference, you make its content available to be reasoned about. Preferences become available for reasoning with.

The purpose of marks is to distinguish between different sort of mental state. One sort of state can be distinguished by the absence of a mark, provided all the others have marks. It is convenient to give beliefs this special status. So from here on, I shall drop the 'yes' marker, and take the content of a belief to be a proposition without a mark.

Marks give us the beginning of an account of first-order reasoning with mental states other than beliefs. Your reasoning will be a process in which you express your mental states to yourself using marked sentences, operate on their contents, and emerge with a new mental state. But this is only the very beginning of an account. The next thing that needs to be done is to make the account realistic. If we are really to use marked sentences in our reasoning, we must have actual marked sentences in our language. Do we?

We do. Natural languages can express beliefs and their contents. They also contain devices that allow them to express many other mental states and their contents. If their contents are indeed propositions with marks, as I am assuming, some of these devices are what I called markers. English uses special constructions or special moods of verbs to serve as markers.

For example, a desire is marked by an optative construction. Robert Browning said 'Oh, to be in England now that April's there!'. This optative sentence designates the proposition that Browning is in England now in April, together with the mark for desire. When Browning said to himself 'Oh, to be in England now that April's there', he expressed his desire to be in England, and also the content of his desire, understood as a proposition with a mark. Translated into my artificial language, he said 'I am in England now that April's there—nice'.

As Jonathan Dancy pointed out to me, English has a marker for preference too. The sentence 'Rather walk than drive' is the English equivalent of my artificial 'I walk—rather—I drive'. It designates the pair of propositions that you walk and that you drive, with the mark for preference.

On the face of it, this construction puts you in a position to reason with your preferences. Suppose you prefer walking to driving and biking to walking, but you do not prefer biking to driving. You do not satisfy the requirement *Transitivity*. But you may say to yourself:

> *Rather walk than drive*
> *Rather bike than walk*
> *So, rather bike than drive.*

When you say each of the first two sentences, you are expressing a preference you have. Saying these sentences to yourself causes you to have a new preference that you did not previously have. By the time you say the third sentence to yourself, you are also expressing this new preference. By causing you to have it, this process has brought you to satisfy *Transitivity*. Intuitively, this seems a plausible instance of reasoning with preferences.

The contents of your preferences are pairs of propositions, with marks attached. I can designate them using sentences in my artificial language. Since I am speaking of you, I shall put them in the second person. The contents are:

> You walk—rather—you drive
> You bike—rather—you walk
> You bike—rather—you drive.

The process I have described satisfies the description of first-order reasoning that I gave in section 3. It is a process whereby some of your mental states give rise to another mental state; the mental states involved have contents; in the course of the reasoning you say to yourself the propositions that constitute these contents, and you reason about these contents. So on the face of it, this is a genuine example of first-order reasoning with preferences.

However, much more needs to be done to make that conclusion secure. For one thing, we need to generalize: are there similar processes that can bring you to satisfy other requirements on preferences? For another, can we find a criterion for correct reasoning with preferences, as opposed to incorrect reasoning? Certainly, if this is to be genuine reasoning, there must be such a distinction.

7. Preferences and beliefs about betterness

But I think the most difficult challenge is to demonstrate that this is really reasoning with *preferences*. When you use a sentence like 'Rather walk than drive' you may well be expressing a belief about betterness, and not a preference—in this case, the belief that walking is better than driving. The betterness in question need not be absolute betterness from the point of view of the universe. It might be betterness for you, or betterness relative to your point of view, or something else.

If your sentences express beliefs rather than preferences, the contents of the reasoning I have described would be the sequence of propositions:

It is better that you walk than that you drive
It is better that you bike than that you walk
So it is better that you bike than that you drive

The process that proceeds by your expressing these propositions to yourself constitutes correct reasoning, because the betterness relation is transitive. If it is better that you walk than that you drive, and better that you bike than that you walk, it is better that you bike than that you drive. But this is theoretical reasoning with beliefs. It is not reasoning with preferences. Perhaps the pattern of reasoning I presented in section 6 is always theoretical reasoning; perhaps it is never reasoning with preferences, as I suggested.

What is the difference between a preference and a belief about betterness? Not very much, possibly. A belief about betterness may satisfy the definition of broad preference that I gave in section 4: a belief that a is better than b may be a mental state that would typically cause you to choose a were you to have a choice between a and b only. I explained that, to define preference in its ordinary sense, we would have to add conditions to this definition of broad preference. I explained that conditions are needed to separate a preference for a over b from an intention to choose a rather than b. It now emerges that we also need conditions to separate a preference for a over b from a belief that a is better than b. But these conditions will be hard to find. The functional role of a belief about betterness may not be very different from the functional role of a preference; it will be hard to separate them.

A belief about betterness does differ from a preference in one respect. It is a state that has a content that is a proposition. The contents of beliefs, being propositions, stand in logical relations to each other. The logical relations among contents induce rational requirements on beliefs. An example is the requirement *Modus ponens*, which derives from the logical relation among propositions known as 'modus ponens'. Moreover, we have reasoning processes for beliefs that allow us to follow up these logical relations, and thereby bring ourselves to satisfy some of the rational requirements on beliefs. These facts are special to beliefs, and seem to separate them from preferences.

But we commonly think there are rational requirements on preferences too, and I have been assuming so in this paper. Moreover, I am now investigating the idea that we have reasoning process for preferences that allow us to bring ourselves to satisfy some of these requirements. If these things are true, it further reduces the functional difference between preferences and beliefs about betterness. Both are governed by rational requirements and, for both, these rational requirements can sometimes be satisfied by reasoning.

Furthermore, there is a case for thinking that the rational requirements on preferences, if they truly exist, derive from the logical relations among propositions about betterness. Why does rationality require your preferences to be transitive? I have mentioned the money-pump argument, but here is another possible explanation. Rationality requires you to prefer a to b if and only if you believe a is better than b. And rationality requires you to believe a is better than c if you believe a is better than b and b is better than c. And this is so in turn because, as a matter of logic, if a is better than b, and b is better than c, then a is better than c. I do not insist this is the correct explanation of the *Transitivity* requirement, but it is a plausible one.

The upshot is that it is hard to distinguish the functional roles of a preferences and a belief about goodness. This explains why many noncognitivists about value think that a belief about betterness is indeed nothing other than a preference. In so far as the two converge, I am inclined in the opposite direction: a preference may be nothing other than a belief about goodness. It may turn out that reasoning with preferences is really nothing other than reasoning with beliefs.[10]

References

Bennett, Jonathan, 'Why is belief involuntary?', *Analysis,* 50 (1990), pp. 87–107.

Bratman, Michael E., *Intention, Plans and Practical Reason*, Harvard University Press, 1987.

Broome, John, 'Does rationality give us reasons?', *Philosophical Issues*, 15 (2005), pp. 321–37.

Broome, John, 'Wide or narrow scope?', *Mind*, forthcoming.

Carroll, Lewis, 'What the tortoise said to Achilles', *Mind*, 4 (1895), pp. 278–80.

Hare, R. M., *The Language of Morals*, Oxford University Press, 1952.

Grice, Paul, *Aspects of Reason*, edited by Richard Warner, Oxford University Press, 2001.

Harman, Gilbert, *Change in View: Principles of Reasoning*, MIT Press, 1986.

Kolodny, Niko, 'Why be rational?' *Mind*, 114 (2005), pp. 509–63.

Pettit, Philip, 'Preference, deliberation and satisfaction', in this volume.

Piller, Christian, 'Content-related and attitude-related reasons for preferences', in this volume.

Rabinowicz, Wlodek, 'Money pump with foresight', in *Imperceptible Harms and Benefits*, edited by Michael J. Almeida, Kluwer 2000, pp. 123–154.

Scanlon, T. M., *What We Owe to Each Other*, Harvard University Press, 1998.

Williams, Bernard, 'Deciding to believe' in his *Problems of the Self*, Cambridge University Press, 1973, pp. 136–51.

[10] This paper has been greatly improved as a result of extremely helpful comments I received from Krister Bykvist and Serena Olsaretti.

Taking unconsidered preferences seriously*

ROBERT SUGDEN

In normative economic analysis, it is conventional to treat each person's preferences as that person's own standard of value, and as the standard by which the effects of public policies on that person should be valued. The proposal that preferences should be treated in this way is usually qualified by two apparently natural conditions—that preferences are internally coherent, and that they reflect the considered judgements of the person concerned. However, there is now a great deal of evidence suggesting that, in many economic environments, preferences of the required kind simply do not exist. It seems that the preferences that govern people's actual behaviour are often incoherent and unstable. This prompts the following question: Is there a defensible form of normative economics which respects each individual's *actual* preferences, whatever form they take? I shall try to show that there is.

1. A contractarian approach to normative analysis

This paper is premised on a contractarian understanding of normative analysis. On this understanding, the object of normative analysis is not to arrive at an all-things-considered judgement about what is valuable for society as a whole, but to look for proposals that each individual can value from his or her own point of view. To follow this approach is to treat social value as *subjective* and *distributed*. To say that social value is subjective is to say that it is not a property of the world, but a perception or attitude on the part of the valuer. To say that social value is distributed is to say that it is not a single measure, expressing a synoptic judgement about what is valuable; it is simply an array of the separate value

*   An early version of this paper was presented at a conference on philosophical aspects of social choice and welfare, held at the University of Caen. I thank participants at this conference, particularly Kaushik Basu, for valuable comments. I also thank Serena Olsaretti for her suggestions as editor.

judgements of the individuals who comprise society. There is, then, no distinction between a person's own standard of value and the standard by which effects on that person are valued.[1]

A contractarian theory needs a way of representing the standard of value of each individual in a society of many individuals. In this context, a broad-brush approach is unavoidable. Clearly, we cannot expect to describe the actual value judgements of particular people: we must be content with a theoretically tractable representation of the standard of value of a typical individual. However, the subjectivity of the contractarian approach requires that this representation be flexible: it should impose as few restrictions as possible on the substantive content of any individual's values.

A contractarian theory is addressed to individuals as reflective citizens. The aim is to recommend proposals for collective action by showing that they promote the values of each citizen, considered separately. There is an implicit presumption that these citizens are willing to engage in the kind of reasoned argument that the theory exemplifies, and are capable of recognising the validity of what has been shown. Thus, the values that are being promoted should be understood as the considered judgements of the relevant individuals, and not merely as pre-reflective hunches. It seems natural, then, to represent each individual's standard of value as having some degree of internal coherence.

However, it is fundamental to the contractarian approach that we (the theorists) take moral psychology as it is, not as we would wish it to be. We must not be tempted to suppose that our own favourite moral positions are the only ones that are capable of being sincerely endorsed by people who have engaged in serious reflection. Nor, since contractarianism is premised on a subjective understanding of value, should we require considered judgements to be supported by reasons which appeal to a conception of moral truth, or which are shared by an imagined community of right-thinking moral agents. Rather, we should think of a person's considered judgements as codifications of his perceptions of value, recognising that those perceptions are products of human psychology and social learning, not insights into a moral universe. When, later in this paper, I speak about finding coherent *formulations* of particular moral intuitions, it is this kind of codification that I have in mind.

How, then, should standards of value be represented in a contractarian theory? The most obvious solution, one might think, is to follow the conventions of normative economics and identify

[1]   I explain and defend this approach in Sugden (1989).

each person's standard of value with his considered preferences. In the next two sections of this paper, I examine this proposal and show how it breaks down when individuals lack stable and coherent preferences. Then I suggest an alternative standard of value, based on considered judgements about opportunity rather than on considered preferences.

2. Considered preference as a standard of value

If a person's preferences are to serve as a standard of value, it seems unexceptionable to require that those preferences should have whatever properties of coherence are intrinsic to the concept of value. In normative economics, these properties are usually presented in purely formal terms. Exactly what is required depends on the nature of the universe X of objects of choice over which preferences are defined. If, for example, X is defined as a finite set of discrete objects, it is normal to require that the binary relation $[\geqslant]$ ('is weakly preferred to') is complete (i.e. for all x, y in X: x $[\geqslant]$ y or y $[\geqslant]$ x) and transitive (i.e. for all x, y, z in X: $[x$ $[\geqslant]$ y and y $[\geqslant]$ $z]$ implies x $[\geqslant]$ z). Additional properties are imposed if X is defined as the set of n-dimensional vectors of non-negative real numbers (interpreted as 'bundles' of n consumption goods), or if it is defined as the set of all probability mixes of some set of 'consequences'.

To illustrate the justification for these restrictions, take the case of transitivity. One might argue that transitivity is intrinsic to the concept of value: if x is at least as valuable as y, and y is at least as valuable as z, then, as a matter of logic, x is at least as valuable as z.[2] It is much less plausible to claim that transitivity is intrinsic to the concept of preference. Whether a person's preferences are transitive or not seems to be an empirical matter. Non-transitive preferences might be a symptom of irrationality, but there is no logical contradiction in supposing their existence. So, if we are to use preferences as a standard of value, we have to be sure that they satisfy transitivity.

[2]   For an argument of this kind, see Broome (1991, pp. 10–12). Broome claims that it is a necessary truth that *all* relations of the form 'is at least as ... as' are transitive. In passing, I must report that I am not persuaded. Broome discusses the relation 'is at least as westerly as' which appears to be a counter-example. Broome tries to persuade us that appearances are deceptive, but in this case I think they are not.

Robert Sugden

It is perhaps misleading to think that what is required here is simply a formal restriction on preferences. We cannot make sense of a formal restriction like transitivity without first postulating a particular universe of objects of choice. The economic theory of choice has content only because, at any given time, there are established conventions about how objects of choice are defined. These conventions reflect the role that preferences play in normative analysis. Objects of choice have to be specified in such a way that it is credible to treat them as carriers of value. For example, suppose that Tom, if given a straight choice between an apple and an orange, would prefer to take the apple. Given a straight choice between the orange and a pear, he would prefer to take the orange. But, given a straight choice between the pear and the apple, he would prefer to take the pear. If we follow the conventions of economics and define $X = \{apple, orange, pear, ...\}$, we have a violation of transitivity. But what if we define X so that it includes options such as 'taking the apple when there is a straight choice between an apple and an orange'? If we do this, Tom's preferences will come out as transitive. However, unless some explanation can be given for why, from Tom's point of view, the value of a particular fruit differs according to the set from which it is chosen, the claim that these preferences express a standard of value seems unpersuasive.[3] It seems that, as a necessary condition for a person's preferences to be treated as a standard of value, they must satisfy appropriate conditions of coherence when defined over a *normatively credible* universe of objects of choice.

A similar argument can be made about the stability or volatility of preferences. The economic theory of choice has content only because a person's preferences can be assumed to be reasonably stable over time. If they did not have that kind of stability, their credibility as carriers of value would be open to question. Suppose that at 10:00 on some day, Jane is offered a choice between pasta and chicken for a meal to be eaten in the evening, and she expresses a strong preference for pasta. At 10:30, she is given the opportunity to reconsider her choice, and she expresses a strong preference for chicken. On one interpretation of these observations, they disconfirm the hypothesis that Jane's choices are governed by coherent preferences. Alternatively, we might say that Jane has one preference ordering at 10:00 and a different one at 10:30. But,

---

[3]   Compare Broome's (1991, pp. 90–107) argument about the individuation of options and the need for 'rational requirements of indifference'.

unless some explanation can be given for why, from Jane's point of view, the value of chicken and pasta as evening meals differs according to the time in the morning from which they are viewed, it seems hard to claim that each of these conflicting preferences expresses her values. Some degree of stability of preference seems to be necessary before preferences can be treated as a standard of value.

This thought provides the justification for a restriction proposed by David Gauthier (1986, pp. 26–38) in formulating his contractarian theory of 'morals by agreement': that preferences must be *stable under experience and reflection*. As Gauthier emphasises, this formulation is consistent with a subjective and distributed conception of value: there is no appeal to any notion of value external to the individual's own perceptions. Nor is there any appeal to counterfactual hypotheses about what an individual would prefer, were she to have true knowledge of the world, as in 'informed desire' theories of value. Gauthier's restriction captures a qualification which, I think, would be accepted by most proponents of the principle that preference is a standard of value.

These qualifications can be brought together as a concept of *considered preference*. I shall say that a person's preferences are considered if they satisfy conventional properties of coherence when defined over a normatively credible universe of objects of choice, and if they are stable under experience and reflection. If considered preferences exist, they can be used as the basis for a theory of subjective and distributed social value: we can assert that each person's standard of value is given by her considered preferences. But do they exist?

3. Do considered preferences exist?

At the conceptual level, there is no guarantee that considered preferences exist at all. One might reasonably assert that, if an agent is capable of autonomous choice, she must have preferences of some sort. That is, she must have attitudes towards the options between which she has to choose, and those attitudes will be revealed in some way in the choices that she actually makes. Those attitudes, we might say, are the agent's preferences. However, there is no conceptual guarantee that those preferences satisfy the conventional coherence requirements when defined over some normatively credible universe of objects of choice. Nor is there any guarantee that they are stable under experience and reflection.

Robert Sugden

Whether preferences have these properties is essentially an empirical question. The viability of the considered preference account of value depends on the truth of the hypothesis that, for most people and for most economically significant choices, considered preferences exist.

For the last twenty-five years, the investigation of this hypothesis has been a central research programme of what has come to be known as *behavioural economics*—that branch of economics which draws on the theoretical ideas and experimental methods of psychology to investigate the actual behaviour of economic agents. As a result of this research programme, we now know that economic agents often do *not* act on considered preferences.

Many highly predictable patterns of behaviour have been discovered which contravene received assumptions about preferences. For example, individuals' decisions in controlled experimental environments show a surprisingly high degree of unexplained stochastic variation: if the same person faces exactly the same binary choice problem twice within a few minutes, the probability that she will choose differently in the two cases is of the order of 25 per cent.[4] If preferences are defined over the normatively relevant domains that economic theory has traditionally used, some of the most fundamental principles of preference coherence—including transitivity, dynamic consistency, and the principle that preferences over lotteries should respect stochastic dominance—are systematically violated. In many cases, preferences are highly sensitive to what appear to be normatively irrelevant matters of presentation. Although many of these violations of standard theory were first observed in laboratory environments, they have been found to occur in 'real' markets too.[5]

Just how serious these 'anomalies' are remains a matter of dispute. While some economists conclude that the received theory is fundamentally flawed, others claim that most anomalies result from errors; given sufficient experience and feedback, it is said, individuals correct those errors and 'discover' their underlying

---

[4] See, for example, Starmer and Sugden (1989) and Hey and Orme (1994, p. 1296).

[5] For surveys of the evidence, see Camerer (1995), Starmer (2000) and Kahneman and Tversky (2000).

preferences.[6] To propose this *discovered preference* hypothesis is, in effect, to propose that considered preferences exist, even if they are not always revealed in choice behaviour (whether in laboratory experiments or in real markets). The evidence on this issue is mixed; while some anomalies do seem to become less frequent as individuals gain experience, others seem much more robust.[7] For the purposes of this paper, it is not necessary to adjudicate these disputes. It is sufficient to recognise that the existence of considered preferences is not a self-evident truth or a well-established empirical fact: it is merely a contested hypothesis. It is surely worth asking what kind of normative economics would be possible if that hypothesis had to be rejected.

Readers who are not familiar with the literature of behavioural economics may find it surprising that apparently unexceptionable principles of rationality are regularly violated. To understand this, one must recognise that, in many cases, the supposed irrationality of these anomalous patterns of behaviour is not visible in any single decision. As an illustration of this general point, consider the phenomenon of 'coherent arbitrariness' reported by Dan Ariely, George Loewenstein and Drazen Prelec (2003).

In one of Ariely et al's experiments, subjects were exposed to an annoying sound and then asked whether, hypothetically, they would repeat the same experience in return for a specified payment. For each person, this hypothetical payment was constructed from the first three digits of her social security number (so that, for example, a person whose number began with 356 was asked to consider a payment of $3.56); subjects knew that this procedure was being used. Following this, subjects were asked to state the minimum amounts of money they would accept as payment for listening to the sound for various lengths of time. 'Prices' were then drawn at random from a distribution, and subjects who had indicated their willingness to listen to the noise at the relevant price were required to do so and were paid the price. This procedure generated a surprising result. subjects whose social security numbers were above the median asked for 60 per cent more payment than those whose numbers were below the median. The implication is that

---

[6] Variants of the discovered preference hypothesis are proposed by Smith (1994) and Plott (1996); the term is Plott's. These hypotheses are discussed by Binmore (1999), Loewenstein (1999), Loomes (1999) and Starmer (1999).

[7] Contrasting evidence on the effect of experience on anomalies can be found in Ariely et al (2003), List (2003) and Loomes et al (2003).

subjects' expressed preferences between money and noise were strongly influenced by the sum of money referred to in the hypothetical payment question, even though it must have been obvious that this carried no information relevant to the task at hand, and even though subjects knew exactly what the experience of noise would be like.

It may seem absurd for a person's preferences to be determined by her social security number but, if we look at the behaviour of any individual subject in this experiment, we see nothing obviously irrational. Consider two typical (but imaginary) subjects. Alan, whose social security number happens to begin with 204, states a willingness-to-accept valuation of $3.55. Betty, whose number begins with 835, states a valuation of $5.76. There is nothing irrational about either valuation, considered in isolation. Probably, neither person is conscious that his or her valuation has been influenced by the irrelevant cue. Viewed in the perspective of rational choice theory, what is wrong with preferences like these is that they are unstable: if examined carefully, they can be found to vary according to factors which seem to have no rational significance.

One might think—indeed, I do think—that such preferences are not *ir*rational at all, but merely *a*rational. If social security numbers have no rational significance for valuations, rationality cannot prescribe valuations which depend on social security numbers. But what if rationality does not prescribe *any* unique valuation? If it is compatible with rationality to value the noise *either* at $3.55 *or* at $5.76, why is it contrary to rationality to report the first valuation if one has one social security number and the second if one has another? But I do not want to get sidetracked into the metaphysics of rationality. What matters is that violations of the principles of rational choice theory need not reveal themselves as obvious pathologies.

Still, the fact remains that the preferences that govern choices in Ariely et al's experiment are not stable under experience and reflection. It may well be that, in cases like this, considered preferences simply do not exist. Given one arbitrary stimulus, people are conscious of one preference; given another, equally arbitrary stimulus, they are conscious of a different one. There may be nothing more to be discovered than this. Clearly, these findings are bad news for the programme of using considered preference as the standard of value. But should we conclude that when people act on *un*considered preferences, it doesn't matter to them whether those preferences are satisfied? I suggest not.

Taking unconsidered preferences seriously

Consider an example from everyday life. It is a hot day. I go into a shop to buy a newspaper. I pass a cabinet displaying chilled cans of sweet drinks but not, unfortunately, chilled unsweetened drinks. The idea of a cold drink is attractive to me (I'm hot and thirsty), but the idea of sweetness is aversive (normally, I dislike sweet drinks). I am conscious of opposing motivational pulls. I do not perceive either pull as obviously stronger than the other, but nor do I perceive them as exactly balanced, as I would if I were choosing between two apparently identical cans of the same brand of drink. I'm just not sure which of the two options ('drink' and 'not drink') to go for. In the end, I go for the drink. Suppose the truth (known to experts in marketing, but not to me) is that people like me are susceptible to the placement of products in display cabinets; had the drinks been on a lower shelf, I would still have seen them, but would not have chosen to buy one. In buying the drink, then, I am not acting on a considered preference. Even though I don't know the marketing theory, I may be conscious that my preferences are unstable: having found it hard to choose between the two options, I may realise that in other, apparently similar circumstances, I might have chosen differently. So is there any value to me in my being able to satisfy my unconsidered preference for the drink?

Speaking for myself, I *do* value such opportunities. To the extent that the economy is structured so that I can satisfy my desires, as I experience them, and however arbitrary and unstable they may be, that is for me something to value. And although the preferences that are being satisfied may be unconsidered, *my valuing the opportunity to satisfy them* is considered: I find that value judgement to be stable under experience and reflection. That judgement may not be shared by everyone, but it is not merely a personal idiosyncrasy. It is the core idea to which generations of economists have appealed when they have argued that competitive markets implement the value of consumer sovereignty, and which is reflected in the business maxim that the customer is always right. Whatever consumers want and are willing to pay for, whether their reasons for wanting it are good, bad or non-existent, producers will find it in their interests to supply. For those of us who value consumer sovereignty, that is one of the great virtues of the market system.

A critic might ask how it can matter to me whether a preference of mine is satisfied, unless I can provide some reason for that preference. Surely (the critic says) what matters to me is that I get what has value, not what I happen to feel a sense of desire for. Preferences that are not stable under experience and reflection are arbitrary mental states; they do not have supporting reasons. Perhaps some higher-order value, such as autonomy, is served by my being free to choose my own actions even in the absence of reasons for choice; but then it is the higher-order value that provides the reason for valuing consumer sovereignty. Merely wanting something (the critic concludes) is not a reason for getting it.

My response is that the critic's demand for reasons is misplaced. As I argued in Section 1, a contractarian approach cannot demand that considered value judgements are justifiable by appeals to reason. When considering a claim about what people value, the contractarian theorist should ask only whether the claim is credible as moral psychology, and whether the alleged standard of value can be formulated in a coherent way. I see nothing incredible in the suggestion that, for many people, being able to satisfy their own desires, as and when they experience them, is something that they perceive as valuable—without their ever imagining that this sense of value needs further rationalisation. Whether this perception can be given a coherent formulation is the subject of this paper.

To avoid misunderstanding, I must make clear that I am not asserting that, for most people, consumer sovereignty always trumps other considerations. One can value consumer sovereignty in general and still recognise certain specific restrictions on one's freedom of choice as being in one's long-term interest. For example, suppose I enjoy moderate consumption of alcohol, but know that this impairs my judgement. Then I might support laws which restrict people's capacity to take decisions with serious long-term consequences while under the influence of alcohol. Everyone will have his or her favourite examples of justified forms of self-constraint. The essential feature of such examples is that, when forming considered judgements about what one values, one disavows certain preferences that one might sometimes wish to act on. All I want to claim is that, for those of us who value consumer sovereignty, such cases are the exception rather than the rule. In the normal run of events, there will be many cases in which one can expect one's preferences to be unstable and yet have no wish to disavow them.

My aim is to consider how this idea might be formulated and, in so doing, to test its conceptual coherence. I do this by taking a case in which a person's preferences are unstable, but in which (for me at least) the intuition in favour of consumer sovereignty remains strong. In this paper, I do not consider the exceptional cases in which there is a considered judgement in favour of self-constraint.[8]

4. Continuing identity: the problem

The focus of my analysis is a stylised model of a simple decision problem for a representative economic agent. I call this model *Joe's problem*, since Joe is the name of my agent. It is constructed to exhibit a transparent violation of the hypothesis that preferences are stable under experience and reflection. My objective is to find a coherent formulation of the idea that the agent values opportunities to act on his unconsidered preferences, even though he may use those opportunities in an apparently inconsistent way.

I begin with the version of the model in which Joe has the greatest freedom of action. There are three time periods. The model concerns Joe's choices with respect to a ticket in a lottery which will be drawn in period 3. The ticket offers a 1 in 100 chance of winning a prize of £1,000. Initially Joe has not entered the lottery, and his only opportunity to do so occurs in period 1; in that period, he has the opportunity to buy the ticket at a cost of £11. If he buys, then in period 2 he has the opportunity to sell back the ticket, but receiving only £9 in exchange. There is no particular significance to these precise probabilities and amounts of money. What matters is that the buying price is higher than the selling price, that Joe might reasonably value the ticket at more than the buying price, but might equally reasonably value it at less than the selling price; and that if he acts on the first valuation in period 1 and on the second in period 2, he will incur an unambiguous loss.

The next feature of the model represents a psychological regularity for which there is solid evidence: other things being equal, people tend to be more willing to take risks in unhappy

---

[8] My hunch is that the analysis presented in Section 5 could be extended to include these cases by making use of the conventional multiple-self approach. Suppose that, at some point in a sequential decision problem, a person acts on a transient preference which, from the perspective of the 'continuing person', he disavows. That action can be treated as if it is made by another person; instead of a single-agent decision problem, we have a game with two players—the continuing person and an alien, transient self. There would be nothing especially original in such an analysis. The real challenge, as I see it, is to analyse cases in which the continuing person does *not* disavow his transient preferences.

moods than in happy ones.[9] For Joe, there are just two possible moods, 'happy' and 'unhappy'. In each period, he is one or other of these moods. Which mood he is in is determined by a random process, independently for each period, such that each mood is experienced with probability 0.5. Joe cannot predict his mood in advance. In the unhappy mood, his attitude to risk is such that he perceives the lottery ticket as more desirable than the certainty of £11. In the happy mood, his attitude to risk is such that he perceives the lottery as less desirable than the certainty of £9. Notice that Joe's happiness or unhappiness, as experienced when he makes decisions about buying or selling the ticket (that is, in periods 1 and 2), is independent of his mood at the time the lottery is drawn (period 3). Thus, his different attitudes to risk—his ex ante perceptions about the merits of risky decisions—are independent of the ex post experiences to which those decisions can lead.

In decision theory, it is standard to represent sequential decision problems of this kind as *decision trees*. Each point in the problem at which a choice is required is represented by a *choice node*, conventionally drawn as a square. Each point at which chance intervenes is represented by a *chance node*, drawn as a circle. If the agent's preferences are different at different times or in different contingencies, this is represented by dividing the agent into two or more *selves*. Each self is then modelled as if it was a distinct agent with its own preferences. In this way, the preferences of each self can be held constant throughout the tree.

Applying this strategy to Joe's problem, we can define two selves, an unhappy and risk-loving *Joe$_1$* and a happy and risk-averse *Joe$_2$*. To avoid unnecessary complications, I assume that Joe's preferences, for any given mood, satisfy the axioms of expected utility theory. Thus, Joe's preferences can be represented by two utility functions, one for each mood. To keep the decision tree as simple as possible, I start the analysis after Joe's mood for period 1 has been determined, and I stipulate that this mood is unhappy. I end the analysis at the end of period 2, before the lottery has been drawn. Payoffs are represented in units of expected utility.

With the model specified in this way, there are three possible outcomes: *either* Joe doesn't buy the ticket, *or* he buys it in period 1 and holds it through period 2, *or* he buys in period 1 and sells in

---

[9]   Reviewing a range of investigations of the role of affect on decision-making, Isen (1999) concludes that positive affect tends to increase risk aversion in relation to decisions that are perceived to involve the possibility of serious loss.

period 2. I stipulate that, for the unhappy Joe_1, the expected utilities of these outcomes are respectively 0, −1 and 2, while for the happy Joe_2, they are 0, −1 and −2. This gives us the tree T_1, shown in Figure 1. For each outcome, the expected utility for Joe_1 is shown, followed by that for Joe_2.

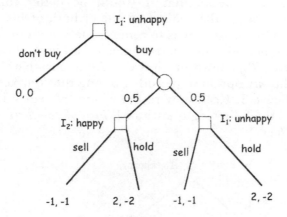

Figure 1: Joe's problem, unconstrained (Tree T_1)

What will Joe do? The standard decision-theoretic analysis uses the *folding-back* (or *backward induction*) algorithm, working out what happens at the most remote nodes of a tree (on the supposition that they are reached) and then working back towards the initial node. So, suppose that Joe_1's second decision node is reached. Risk-loving Joe_1 will then choose *hold* (with an expected utility of 2) rather than *sell* (−1). Next, suppose that Joe_2's decision node is reached. Risk-averse Joe_2 will choose *sell* (−1) rather than *hold* (−2). Finally, consider Joe_1 at the initial node, and assume that he can replicate the analysis we have just been through. So Joe_1 knows that if he chooses *buy*, there is a 0.5 probability that Joe_2 will *sell*, giving Joe_1 a payoff of −1, and a 0.5 probability that Joe_1 will *hold*, giving a payoff of 2. From this, it follows that the expected payoff to Joe_1 from *buy* is 0.5. Since this is greater than the payoff of *don't buy*, Joe_1 will *buy*. So the answer to the original question is that in period 1, Joe will *buy*; in period 2, he will *sell* if he is happy but *hold* if he is unhappy.[10]

---

[10]   It might be objected that the folding-back analysis attributes too much rationality to the agent. However, the outcome of the analysis is just the same if Joe is *myopic*—that is, if each self acts as if its own preferences

Robert Sugden

Notice that, with probability 0.5, Joe$_1$'s choice in period 1 is undone by Joe$_2$'s choice in period 2. This combination of actions leads to an unambiguous loss. (More formally, the outcome of *buy* followed by *sell* is strictly worse than the outcome of *don't buy*, whether evaluated in terms of Joe$_1$'s preferences or in terms of Joe$_2$'s.) Does this imply that it would be better for Joe, as a continuing person, if the choices of one or both of his selves were constrained? One possibility is to remove the *sell* option in period 2, so that Joe$_1$'s period 1 decision cannot be undone. This gives the contracted tree T_2, shown in Figure 2. An alternative possibility is to remove the *buy* option in period 1, giving the contracted tree T_3, shown in Figure 3. I can now reveal where this story is leading. I want to pose the following question: *Which of the three trees is most valuable to Joe?*

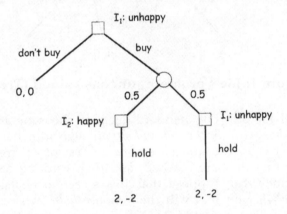

Figure 2: Joe's problem with a constraint (Tree T_2)

It seems natural to say that the principle of consumer sovereignty favours the unconstrained tree T_1. If Joe is to be a sovereign consumer, he should be free to buy and sell as he chooses. T_2 removes an options to sell, while T_3 removes an option to buy. Each of these constraints prevents Joe from choosing to do one thing in period 1 and then choosing to undo it in period 2. Of course, he would incur a cost in changing his mind in this way. Still,

---

will determine behaviour at all subsequent nodes. The myopic Joe$_1$ will *buy*, expecting both Joe$_1$ and Joe$_2$ to *hold* (since that is the best action from Joe$_1$'s point of view); but while the myopic Joe$_1$ will indeed *hold*, the myopic Joe$_2$ will *sell*.

222

if we are to treat him as a sovereign consumer, we must surely allow him the privilege of changing his mind, provided he is willing to pay the price of doing so. The problem is to find a way of saying that this form of sovereignty is valuable *to Joe*—of saying that, for Joe, T_1 is the most valuable of the three trees. That is the problem I shall now try to solve.

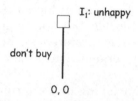

Figure 3: Joe's problem with a different constraint (Tree T_3)

In thinking about this issue, we immediately confront the difficulty that we need to define the continuing Joe for whom trees can have value. On what I take to be the most conventional understanding of multiple-selves models in decision theory, there is no such entity. Of course, there is Joe the continuing human being; but, since preference is the standard of value, an entity can be a locus of value only if it has stable preferences. The only loci of value are Joe_1 and Joe_2. Taking the viewpoint of a given self, we can rank the trees in terms of their outcomes, as evaluated by that self's preferences. Following this approach, we can say that, for Joe_1, the most valuable tree is T_2. (This gives Joe_1 an expected payoff of 2, compared with 0.5 from T_1 and zero from T_3.) For Joe_2, the most valuable tree is T_3. (This gives Joe_2 an expected payoff of zero, compared with –1.5 from T_1 and –2 from T_2.) Each self values the imposition of constraints on the other: Joe_1 wants to prevent Joe_2 from selling, while Joe_2 wants to prevent Joe_1 from buying. There seems to be no other Joe for whom the absence of constraints can be valuable: there seems to be no continuing person for whom T_1 is the most valuable tree.

One way of trying to define a continuing person is to appeal to *metapreferences*—that is, preferences over preferences. The idea is that there is a continuing Joe who in some sense prefers, or identifies with, the preferences of one of his selves even while he is acting on the preferences of the other. In recognition of the fact that this continuing Joe is the locus of metapreferences, let us call him Joe^M. We might suppose that Joe^M identifies with the

223

preferences of the happy and risk-averse Joe_2, and treats Joe_1's inclination to act contrary to those preferences as weakness of will. On this account, the most valuable tree for Joe^M is T_3. Conversely, if Joe^M identifies with Joe_1, the most valuable tree is T_2. Notice that, whatever we assume about Joe^M's metapreferences, T_1 cannot be the most valuable tree. To put this conclusion another way, the special feature of T_1 is that it allows (and, given the actual preferences of Joe_1 and Joe_2, can induce) the sequence of actions in which *buy* is followed by *sell*; but Joe^M cannot identify with this sequence. Whatever his metapreferences, he must attribute one of the two actions in that sequence to a self whose preferences he disavows.[11]

A different way of conceiving of a continuing Joe is as the *set* of selves $\{Joe_1, Joe_2\}$, and to treat the welfare of this entity (let us call it Joe^S) as a weighted average of the utilities of its component selves, on the analogy of a utilitarian social welfare function. Formally, let U^S be the welfare of Joe^S and let u_1 and u_2 be the utilities of Joe_1 and Joe_2; then $U^S = \alpha u_1 + (1-\alpha)u_2$, where α (the weight given to Joe_1) is in the interval $0 < \alpha < 1$. It is easy to work out that if $\alpha > 0.5$, the best tree for Joe^S is T_2; if $\alpha < 0.5$, the best tree is T_3; if $\alpha = 0.5$, T_2 and T_3 are jointly best. There is no value of α at which T_1 is best. That is because, whatever relative weights Joe^S gives to the utilities of his two selves, the outcome of the sequence in which *buy* is followed by *sell* is inferior to that of *don't buy*. For Joe^S, the fact that T_1 can induce this sequence is a reason for rejecting it in favour of one of the other trees.

Summing up the argument so far, conventional decision-theoretic analysis seems to be unable to represent the idea of a continuing Joe for whom T_1 is the most valuable tree. But, for me, the intuition persists that, if Joe values his sovereignty as a consumer, he can see T_1 as the most valuable tree. The problem remains: we need to find a way of representing that intuition as a coherent theoretical principle.

---

[11] It has been suggested to me that the continuing Joe might have a preference for *spontaneity*, in the sense that he prefers to be the sort of person who acts on the preferences of the moment. This is not a metapreference in the standard theoretical sense of the term—that is, a higher-order preference *between alternative preference relations*. My hunch is that the most convincing analysis of a 'preference for spontaneity' would be very similar to my analysis of the value of consumer sovereignty.

5. Continuing identity: a solution

I suggest that we need a radically different conception of the continuing person. We should think of the continuing Joe—let us call him Joe*—as the *composition* of the selves which perform the various parts of whatever sequence of actions is in fact performed. For theorists who insist on modelling identity in terms of some kind of preference relation, this idea may seem strange. But, viewed from outside the framework of decision theory, it seems a very natural way of thinking of identity. The continuing Joe* is just whatever Joe the human being is over time. What the continuing Joe* does is just whatever Joe does over time; what the continuing Joe* values is just whatever Joe values over time. In this perspective, it becomes clear how the continuing person can value the absence of constraints on his present and future actions.

Suppose the decision problem is T_1. In period 1, Joe_1 wants to choose, and does choose, *buy*. Since Joe* *is* Joe_1 at this moment, it is also true that Joe* wants to choose, and does choose, *buy*. In period 2, let us suppose, chance selects the happy mood. Then Joe_2 is the agent, and he wants to choose, and does choose, *sell*. Since Joe* *is* Joe_2 at this moment, it is also true that Joe* wants to choose, and does choose, *sell*. So Joe* wants and chooses to *buy* in period 1 and to *sell* in period 2. In allowing this sequence of actions, T_1 gives Joe* an opportunity to do something that he wants to do. If Joe* values opportunities to do as he wants, this feature of T_1 has value for him.

Consider how, at the end of period 2, Joe (the human being) might reflect on the actions he has taken. A conventional decision theorist might point out to him that he has acted on preferences that are not stable under experience and reflection, and that in consequence he has incurred an unambiguous loss—he has bought dear and sold cheap. Joe can concede this, yet still see both buying and selling as *his* autonomously chosen actions: he wanted to buy, and he bought; he wanted to sell, and he sold. He does not have to disown either of those actions as the work of an alien self, or as the result of weakness of will. While recognising that he has acted on unconsidered preferences, he can say that he has done what he wanted to do, when he wanted to do it. Without asserting that those preferences are his standard of value, he can say that he values the opportunity to act on them; and this can be a considered judgement on his part. All this becomes coherent if 'he' is understood as the continuing Joe*.

Robert Sugden

I now offer a sketch of how we might represent and generalise the idea that, for the continuing Joe*, T_1 is the most valuable of the three trees. The first step is to recognise that the standard of value for Joe* is not preference itself, but the opportunity to act on preferences, as and when they are felt. For my purposes, I do not need to use the information contained in the payoffs of Joe_1 and Joe_2. It is more useful to conduct the analysis in terms of *outcomes*. There are three relevant outcomes. One outcome, which results from *don't buy*, is that Joe keeps his status quo level of wealth and doesn't participate in the lottery. I denote this outcome x. The second possible outcome, denoted y, is that Joe doesn't participate in the lottery and loses £2 of his status quo wealth; this results from *buy* followed by *sell*. The third possible outcome, denoted z, is that Joe gives up £9 of his status quo wealth and participates in the lottery; this results from *buy* followed by *hold*.

It is an important part of the problem that y is 'unambiguously' worse than x. One way of understanding this idea is to use the concept of *potential preference*.[12] To say that some preference is 'potentially' the preference of a particular agent is to say that the agent *might* have that preference. If an agent's preferences are unstable, we can think of him at any given time as acting on some preference relation drawn (perhaps arbitrarily) from some fixed set of potential preference relations. If every potential preference relation ranks x above y, then x can be said to be unambiguously better than y.

To represent this idea, I do not need to model the set of potential preference relations explicitly, although I make the implicit assumption that each potential preference relation is complete and transitive (that is, that each of these relations is an ordering). Instead, I define a relation $\geq_*$ of *weak dominance* on the set of outcomes; $v \geq_* w$ is read as 'v weakly dominates w', and is interpreted as indicating that v is ranked at least as highly as w by every potential preference ordering. I stipulate that this relation is reflexive (that is, for every outcome v, $v \geq_* v$), but I do not require it to be complete. Given my interpretation of dominance, these properties are immediate implications of the assumption that each potential preference relation is complete and transitive. If v weakly dominates w but w does not weakly dominate v, I shall say that v *strictly dominates* w, denoted $v >_* w$. If each of v and w weakly dominates the other, I shall say that they are *dominance-equivalent*, denoted $v =_* w$.

---

[12] I discuss the concept of potential preference in Sugden (1998).

I now need a notation for representing decision problems that are confronted by a single continuing agent but which extend over time. When dealing with decision problems which require single acts of choice at one moment in time, it is conventional to represent each such problem as a set of outcomes (the *opportunity set* or *menu*); the idea is that the agent is able to choose one outcome from this set. Of course, such a problem can also be represented as a decision tree with a single choice node, but representing it as a set of outcomes is simpler and more compact. It is possible to extend the set-theoretic notation to represent sequences of choices by using *nested sets*.[13] This idea is most easily explained by examples.

In this new notation, the decision problem that was previously represented by the tree T_1 is denoted by the nested set $S_1 = \{\{x\}, \{y, z\}\}$. The outer pair of curly brackets defines the choice facing the agent in period 1. This is a choice between the elements of the set that is specified by that pair of brackets—that is, the elements $\{x\}$, corresponding with *don't buy*, and $\{y, z\}$, corresponding with *buy*. Each of these elements is a (possibly degenerate) choice problem that will be confronted in period 2, if the relevant action is chosen in period 1. The singleton $\{x\}$ represents the fact that, if *don't buy* is chosen in period 1, there is no choice to be made in period 2, and the outcome will be x. The set $\{y, z\}$ represents the fact that, if *buy* is chosen in period 1, there will be a further choice to be made in period 2, between one action (*sell*) which leads to y and another (*hold*) which leads to z. Similarly, the decision problem previously represented by the tree T_2 is denoted by the nested set $S_2 = \{\{x\}, \{z\}\}$, while the decision problem previously represented by T_3 is denoted by the nested set $S_3 = \{\{x\}\}$.

Notice that, in this notation, each matched pair of curly brackets is associated with a specific time period; the succession of periods is represented by successively 'deeper' nesting of sets. Every outcome is nested within as many pairs of brackets as there are periods in the analysis (two in each of the variants of Joe's problem). The number of pairs of brackets within which each outcome is nested is the *depth* of the relevant nested set; thus S_1, S_2 and S_3 all have depth 2. The elements of each of these nested sets are themselves nested sets, but with depth 1. In general, a nested set of depth n (where n

---

[13] The idea of representing decision problems as nested sets derives from Cubitt and Sugden (2001). However, the current analysis differs from that of Cubitt and Sugden by attributing decision nodes to specific time periods.

> 1) is a set of nested sets, each of which has depth n—1; a nested set of depth 1 is a set of outcomes.

Using this notation, I now propose a principle for inducing a dominance relation among nested sets from the dominance relation among outcomes. I begin by considering nested sets of depth 1. I define a relation $\geq_*$ of weak dominance among such sets in the following way:

Dominance Extension Rule (for nested sets of depth 1) For any nested sets R and S of depth 1: $R \geq_* S \Leftrightarrow (\forall v \in S) (\exists w \in R)\, w \geq_* v$.

Strict dominance and dominance equivalence are defined from weak dominance as before.

According to the Dominance Extension Rule, R weakly dominates S if every outcome in S is weakly dominated by some outcome in R. Thus, to say that R dominates S is to say that, for each potential preference ordering, for each outcome v in S, there is some outcome w in R such that w is at least as preferred as v. Given that dominance with respect to outcomes has been defined in terms of agreement among potential preferences, the Dominance Extension Rule is very natural.

For example, consider the outcomes x, y and z, as defined for Joe's problem. Recall that all potential preference orderings rank x strictly above y, but there is no agreement among these orderings about the ranking of x and z, or of y and z. Thus, x strictly dominates y, but there is no relation of dominance between x and z or between y and z. By the Dominance Extension Rule, $\{x, y\} =_* \{x\}$. Since y is weakly dominated by x, the best element of $\{x, y\}$ can be no better than the only element of $\{x\}$, whichever potential preference ordering we base our judgement on. In contrast, the same rule implies $\{y, z\} >_* \{z\}$. Since y is not weakly dominated by z, there is at least one potential preference ordering such that the best element of $\{y, z\}$ is better than z, while z obviously cannot be better than the best element of $\{y, z\}$.

It is straightforward to prove that, if the weak dominance relation $\geq_*$ is reflexive and transitive on the set of outcomes, it is also reflexive and transitive on the set of nested sets of depth 1, when that extension is as defined by the Dominance Extension Rule.[14] Because the formal properties of the weak dominance

---

[14] It is immediately obvious that if $\geq_*$ is reflexive on the set of outcomes, the Dominance Extension Rule implies that $\geq_*$ is reflexive on the set of nested sets of depth 1. To prove that transitivity is transmitted in a similar way, let Q, R and S be nested sets of depth 1, and suppose $Q \geq_* R$ and $R \geq_* S$. By the Dominance Extension Rule, $(\forall x \in S) (\exists y \in R)\, y$

relation are preserved as we move from rankings of outcomes to rankings of nested sets of depth 1, we can use the same method to extend the weak dominance relation from nested sets of depth 1 to nested sets of depth 2, and so on indefinitely. Formally, I define:

Dominance Extension Rule (for nested sets of depth $d > 1$) Let S and T be nested sets of depth d, where $d > 1$; notice that the elements of S and T are nested sets of depth $d—1$. For all such S, T: $S \geq_* T \Leftrightarrow (\forall V \in T) (\exists W \in S) W \geq_* V$.

We can now apply the Dominance Extension Rule to the three nested sets of Joe's problem, that is $S_1 = \{\{x\}, \{y, z\}\}$, $S_2 = \{\{x\}, \{z\}\}$ and $S_3 = \{\{x\}\}$. First, compare S_2 and S_3. Both sets have the common element $\{x\}$, but S_2 has the additional element $\{z\}$. Since z neither dominates nor is dominated by x, the Dominance Extension Rule, applied at depth 1, implies that $\{z\}$ neither dominates nor is dominated by $\{x\}$. Thus, when the rule is applied at depth 2, we have $S_2 >_* S_3$. Now compare S_1 and S_2. Each of these sets contains two elements. One element, $\{x\}$, is common to both. The difference is that S_1 also contains $\{y, z\}$ while S_2 also contains $\{z\}$. I have already shown that the Dominance Extension rule, applied at depth 1, implies $\{y, z\} >_* \{z\}$. Thus, when the rule is applied at depth 2, we have $S_1 >_* S_2$. By transitivity, we have $S_1 >_* S_3$. On this analysis, the intuition of consumer sovereignty is vindicated: the absence of constraints on Joe's choices is unambiguously valuable to Joe.[15]

To see why the nested-set analysis delivers this result, consider the sequence of choices (*buy*, *sell*). Because this path leads to a dominated outcome (namely, y), conventional analyses imply that the existence of this path has no positive value; if (because of Joe's

---

$\geq_* x$, and $(\forall y \in R) (\exists z \in Q) z \geq_* y$. Therefore $(\forall x \in S) (\exists z \in Q$ and $y \in R)$ $(z \geq_* y$ and $y \geq_* x)$. Because $\geq_*$ is transitive on the set of outcomes, this implies $(\forall x \in S) (\exists z \in Q) (z \geq_* x)$. So by the Dominance Extension Rule, $Q \geq_* S$.

[15] The reader may wonder if it would be even more valuable to Joe* to be able to choose which of the three decision problems to face. According to my analysis, the answer is 'No'. Since $\{S_1\}$ weakly dominates both S_2 and S_3, the Dominance Extension Rule applied at depth 3 implies $S_1 =_*$ $\{S_1, S_2, S_3\}$. More generally: from the viewpoint of one's continuing self, an opportunity to impose constraints on oneself has zero value. This seems to be an inescapable implication of the conception of value that I am proposing. If constraints on a person's actions cannot have positive value for him, then an opportunity to impose constraints on oneself cannot have positive value either.

inconsistency over time) it might in fact be chosen, its existence has negative value. The interests of the continuing Joe^M or Joe^S would then be best served by removing this apparently undesirable path, contracting the decision problem either to S_2 or to S_3. On the nested-set analysis, in contrast, this path is treated as the combination of two choices, each of which the continuing Joe* might want to make, and so has positive value. In period 1, Joe* has a choice between the actions *buy* and *don't buy*. *Don't buy* leads to $\{x\}$, while *buy* leads to $\{y, z\}$. Since neither of these sets dominates the other, each action is one that Joe* might want to take. The existence of each of these options, therefore, is valuable to Joe*. To remove the path leading to $\{y, z\}$, contracting the problem to S_3, would be to remove something of value. Now, suppose Joe* has chosen *buy* in period 1. In period 2, he faces a choice between y and z. Neither outcome dominates the other. Since each option is one that Joe* might wish to choose, the existence of each of them is valuable to him; to remove the path leading to y (contracting the problem to S_2) would again be to remove something of value.

6. Conclusion

Normative economics has been built on the assumption that each person has consistent and stable preferences, and has used these assumed preferences as the standard of value for that person. However, in the light of the recent findings of behavioural economics, it is no longer possible to treat this assumption either as a self-evident truth about human reason or as a well-established fact about how real economic agents think and act. This paper has asked whether it is possible to preserve the idea that there is value in respecting individuals' actual preferences, even if those preferences are inconsistent and unstable.

I have argued that each of us can value being free to act on his or her own preferences, considered or unconsidered, as and when we experience them. This is a kind of freedom that competitive markets are highly effective in providing, at least in relation to private goods and for individuals who are endowed with transferable goods that other people value.[16] Such a robust understanding of the value of opportunity may not be to everyone's

---

[16]   I argue this in Sugden (2004).

taste, but I hope that at least I have persuaded the reader that those of us who do find it attractive can endorse it coherently and clear-sightedly.

References

Ariely, Dan, George Loewenstein and Drazen Prelec (2003). 'Coherent arbitrariness': stable demand curves without stable preferences. *Quarterly Journal of Economics* 118: 73–105.

Binmore, Ken (1999). Why experiment in economics? *Economic Journal* 109: F16-F24.

Broome, John (1991). *Weighing Goods*. Oxford: Blackwell.

Camerer, Colin (1995). Individual decision making. In John Kagel and Alvin Roth (eds), *The Handbook of Experimental Economics*. Princeton, N.J.: Princeton University Press, pp. 587–703.

Cubitt, Robin and Robert Sugden (2001). On money pumps. *Games and Economic Behavior* 37: 121–160.

Gauthier, David (1986). *Morals by Agreement*. Oxford: Clarendon Press.

Hey, John and Chris Orme (1994). Investigating generalizations of expected utility theory using experimental data. *Econometrica* 62: 1291–1326.

Isen, A.M. (1999). Positive affect. In T. Dalgleish and M. Power (eds), *Handbook of Cognition and Emotion*. London: Wiley and Sons.

Kahneman, Daniel and Amos Tversky, eds (2000). *Choices, Values and Frames*. Cambridge: Cambridge University Press.

List, John (2003). Does market experience eliminate market anomalies? *Quarterly Journal of Economics* 118: 41–71.

Loewenstein, George (1999). Experimental economics from the viewpoint of behavioural economics. *Economic Journal* 109: F25–34.

Loomes, Graham (1999). Some lessons from past experiments and some challenges for the future. *Economic Journal* 109: F35-F45.

Loomes, Graham, Chris Starmer and Robert Sugden (2003). Do anomalies disappear in repeated markets? *Economic Journal* 113: C 153–166.

Plott, Charles (1996). Rational individual behaviour in markets and social choice processes: the discovered preference hypothesis. In Kenneth J. Arrow, Enrico Colombatto, Mark Perlman and Christian Schmidt (eds), *The Rational Foundations of Economic Behaviour*. Basingstoke: Macmillan, pp. 225–250.

Smith, Vernon (1994). Economics in the laboratory. *Journal of Economic Perspectives* 8: 113–131.

Starmer, Chris (1999). Experimental economics: hard science or wasteful tinkering? *Economic Journal* 109: F5-F15.

Robert Sugden

Starmer, Chris (2000). Developments in non-expected utility theory: the hunt for a descriptive theory of choice under risk. *Journal of Economic Literature* 38: 332–382.

Starmer, Chris and Robert Sugden (1989). Violations of the independence axiom in common ratio problems: an experimental test of some competing hypotheses. *Annals of Operations Research* 19: 79–102.

Sugden, Robert (1989). Maximizing social welfare: is it the government's business? In Alan Hamlin and Philip Pettit (eds), *The Good Polity* (Oxford: Basil Blackwell).

Sugden, Robert (1998). The metric of opportunity. *Economics and Philosophy* 14: 307–337.

Sugden, Robert (2004). The opportunity criterion: consumer sovereignty without the assumption of coherent preferences. *American Economic Review* 94: 1014–1033

Preferences, Paternalism, and Liberty

CASS R. SUNSTEIN

RICHARD H. THALER

Our goal in this chapter is to draw on empirical work about preference formation and welfare to propose a distinctive form of paternalism, libertarian in spirit, one that should be acceptable to those who are firmly committed to freedom of choice on grounds of either autonomy or welfare. Indeed, we urge that a kind of 'libertarian paternalism' provides a basis for both understanding and rethinking many social practices, including those that deal with worker welfare, consumer protection, and the family.

In the process of defending these claims, we intend to make some objections to widely held beliefs about both freedom of choice and paternalism. Our major emphasis is on the fact that in many domains, people lack clear, stable, or well-ordered preferences. What they choose is strongly influenced by details of the context in which they make their choice, for example default rules, framing effects (that is, the wording of possible options), and starting points. These contextual influences render the very meaning of the term 'preferences' unclear. If social planners are asked to respect preferences, or if they are told that respect for preferences promotes well-being, they will often be unable to know what they should do.

Consider the question whether to undergo a risky medical procedure. When people are told, 'Of those who undergo this procedure, 90 percent are still alive after five years,' they are far more likely to agree to the procedure than when they are told, 'Of those who undergo this procedure, 10 percent are dead after five years' (Redelmeier, Rozin, & Kahneman, 1993, p. 73). What, then, are the patient's 'preferences' with respect to this procedure? Repeated experiences with such problems might be expected to eliminate this framing effect, but doctors too are vulnerable to it. Or consider the question of savings for retirement. It is now clear that if an employer requires employees to make an affirmative election in favor of savings, with the default rule devoting 100 percent of wages to current income, the level of savings will be far lower than if the employer adopts an automatic enrollment program from which employees are freely permitted to opt out

(Choi et al., 2002, p. 70; Madrian & Shea, 2001, pp. 1149–1150). Can workers then be said to have well-defined preferences about how much to save? This simple example can be extended to many situations involving the behavior of workers, consumers, voters, and family members.

As the savings problem illustrates, the design features of both legal and organizational rules have surprisingly powerful influences on people's choices. Preferences are formed in part by reference to those influences. We urge that the relevant rules should be chosen with the explicit goal of improving the welfare of the people affected by them. The libertarian aspect of our strategies lies in the straightforward insistence that, in general, people should be free to opt out of specified arrangements if they choose to do so. To borrow a phrase, libertarian paternalists urge that people should be 'free to choose' (Friedman & Friedman, 1980). Hence we do not aim to defend any approach that blocks individual choices.

The paternalistic aspect consists in the claim that it is legitimate for private and public institutions to attempt to influence people's choices and preferences, even when third-party effects are absent. In other words, we argue for self-conscious efforts, by private and public institutions, to steer people's choices in directions that will improve the choosers' own welfare. In our understanding, a policy therefore counts as 'paternalistic' if it attempts to influence the choices of affected parties in a way that will make choosers better off (see also VanDeVeer 986, p. 22). Drawing on some well-established findings in behavioral economics and cognitive psychology, we emphasize the possibility that in some cases individuals make inferior decisions in terms of their own welfare—decisions that they would change if they had complete information, unlimited cognitive abilities, and no lack of self-control (Jolls, Sunstein, & Thaler, 1998, pp. 1477–1479). In addition, the notion of libertarian paternalism can be complemented by that of *libertarian benevolence*, by which plan design features such as default rules, framing effects, and starting points are enlisted in the interest of vulnerable third parties. We shall devote some discussion to this possibility.

Libertarian paternalism is a relatively weak and nonintrusive type of paternalism, because choices are not blocked or fenced off. In its most cautious forms, libertarian paternalism imposes trivial costs on those who seek to depart from the planner's preferred option. But the approach we recommend nonetheless counts as paternalistic, because private and public planners are not trying to track people's anticipated choices, but are self-consciously attempting to move people in welfare-promoting directions. It follows that one of our principal targets is the dogmatic anti-paternalism of numerous analysts of law and policy. We believe that this dogmatism is based on a combination of a false assumption and two misconceptions.

The false assumption is that almost all people, almost all of the time, make choices that are in their best interest or at the very least are better, by their own lights, than the choices that would be made by third parties. This claim is either tautological, and therefore uninteresting, or testable. We claim that it is testable and false, indeed obviously false. In fact, we do not think that anyone believes it on reflection. Suppose that a chess novice were to play against an experienced player. Predictably the novice would lose precisely because he made inferior choices—choices that could easily be improved by some helpful hints. More generally, how well people choose is an empirical question, one whose answer is likely to vary across domains.

As a first approximation, it seems reasonable to say that people make better choices in contexts in which they have experience and good information (say, choosing ice cream flavors) than in contexts in which they are inexperienced and poorly informed (say, choosing among medical treatments or investment options). So long as people are not choosing perfectly, it is at least possible that some policy could make them better off by improving their decisions.

The first misconception is that preferences predate social contexts and hence that there are viable alternatives to paternalism. In many situations, some organization or agent *must* make a choice that will affect the behavior of some other people. There is, in those situations, no alternative to a kind of paternalism—at least in the form of an intervention that affects what people choose and often even what they prefer. We are emphasizing, then, the possibility that people's preferences, in certain domains and across a certain range, are influenced by the choices made by planners (even those who do not understand themselves as such).

As a simple example, consider the cafeteria at some organization. The cafeteria must make a multitude of decisions, including which foods to serve, which ingredients to use, and in what order to arrange the choices. Suppose that the director of the cafeteria notices that customers have a tendency to choose more of the items that are presented earlier in the line. How should the director decide in what order to present the items? To simplify, consider some alternative strategies that the director might adopt in deciding which items to place early in the line:

1. She could make choices that she thinks would make the customers best off, all things considered.
2. She could make choices at random.
3. She could choose those items that she thinks would make the customers as obese as possible.
4. She could give customers what she thinks they would choose on their own.

Option 1 appears to be paternalistic, but would anyone advocate options 2 or 3? Option 4 is what many anti-paternalists would favor, but it is much harder to implement than it might seem. Across a certain domain of possibilities, consumers will often lack well-formed preferences, in the sense of preferences that are firmly held and preexist the director's own choices about how to order the relevant items. If the arrangement of the alternatives has a significant effect on the selections the customers make, then their true 'preferences' do not formally exist.

The second misconception is that paternalism always involves coercion. As the cafeteria example illustrates, the choice of the order in which to present food items does not coerce anyone to do anything, yet one might prefer some orders to others on grounds that are paternalistic in the sense that we use the term. Would anyone object to putting the fruit and salad before the desserts at an elementary school cafeteria if the result were to increase the consumption ratio of apples to Twinkies? Is this question fundamentally different if the customers are adults? Since no coercion is involved, we think that some types of paternalism should be acceptable to even the most ardent libertarian. This point has large implications for planners who are seeking to promote social welfare.

Once it is understood that some organizational decisions are inevitable, that preferences are endogenous to social situations, that a form of paternalism cannot be avoided, and that the alternatives to paternalism (such as choosing options to make people worse off) are unattractive, we can abandon the less interesting question of whether to be paternalistic or not, and turn to the more constructive question of how to choose among the possible choice-influencing options.

Preferences, Paternalism, and Liberty

I. The Rationality of Choices

The presumption that individual choices should be respected is often based on the claim that people do an excellent job of making choices that promote their welfare, or at least that they do a far better job than third parties could possibly do.[1] As far as we can tell, there is little empirical support for this claim, at least if it is offered in this general form. Consider the issue of obesity. Rates of obesity in the United States are now approaching 20 percent, and over 60 percent of Americans are considered either obese or overweight. These numbers reflect a 61 percent increase in obesity from 1991 to 2001, with 38.8 million Americans now qualifying as obese (Centers for Disease Control and Prevention, 2003). There is a great deal of evidence that obesity causes serious health risks, frequently leading to premature death (Calle, Thun, Petrelli, Rodriguez, & Heath, 1999; National Institute of Diabetes & Digestive & Kidney Diseases, 2001). It is quite fantastic to suggest that everyone is choosing the optimal diet, or a diet that is preferable to what might be produced with third-party guidance.

Of course, rational people care about the taste of food, not simply about health, and we do not claim that everyone who is overweight is necessarily failing to act rationally. It is the strong claim that all or almost all Americans are choosing their diet *optimally* that we reject as untenable. What is true for diets is true as well for much other risk-related behavior, including smoking and drinking, which produce many thousands of premature deaths each year (Sunstein, 2002, pp. 8–9). In these circumstances, people's

---

[1] It is not always based on this claim. Some of the standard arguments against paternalism rest not on consequences but on autonomy—on a belief that people are entitled to make their own choices even if they err. Thus Mill (1972, p. 69) advances a mix of autonomy-based and consequentialist claims. Our principal concern here is with welfare and consequences, though as we suggest below, freedom of choice is sometimes an ingredient in welfare. We do not disagree with the view that autonomy has claims of its own, but we believe that it would be fanatical, in the settings that we discuss, to treat autonomy, in the form of freedom of choice, as a kind of trump not to be overridden on consequentialist grounds. In any case, the autonomy argument is undermined by the fact, discussed in Part II, that sometimes preferences and choices are a function of given arrangements. Most importantly, we think that respect for autonomy is adequately accommodated by the libertarian aspect of libertarian paternalism, as discussed below.

choices cannot reasonably be thought, in all domains, to be the best means of promoting their well-being.

On a more scientific level, research by psychologists and economists over the past three decades has raised questions about the rationality of many of our judgments and decisions. People fail to make forecasts that are consistent with Bayes's rule (Grether, 1980); use heuristics that can lead them to make systematic blunders (Kahneman & Frederick, 2002, p. 53; Tversky & Kahneman, 1973; Tversky & Kahneman, 1974); exhibit preference reversals (that is, they prefer A to B *and* B to A) (Thaler, 1992, pp. 79–91; Sunstein, Kahneman, Schkade, & Ritov, 2002); suffer from problems of self-control (Frederick, Loewenstein, & O'Donoghue, 2002, pp. 367–368); and make different choices depending on the framing of the problem (Camerer, 2000, pp. 294–295; Johnson, Hershey, Meszaros, & Kunreuther, 2000, pp. 224, 238). It is possible to raise questions about some of these findings and to think that people may do a better job of choosing in the real world than they do in the laboratory. But studies of actual choices reveal many of the same problems, even when the stakes are high (De Bondt & Thaler, 1990; Shiller, 2000, pp. 135–147; Camerer & Hogarth, 1999).

We do not intend to outline all of the relevant evidence here, but consider an illustration from the domain of savings behavior. Benartzi and Thaler (2002) have investigated how much investors like the portfolios they have selected in their defined contribution savings plans. Employees volunteered to share their portfolio choices with the investigators by bringing a copy of their most recent statement to the lab. They were then shown the probability distributions of expected retirement income for three investment portfolios simply labeled A, B, and C. Unbeknownst to the subjects, the three portfolios were their own and portfolios mimicking the average and median choices of their fellow employees. The distributions of expected returns were computed using the software of Financial Engines, the financial information company founded by William Sharpe. On average, the subjects rated the average portfolio equally with their own portfolio, and judged the median portfolio to be significantly more attractive than their own. Indeed, only 20 percent of the subjects preferred their own portfolio to the median portfolio. Apparently, people do not gain much, by their own lights, from choosing investment portfolios for themselves.

Or consider people's willingness to take precautions. In general, the decision to buy insurance for natural disasters is a product not of a systematic inquiry into the likely effects on individual welfare, but of recent events (Slovic, Kunreuther, & White, 1974, p. 14; Kunreuther, 1996, pp. 174–178). If floods have not occurred in the immediate past, people who live on flood plains are far less likely to purchase insurance (Kunreuther, 1996, pp. 176–177). In the aftermath of an earthquake, the level of insurance coverage for earthquakes rises sharply—but it declines steadily from that point, as vivid memories recede (Kunreuther, 1996, pp. 176–177; Slovic et al., 1974, p. 14). Findings of this kind do not establish that people's choices are usually bad or that third parties can usually do better. But they do show that some of the time, people do not choose optimally even when the stakes are high.

It is true that people sometimes respond to their own bounded rationality by, for example, hiring agents or delegating decisions to others (Sunstein & Ullman-Margalit, 1999). It is also true that learning frequently enables people to overcome their own limitations. But many of the most important decisions (for example, buying a home or choosing a spouse) are made infrequently and typically without the aid of impartial experts. The possibilities of delegation and learning are insufficient to ensure that people's choices always promote their welfare or that they always choose better than third parties would.

In any event, our emphasis here is not on blocking choices, but on strategies that move people in welfare-promoting directions while also allowing freedom of choice. Evidence of bounded rationality and problems of self-control is sufficient to suggest that such strategies are worth exploring. Of course many people value freedom of choice as an end in itself, but they should not object to approaches that preserve that freedom while also promising to improve people's lives.

II. Is Paternalism Inevitable? On the Endogeneity of Preferences

A few years ago, the tax law was changed so that employees could pay for employer-provided parking on a pre-tax basis (Energy Policy Act of 1992, 2000). Previously, such parking had to be paid for with after-tax dollars. Our employer, and the employer of some of our prominent anti-paternalist colleagues, sent around an announcement of this change in the law, and adopted the following policy: Unless the employee notified the payroll department, deductions for parking would be taken from pre-tax rather than post-tax income. In other words, the University of Chicago decided that the default option would be to pay for parking with pre-tax dollars, but employees could opt out of this arrangement and pay with after-tax dollars. Call this choice Plan A. An obvious alternative, Plan B, would be to announce the change in the law and tell employees that if they want to switch to the new pre-tax plan they should return some form electing this option. The only difference between the two plans is the default. Under Plan A the new option is the default, whereas under Plan B the status quo is the default. We will refer to the former as an 'opt-out' strategy and the latter as an 'opt-in' strategy.

How should the university choose between opt-in and opt-out? In the parking example, it seems to be the case that every employee would prefer to pay for parking with pre-tax dollars rather than after-tax dollars. Since the cost savings are substantial (parking costs as much as $1200 per year) and the cost of returning a form is trivial, standard economic theory predicts that the university's choice will not really matter. Under either plan, all employees would choose (either actively under Plan B or by default under Plan A) the pre-tax option. In real life, however, had the university adopted Plan B, we suspect that many employees, especially faculty members (and probably including the present authors), would still have that form buried somewhere in their offices and would be paying substantially more for parking on an after-tax basis. In short, the default plan would have had large effects on behavior.

Throughout we shall be drawing attention to the effects of default plans on choices. Often those plans will be remarkably 'sticky.' Often people's choices, and even their valuations, are endogenous to the social context, including default rules. This point raises a serious problem for those who reject paternalism in the name of liberty, and who argue that people should be permitted to choose in accordance with their preferences.

A Savings and Employers

1. Data and default rules

Our conjecture that default plans affect outcomes is supported by the results of numerous experiments documenting a 'status quo' bias (Kahneman, Knetsch, & Thaler, 1991, pp. 197–199; Samuelson & Zeckhauser, 1988). The existing arrangement, whether set out by private institutions or by government, is often robust. One illustration of this phenomenon comes from studies of automatic enrollment in 401(k) employee savings plans (Choi et al., 2002, p. 70; Madrian & Shea, 2001, pp. 1149–1150), and we now elaborate the brief account with which we began. Most 401(k) plans use an opt-in design. When employees first become eligible to participate in the 401(k) plan, they receive some plan information and an enrollment form that must be completed in order to join. Under the alternative of automatic enrollment, employees receive the same information but are told that unless they opt out, they will be enrolled in the plan (with default options for savings rates and asset allocation). In companies that offer a 'match' (the employer matches the employee's contributions according to some formula, often a 50 percent match up to some cap), most employees eventually do join the plan, but enrollments occur much sooner under automatic enrollment. For example, Madrian and Shea found that initial enrollments jumped from 49 percent to 86 percent (Madrian & Shea, 2001, pp. 1158–1159), and Choi et al. (2002, pp. 76–77) found similar results.[2]

Should the adoption of automatic enrollment be considered paternalistic? And if so, should it be seen as a kind of officious meddling with employee preferences? We answer these questions yes and no respectively. If employers think (correctly, we believe) that most employees would prefer to join the 401(k) plan if they took the time to think about it and did not lose the enrollment form, then by choosing automatic enrollment, they are acting paternalistically by our definition of the term. They are not attempting to protect against harms to third parties, but to steer employees' choices in directions that will, in the view of employers, promote employees' welfare. Since no one is forced to do anything, we think that this steering should be considered unobjectionable

---

[2]   In a separate phenomenon, the default rule also had a significant effect on the chosen contribution rate (Madrian & Shea, pp. 116). The default contribution rate (3 percent) tended to stick; a majority of employees maintained that rate even though this particular rate was chosen by around 10 percent of employees hired before the automatic enrollment. The same result was found for the default allocation of the investment: While less than 7 percent of employees chose a 100 percent investment allocation to the money market fund, a substantial majority (75 percent) of employees stuck with that allocation when it was the default rule. The overall default rate (participation in the plan, at a 3 percent contribution rate, investing 100 percent in the money market fund) was 61 percent, but only 1 percent of employees chose this set of options prior to their adoption as defaults.

even to committed libertarians. The employer must choose some set of rules, and either plan affects employees' choices. No law of nature says that in the absence of an affirmative election by employees, 0 percent of earnings will go into a retirement plan. Because both plans alter choices, neither one can be said, more than the other, to count as a form of objectionable meddling.

2. Skeptics

Skeptical readers, insistent on freedom of choice, might be tempted to think that there is a way out of this dilemma. Employers could avoid choosing a default if they *required* employees to make an active choice, either in or out. Call this option *required active choosing*. Undoubtedly required active choosing is attractive in some settings, but a little thought reveals that this is not at all a way out of the dilemma. On the contrary, required active choosing is simply another option among many that the employer can elect. In fact the very requirement that employees make a choice has a strong paternalistic element. Some employees may not want to have to make a choice (and might make a second-order choice not to have to do so). Why should employers force them to choose?

Required active choosing honors freedom of choice in a certain respect; but it does not appeal to those who would choose not to choose, and indeed it will seem irritating and perhaps unacceptably coercive by their lights. In some circumstances, required choosing will not even be feasible. In any case, an empirical question remains: What is the effect of forced choosing? Choi et al. (2002, pp. 77, 86) find that required active choosing increases enrollments relative to the opt-in rule, though not by as much as automatic enrollment (opt-out). Our discussion in Part III below offers some suggestions about the circumstances in which it makes most sense to force people to choose.

Other skeptics might think that employers should avoid paternalism by doing what most employees would want employers to do. On this approach, a default rule can successfully avoid paternalism if it tracks employees' preferences. Sometimes this is a plausible solution. But what if many or most employees do not have stable or well-formed preferences, and what if employee choices are inevitably a product of the default rule? In such cases, it is meaningless to ask what most employees would do. The choices employees will make depend on the way the employer frames those choices. Employee 'preferences,' as such, do not exist in those circumstances.

We think that savings is a good example of a domain in which preferences are likely to be ill-defined. Few households have either the knowledge or inclination to calculate their optimal life-cycle savings rate, and even if they were to make such a calculation, its results would be highly dependent on assumptions about rates of return and life expectancies. In light of this, actual behavior is highly sensitive to plan design features.

B. Government

Some enthusiasts for free choice might be willing to acknowledge these points and hence to accept private efforts to steer people's choices in what seem to be the right directions. Market pressures, and the frequently wide range of possible options, might be thought to impose sufficient protection against objectionable steering. But our emphasis has been on the inevitability of paternalism, and on this count, the same points apply to some choices made by governments in establishing legal rules.

1. Default rules

Default rules of some kind are inevitable, and much of the time those rules will affect preferences and choices (Sunstein, 2002b; Korobkin, 1998). In the neglected words of a classic article (Calabresi & Melamed, 1972, pp. 1090–1091):

> [A] minimum of state intervention is always necessary ... When a loss is left where it falls in an auto accident, it is not because God so ordained it. Rather it is because the state has granted the injurer an entitlement to be free of liability and will intervene to prevent the victim's friends, if they are stronger, from taking compensation from the injurer.

If the entitlement-granting rules seem invisible, and seem to be a simple way of protecting freedom of choice, it is because they appear so sensible and natural that they are not taken to be a legal allocation at all. But this is a mistake. What we add here is that when a default rule affects preferences and behavior, it has the same effect as employer presumptions about savings plans. This effect is often both unavoidable and significant. So long as people can contract around the default rule, it is fair to say that the legal system is protecting freedom of choice, and in that sense complying with libertarian goals.

Consumers, workers, and married people,[3] for example, are surrounded by a network of legal allocations that provide the background against which agreements are made. As a matter of employment law, and consistent with freedom of contract, workers might be presumed subject to discharge 'at will,' or they might be presumed protected by an implied right to be discharged only 'for cause.' They might be presumed to have a right to vacation time, or not. They might be presumed protected by safety requirements, or the employer might be free to invest in safety as he wishes, subject to market pressures. In all cases, the law must establish whether workers have to 'buy' certain rights from employers or vice versa (Sunstein, 2001, pp. 208–212). Legal intervention, in this important sense, cannot be avoided. The same is true for consumers, spouses, and all others who are involved in legal relationships. Much of the time, the legal background matters, even if transaction costs are zero, because it affects choices and preferences, as demonstrated by Korobkin (1998, pp. 633–64) and Kahneman et al. (1991, pp. 194–204). Here, as in the private context, a form of paternalism is unavoidable.

In the context of insurance, an unplanned, natural experiment showed that the default rule can be very 'sticky' (Camerer, 2000, pp. 294–95; Johnson et al., 2000, p. 238). New Jersey created a system in which the default insurance program for motorists included a relatively low premium and no right to sue; purchasers were allowed to deviate from the default program and to purchase the right to sue by choosing a program with that right and also a higher premium. By contrast, Pennsylvania offered a default program containing a full right to sue and a relatively high premium; purchasers could elect to switch to a new plan by 'selling' the more ample right to sue and paying a lower premium. In both cases, the default rule tended to stick. A strong majority accepted the default rule in both states, with only about 20 percent of New Jersey drivers acquiring the full right to sue, and 75 percent of Pennsylvanians retaining that right (Johnson et al., 2000, p. 238). There is no reason to think that the citizens of Pennsylvania have systematically different preferences from the citizens of New Jersey. The default plan is what produced the ultimate effects.

[3] Okin (1989) is a good source of general information on marriage and legal rules.

Indeed, controlled experiments find the same results, showing that the value of the right to sue is much higher when it is presented as part of the default package (Johnson et al., 2000, pp. 235–238).

In another example, a substantial effect from the legal default rule was found in a study of law student reactions to different state law provisions governing vacation time from firms (Sunstein, 2002b, pp. 113–114). The study was intended to be reasonably realistic, involving as it did a pool of subjects to whom the underlying issues were hardly foreign. Most law students have devoted a good deal of time to thinking about salaries, vacation time, and the tradeoffs between them. The study involved two conditions. In the first, state law guaranteed two weeks of vacation time, and students were asked to state their median willingness to pay (in reduced salary) for two extra weeks of vacation. In this condition, the median willingness to pay was $6,000. In the second condition, state law provided a mandatory, non-waivable two-week vacation guarantee, but it also provided employees (including associates at law firms) with the right to two additional weeks of vacation, a right that could be 'knowingly and voluntarily waived.' Hence the second condition was precisely the same as the first, except that the default rule provided the two extra weeks of vacation. In the second condition, students were asked how much employers would have to pay them to give up their right to the two extra weeks. All by itself, the switch in the default rule more than doubled the students' responses, producing a median willingness to accept of $13,000.

We can imagine countless variations on these experiments. For example, the law might authorize a situation in which employees have to opt into retirement plans, or it might require employers to provide automatic enrollment and allow employees to opt out. Both systems would respect the freedom of employees to choose, and either system would be libertarian in that sense. In the same vein, the law might assume that there is no right to be free from age discrimination in employment, permitting employees (through individual negotiation or collective bargaining) to contract for that right. Alternatively, it might give employees a nondiscrimination guarantee, subject to waiver via contract. Our suggestion here is that one or another approach is likely to have effects on the choices of employees. This is the sense in which paternalism is inevitable, from government no less than from private institutions.

2. Anchors

In emphasizing the absence of well-formed preferences, we are not speaking only of default rules. Consider the crucial role of 'anchors,' or starting points, in contingent valuation studies, an influential method of valuing regulatory goods such as increased safety and environmental protection (Bateman & Willis, 1999). Such studies, used when market valuations are unavailable, attempt to ask people their 'willingness to pay' for various regulatory benefits. Contingent valuation has become prominent in regulatory theory and practice. Because the goal is to determine what people actually want, contingent valuation studies are an effort to elicit, rather than to affect, people's values. Paternalism, in the sense of effects on preferences and choices, is not supposed to be part of the picture. But it is extremely difficult for contingent valuation studies to avoid constructing the very values that they are supposed to discover (Payne, Bettman, & Schkade, 1999). The reason is that in the contexts in which such studies are used, people do not have clear or well-formed preferences, and hence it is unclear that people have straightforward 'values' that can actually be found. Hence some form of paternalism verges on the inevitable: Stated values will often be affected, at least across a range, by how the questions are set up.

Perhaps the most striking evidence to this effect comes from a study of willingness to pay to reduce annual risks of death and injury in motor vehicles (Jones-Lee & Loomes, 2001, pp. 208–212). The authors of that study attempted to elicit both maximum and minimum willingness to pay for safety improvements. People were presented with a statistical risk and an initial monetary amount, and asked whether they were definitely willing or definitely unwilling to pay that amount to eliminate the risk, or if they were 'not sure.' If they were definitely willing, the amount displayed was increased until they said that they were definitely unwilling. If they were unsure, the number was moved up and down until people could identify the minimum and maximum.

The authors were not attempting to test the effects of anchors; on the contrary, they were alert to anchoring only because they 'had been warned' of a possible problem with their procedure, in which people 'might be unduly influenced by the first amount of money that they saw displayed.' To solve that problem, the study allocated people randomly to two subsamples, one with an initial display of 25 pounds, the other with an initial display of 75 pounds. The authors hoped that the anchoring effect would be small, with no significant consequences for minimum and maximum values. But their hope was dashed. *For every level of risk, the minimum willingness to pay was higher with the 75 pound starting point than the maximum willingness to pay with the 25 pound starting point!* For example, a reduction in the annual risk of death by 4 in 100,000 produced a *maximum* willingness to pay of 149 pounds with the 25 pound starting value, but a *minimum* willingness to pay of 232 pounds with the 75 pound starting value (and a maximum, in that case, of 350 pounds). The most sensible conclusion is that people are sometimes uncertain about appropriate values, and whenever they are, anchors have an effect—sometimes a startlingly large one.

It is not clear how those interested in eliciting (rather than affecting) values might respond to this problem. What is clear is that in the domains in which contingent valuation studies are used, people often lack well-formed preferences, and starting points have important consequences for behavior and choice.

3. Framing

We have suggested that in the important context of medical decisions, framing effects are substantial (Redelmeier et al., 1993, p. 73). Apparently, most people do not have clear preferences about how to evaluate a procedure that leaves 90 percent of people alive (and 10 percent of people dead) after a period of years. A similar effect has been demonstrated in the area of obligations to future generations (Frederick, 2003), a much-disputed policy question (Revesz, 1999, pp. 987–1016; Morrison, 1998). This question does not directly involve paternalism, because those interested in the valuation of future generations are not attempting to protect people from their own errors. But a regulatory system that attempts to track people's preferences would try to measure intergenerational time preferences, that is, to elicit people's judgments about how to trade off the protection of current lives and future lives (Revesz, 1999, pp. 996–1007).

Hence an important question, asked in many debates about the issue, is whether people actually make such judgments and whether they can be elicited. And indeed, an influential set of studies finds that people value the lives of those in the current generation far more than the lives of those in future generations (Cropper, Aydede, & Portney, 1994; Cropper, Aydede, & Portney, 1992, p. 472). From a series of surveys, Maureen Cropper and her coauthors (1994) suggest that people are indifferent between saving

1 life today and saving 44 lives in 100 years. They make this suggestion on the basis of questions asking people whether they would choose a program that saves '100 lives now' or a program that saves a substantially larger number '100 years from now.'

But it turns out that other descriptions of the same problem yield significantly different results (Frederick, 2003). Here, as in other contexts, it is unclear whether people actually have well-formed preferences with which the legal system can work. For example, most people consider 'equally bad' a single death from pollution next year and a single death from pollution in 100 years—implying no preference for members of the current generation. In another finding of no strong preference for the current generation, people are equally divided between two programs: one that will save 55 lives now and 105 more lives in 20 years; and one that will save 100 lives now and 50 lives 25 years from now. It is even possible to frame the question in such a way as to find that future lives are valued more, not less, highly than current lives. The most sensible conclusion is that people do not have robust, well-ordered intergenerational time preferences. If so, it is not possible for government to track those preferences, because they are an artifact of how the question is put. The point applies in many contexts. For example, people are unlikely to have context-free judgments about whether government should focus on statistical lives or statistical life-years in regulatory policy; their judgments will be much affected by the framing of the question (Sunstein, 2004).

C. Why Effects on Choice Can Be Hard to Avoid

1. Explanations

Why, exactly, do default rules, starting points, and framing effects have such large effects? To answer this question, it is important to make some distinctions.

a) Suggestion

In the face of uncertainty about what should be done, people might rely on one of two related heuristics: do what most people do, or do what informed people do. Choosers might think that the default plan or value captures one or the other. In many settings, any starting point will carry some informational content and will thus affect choices. When a default rule affects behavior, it might well be because it is taken to carry information about how sensible people usually organize their affairs. Notice that in the context of savings, people might have a mild preference for one or another course, but the preference might be overcome by evidence that most people do not take that course. Some workers might think, for example, that they should not enroll in a 401(k) plan and have a preference not to do so; but the thought and the preference might shift with evidence that the employer has made enrollment automatic.

With respect to savings, the designated default plan apparently carries a certain legitimacy for many employees, perhaps because it seems to have resulted from some conscious thought about what makes most sense for most people (Madrian & Shea, 2001). This interpretation is supported by the finding that the largest effects from the new default rule are shown by women and African-Americans. We might speculate that members of such groups tend to be less confident in their judgments in this domain and may have less experience in assessing different savings plans.

b) Inertia

A separate explanation points to inertia. Any change from the default rule or starting value is likely to require some action. Even a trivial action, such as filling in some form and returning it, can leave room for failures due to memory lapses, sloth, and procrastination. Many people wait until the last minute to file their tax return, even when they are assured of getting a refund. Madrian & Shea (2001, p. 1171) note that, under automatic enrollment, individuals become 'passive savers' and 'do nothing to move away from the default contribution rate.' The power of inertia should be seen as a form of bounded rationality. Although the costs of switching from the default rule or the starting point can be counted as transaction costs, the fact that large behavioral changes are observed even when such costs are tiny suggests that a purely rational explanation is difficult to accept.

c) Endowment effect

A default rule might create a 'pure' endowment effect. It is well known that people tend to value goods more highly if those goods have been initially allocated to them than if those goods have been initially allocated elsewhere (Korobkin, 1998; Thaler, 1991). And it is well known that, in many cases, the default rule will create an endowment effect (Kahneman et al., 1991, pp. 197–199; Samuelson & Zeckhauser, 1998). When an endowment effect is involved, the initial allocation, by private or public institutions, affects people's choices simply because it affects their valuations.

d) Ill-formed preferences

In the cases we have discussed, people's preferences are ill-formed and murky. Suppose, for example, that people are presented with various payouts and risk levels for various pension plans. They might be able to understand the presentation; there might be no confusion. But people might not have a well-defined preference for, or against, a slightly riskier plan with a slightly higher expected value. In these circumstances, their preferences might be endogenous to the default plan simply because they lack well-formed desires that can be accessed to overrule the default starting points. In unfamiliar situations, it is especially unlikely that well-formed preferences will exist. The range of values in the highway safety study is likely a consequence of the unfamiliarity of the context, which leaves people without clear preferences from which to generate numbers. The effects of framing on intergenerational time preferences attest to the fact that people do not have unambiguous judgments about how to trade off the interests of future generations with those of people now living.

2. The inevitability of paternalism

For present purposes, the choice among these various explanations does not greatly matter. The central point is that effects on individual choices are often unavoidable. Of course it is usually good not to block choices, and we do not mean to defend non-libertarian paternalism here. But in an important respect the anti-paternalist position is incoherent, simply because there is no way to avoid effects on behavior and choices. The task for the committed libertarian is, in the midst of such effects, to preserve freedom of choice.

Because framing effects are inevitable, it is hopelessly inadequate to say that when people lack relevant information the best response is to provide it. In order to be effective, any effort to inform people must be rooted in an understanding of how people actually think. Presentation makes a great deal of difference: The behavioral consequences of otherwise identical pieces of information depend on how they are framed.

Consider one example from the realm of retirement savings. Benartzi and Thaler (1999) asked participants in a defined contribution savings plan to imagine that they had only two investment options, Fund A and Fund B, and asked them how they would allocate their investments between these two funds. (The two funds were, in fact, a diversified stock fund and an intermediate term bond fund.) All subjects were given information about the historic returns on these funds. However, one group was shown the distribution of annual rates of return, whereas another group was shown simulated thirty-year rates of return. The long-term rates of return were derived from the annual rates of return (by drawing years at random from history), and so the two sets of information were, strictly speaking, identical. Nevertheless, participants elected to invest about 40 percent of their money in equities when shown the annual returns and 90 percent when shown the long-term rates of return. The lesson from this example is that plan sponsors cannot avoid influencing the choices their participants make simply by providing information. The way they display the information will, in some situations, strongly alter the choices people make.

The point that the presentation of information influences choice is a general one. In the face of health risks, for example, some presentations of accurate information might actually be counter-productive, because people might attempt to control their fear by refusing to think about the risk at all. In empirical studies, 'some messages conveying identical information seemed to work better than others, and . . . some even appeared to backfire' (Caplin, 2003, p. 443). When information campaigns fail altogether, it is often because those efforts 'result in counterproductive defensive measures.' Hence the most effective approaches go far beyond mere disclosure and combine 'a frightening message about the consequences of inaction with an upbeat message about the efficacy of a proposed program of prevention' (Caplin, 2003, p. 442).

There are complex and interesting questions here about how to promote welfare. If information greatly increases people's fear, it will to that extent reduce welfare—in part because fear is unpleasant, in part because fear has a range of ripple effects producing social costs. We do not speak to the welfare issue here. Our only suggestions are that if people lack information, a great deal of attention needs to be paid to information processing, and

251

Richard H. Thaler

that without such attention, information disclosure might well prove futile or counterproductive. And to the extent that those who design informational strategies are taking account of how people think and are attempting to steer people in desirable directions, their efforts will inevitably have a paternalistic dimension.

D. Beyond the Inevitable (But Still Libertarian)

The inevitability of paternalism is most clear when the planner has to choose starting points or default rules. But if the focus is on welfare, it is reasonable to ask whether the planner should go beyond the inevitable, and whether such a planner can also claim to be libertarian.

In the domain of employee behavior, there are many imaginable illustrations. Employees might be automatically enrolled in a 401(k) plan, with a right to opt out, but employers might require a waiting period, and perhaps a consultation with an adviser, before the opt-out could be effective. Thaler and Benartzi (in press) have proposed a method of increasing contributions to 401(k) plans that also meets the libertarian test. Under the Save More Tomorrow plan, now in place in many institutions, employees are invited to sign up for a program in which their contributions to the savings plan are increased annually whenever they get a raise. Once employees join the plan, they stay in until they opt out or reach the maximum savings rate. In the first company to use this plan, the employees who joined increased their savings rates from 3.5 percent to 11.6 percent in a little over two years (three raises). Very few of the employees who join the plan drop out.

It should now be clear that the difference between libertarian and non-libertarian paternalism is not simple and rigid. The libertarian paternalist insists on preserving choice, whereas the non-libertarian paternalist is willing to foreclose choice. But in all cases, a real question is the cost of exercising choice, and here there is a continuum rather than a sharp dichotomy. A libertarian paternalist who is especially enthusiastic about free choice would be inclined to make it relatively costless for people to obtain their preferred outcomes. (Call this a *libertarian* paternalist.) By contrast, a libertarian paternalist who is especially confident of his welfare judgments would be willing to impose real costs on workers and consumers who seek to do what, in the paternalist's view, would not be in their best interests. (Call this a libertarian *paternalist*.)

Rejecting both routes, a non-libertarian paternalist would attempt to block certain choices. But notice that almost any such attempt will amount, in practice, to an effort to impose high costs on those who try to make those choices. Consider a law requiring drivers to wear seat belts. If the law is enforced, and a large fine is imposed, the law is non-libertarian even though determined violators can exercise their freedom of choice—at the expense of the fine. But as the expected fine approaches zero, the law approaches libertarianism.

III. How to Choose: Preference Formation and Welfare

How should sensible planners choose among possible systems, given that some choice is necessary? The promotion of human well-being should be a principal goal, but it is far from clear how to do so. We suggest two approaches. If feasible, a comparison of possible rules should be done using a form of cost-benefit analysis, one that pays serious attention to welfare effects. In many cases, however, such analyses will be both difficult and expensive. As an alternative, we offer some rules of thumb that might be adopted to choose among various options.

A. Costs and Benefits

The goal of a cost-benefit study would be to measure the full ramifications of any design choice. In the context at hand, the cost-benefit study cannot be based on the economists' measure of willingness to pay (WTP), because WTP will be a function of the default rule (Kahneman et al., 1991, pp. 202–203; Korobkin, 1998, pp. 636–641). What is necessary is a more open-ended (and inevitably somewhat subjective) assessment of the welfare consequences. To illustrate, take the example of automatic enrollment. Under automatic enrollment, some employees, who otherwise would not join the plan, will now do so. Presumably, some are made better off (especially if there is an employer match), but some may be made worse off (for example, those who are highly liquidity-constrained and do not exercise their right to opt out). A cost-benefit analysis would attempt to evaluate these gains and losses.

If the issue were only enrollment, we think it highly likely that the gains would exceed the losses. Because of the right to opt out,

Richard H. Thaler

those who need the money immediately are able to have it. In principle one could also compare the costs of foregone current consumption and the benefits of increased consumption during retirement, though this is, admittedly, difficult to do in practice. It is also possible to make inferences from actual choices about welfare. For example, most employees do join the plan eventually, and very few drop out if automatically enrolled (Choi et al., 2002, p. 78; Madrian & Shea, 2001, pp. 1158–1161). These facts suggest that, at least on average, defaulting people into the plan will mostly hasten the rate at which people join the plan, and that the vast majority of those who are so nudged will be grateful.

Some readers might think that our reliance on behavior as an indication of welfare is inconsistent with one of our central claims—that choices do not necessarily coincide with welfare. But in fact, there is no inconsistency. Compare rules calling for mandatory cooling-off periods. The premise of such rules is that people are more likely to make good choices when they have had time to think carefully and without a salesperson present. Similarly, it is reasonable to think that if, on reflection, workers realized that they had been 'tricked' into saving too much, they might take the effort to opt out. The fact that very few participants choose to opt out supports (though it does not prove) the claim that they are helped by a system that makes joining easy.

Once the other effects of automatic enrollment are included, the analysis becomes cloudier. Any plan for automatic enrollment must include a specified default savings rate. Some of those automatically enrolled at a 3 percent savings rate—a typical default in automatic enrollment—would have chosen a higher rate if left to their own devices (Choi et al., 2002, pp. 78–79). If automatic enrollment leads some or many people to save at a lower rate than they would choose, the plan might be objectionable for that reason. Hence we are less confident that this more complete cost-benefit analysis would support the particular opt-out system, though a higher savings rate might well do so. A more sophisticated plan, avoiding some of these pitfalls, is discussed below.

Similar tradeoffs are involved with another important issue: the appropriate default rule for organ donations. In many nations— Austria, Belgium, Denmark, Finland, France, Italy, Luxembourg, Norway, Singapore, Slovenia, and Spain—people are presumed to consent to allow their organs to be used, after death, for the benefit of others; but they are permitted to rebut the presumption, usually through an explicit notation to that effect on their drivers' licenses (Presumed Consent Foundation, Inc., 2003b). In the United States,

254

by contrast, those who want their organs to be available for others must affirmatively say so, also through an explicit notation on their drivers' licenses. The result is that in 'presumed consent' nations over 90 percent of people consent to make their organs available for donation, whereas in the United States, where people have to take some action to make their organs available, only 28 percent elect to do so (Presumed Consent Foundation, Inc., 2003b; Mardfin, 1998). We hypothesize that this dramatic difference is not a product of deep cultural differences, but of the massive effect of the default rule. Hence we would predict that a European-style opt-out rule in the United States would produce donation rates similar to those observed in the European countries that use this rule. Note in this regard that by one report, over 85 percent of Americans support organ donation—a statistic that suggests opt-outs would be relatively rare (Presumed Consent Foundation, Inc., 2003a).

A recent study strongly supports this prediction. Suggesting that preferences are constructed by social frames, Johnson and Goldstein (2004; Chapter 39) urge that with respect to organ donation, people lack stable preferences and that their decisions are very much influenced by the default rule. A controlled online experiment showed a substantial effect from the default rule: The opt-in system created a 42 percent consent rate, about half of the 82 percent rate for an opt-out system. The real-world evidence is even more dramatic. Presumed consent nations show consent rates ranging from a low of 85.9 percent (Sweden) to a high of 100 percent (Austria), with a median of 99 percent. The default also produces a significant, though less dramatic, increase in actual donations, meaning that many people are saved as a result of the presumed consent system.[4] There is reason to believe that in the United States, a switch in the default rule could save thousands of lives.

The default rules for organ donation do not fit the usual definition of paternalism. The issue is the welfare of third parties, not of choosers. Here we are speaking not of libertarian paternalism, but of libertarian benevolence: an approach that

---

[4] Many factors determine how many organs are actually made available and used for transplants. The transplant infrastructure is certainly important, and fewer organs will be available if family members and heirs can veto transplants, even under a presumed consent regime. Johnson and Goldstein estimate that switching to an opt-out system increases organs actually used by 16 percent, holding everything else constant.

attempts to promote benevolence, and to assist vulnerable people, without mandating behavior in any way. We suggest that changes in default rules, or a system of Give More Tomorrow, could produce large increases in public assistance—and that such approaches could do so in a way that avoids coercion. With respect to behavior, the analysis of libertarian benevolence is quite similar to that of libertarian paternalism. One of the advantages of that analysis is the demonstration that when third-party interests are at stake, the default rule will matter a great deal. It follows that planners can often deliver significant benefits to third parties simply by switching the default rule. In the case of organ donation, this is what we observe.

Does one or another default rule promote welfare? At first glance, the opt-out rule common in Europe seems better, simply because it should save a large number of lives without compromising any other important value. The most that can be said against the opt-out rule is that through inertia, perceived social pressure, or confusion, some people might end up donating their organs when they would not, all things considered, prefer to do so ex ante. (Their ex post preferences are difficult to infer!) If this objection (or some other) seems forceful, an alternative would be to require active choices—for example, to mandate, at the time of applying for a driver's license, that applicants indicate whether they want to allow their organs to be used for the benefit of others. We make only two claims about this example. First, the evaluative question turns in large part on empirical issues of the sort that it would be both possible and useful to investigate. Second, the opt-in approach is unlikely to be best.

B. Rules of Thumb

In many cases, the planner will be unable to make a direct inquiry into welfare, either because too little information is available or because the costs of conducting the analysis are not warranted. The committed anti-paternalist might say, in such cases, that people should simply be permitted to choose as they see fit. We hope that we have said enough to show why this response is unhelpful. What people choose often depends on the starting point, and hence the starting point cannot be selected by asking what people choose. In these circumstances, the libertarian paternalist would seek indirect proxies for welfare—methods that test whether one or another approach promotes welfare without relying on guesswork about that question. We suggest three possible methods.

First, the libertarian paternalist might select the approach *that the majority would choose if explicit choices were required and revealed.* In the context of contract law, this is the most familiar inquiry in the selection of default rules (Ayres & Gertner, 1989, pp. 90–91)—provisions that govern contractual arrangements in the absence of express decisions by the parties. Useful though it is, this market-mimicking approach raises its own problems. Perhaps the majority's choices would be insufficiently informed, or a reflection of bounded rationality or bounded self-control. Perhaps those choices would not, in fact, promote the majority's welfare. At least as a presumption, however, it makes sense to follow those choices if the planner knows what they would be. A deeper problem is that the majority's choices might themselves be a function of the starting point or the default rule. If so, the problem of circularity dooms the market-mimicking approach. But in some cases, at least, the majority might go one way or the other regardless of the starting point; and to that extent, the market-mimicking strategy is workable. Note that in the cafeteria example, some options would not fit with the majority's ex ante choices (healthy but terrible-tasting food, for example), and that for savings, some allocations would certainly violate the choices of ordinary workers (say, an allocation of 30 percent or more to savings). In fact a clear understanding of majority choices might well support a default rule that respects those choices even if the planner thinks that an inquiry into welfare would support another rule. At the very least, planners should be required to have real confidence in their judgment if they seek to do something other than what a suitably informed majority would find to be in its interest.

Second, the libertarian paternalist might select the approach that we have called required active choices, one *that would force people to make their choices explicit.* This approach might be chosen if the market-mimicking strategy fails, either because of the circularity problem or because the planner does not know which approach would in fact be chosen by the majority. We have seen the possibility of requiring active choices in the context of retirement plans and organ donations; it would be easy to multiply examples. In the law of contract, courts sometimes choose 'penalty defaults'—default rules that penalize the party in the best position to obtain a clear statement on the question at hand, and hence create an incentive for clarity for the person who is in the best position to produce clarity (Ayres & Gertner, 1989, pp. 101–106).

Richard H. Thaler

Libertarian paternalists might go along the same track; in fact penalty defaults can be seen as a form of libertarian paternalism.

Here too, however, there is a risk that the choices that are actually elicited will be inadequately informed or will not promote welfare. In the case of retirement plans, for example, forced choices have been found to produce higher participation rates than requiring opt-ins, but lower rates than requiring opt-outs (Choi et al., 2002, pp. 77, 86). If it is likely that automatic enrollment promotes people's welfare, perhaps automatic enrollment should be preferred over requiring active choices. The only suggestion is that where social planners are unsure how to handle the welfare question, they might devise a strategy that requires people to choose.

Third, the libertarian paternalist might select the approach *that minimizes the number of opt-outs.* Suppose, for example, that when drivers are presumed to want to donate their organs to others, only 10 percent opt out, but that when drivers are required to signal their willingness to donate their organs to others, 30 percent opt in. This is an ex post inquiry into people's preferences, in contrast to the ex ante approach favored by the market-mimicking strategy. With those numbers, there is reason to think that the presumption in favor of organ donation is better, if only because more people are sufficiently satisfied to leave it in place.

IV How Much Choice Should Be Offered?

It is far beyond our ambition here to venture a full analysis of the question of how much choice to offer individuals in various domains (Loewenstein, 2000, pp. 89–94; Dworkin, 1988, pp. 62–81). Instead, we identify some questions that a libertarian paternalist might ask to help decide how much (reasonable) choice to offer. Any such libertarian would obviously want to reduce the frequency and severity of errors, and the costs of making decisions. If an approach increases the costs of decisions for choosers, there is less reason to adopt it, and it should be selected only if it is likely to improve the match of choices to actual welfare. If an approach increases errors and their costs by leading people to make choices that do not promote their welfare, that is a strong point against it. We now trace some considerations that help answer the question whether more choices would increase the costs of errors and the costs of decisions.

Preferences, Paternalism, and Liberty

A. Do Choosers Have Informed Preferences?

In some domains, consumers and workers are highly informed—so much so that they will not even be influenced by default rules. Most adults have experimented enough over the course of their lives to have a good sense of what flavors of ice cream they like. They can do a decent job of picking even in a shop offering dozens of flavors. If the default option is asparagus-flavored ice cream, they will be unlikely to choose it, and might well be annoyed. But when faced with a menu listing many unfamiliar foods in a foreign country, customers would be unlikely to benefit from being required to choose among them, and they might prefer a small list or ask the waiter for a default suggestion (for example, what do other tourists like?). In such settings, clever restaurants catering to tourists often offer a default 'tourist menu.' Many actual choices fall between the poles of ice cream flavors and foreign menus. When information is limited, a menu of countless options increases the costs of decisions without increasing the likelihood of accuracy. But when choosers are highly informed, the availability of numerous options decreases the likelihood of error and does not greatly increase decision costs, simply because informed choosers can more easily navigate the menu of options.

B. Is the Mapping from Options to Preferences Transparent?

If we order a coffee ice cream cone, we have a pretty good idea what we will consume. If we invest $10,000 in a mix of mutual funds, we have little idea (without the aid of sophisticated software) what a change in the portfolio will do to our distribution of expected returns in retirement. When we choose between health plans, we may not fully understand all the ramifications of our choice. If I get a rare disease, will I be able to see a good specialist? How long will I have to wait in line? When people have a hard time predicting how their choices will end up affecting their lives, they have less to gain from having numerous options from which to choose. If it is hard to map from options to preferences, a large set of choices is likely to be cognitively overwhelming, and thus to increase the costs of decisions without also increasing welfare by reducing errors.

Richard H. Thaler

C. How Much Do Preferences Vary across Individuals?

Some people smoke; others hate the smell of smoke. Some people like hard mattresses; others like soft ones. How do hotels deal with this problem? Most choose to cater to differences in tastes with respect to smoking but not with respect to mattresses. The mattress that appeals to the median hotel guest seems to be good enough to satisfy most customers, but the threat of a smoky room (or a night without cigarettes) is enough to scare customers away. Here is a case in which many people have well-formed preferences that trump default rules. Many planners, both private and public, must make similar tradeoffs. Since offering choice is costly, sensible planners make multiple choices available when people's preferences vary most. The argument for a large option set is thus strongest in cases of preferences that are both clear and heterogeneous. In such cases, people's welfare is likely to be promoted if each can choose as he sees fit, and homogeneity will lead to inaccuracy and thus widespread error costs.

D. Do Consumers Value Choosing for Themselves As An Intrinsic Good?

Freedom of choice is itself an ingredient in welfare. In some situations people derive welfare from the very act of choosing. But sometimes it is a chore to have to choose, and the relevant taste can differ across individuals. (One of us derives pleasure from reading and choosing from a wine list; the other finds that enterprise basically intolerable.) A more serious example comes from evidence that many patients do not want to make complex medical decisions and would prefer their doctors to choose for them (Schneider, 1998, pp. 35–46). The point very much bears on the decision whether to force explicit choices or instead to adopt a default rule that reflects what the majority wants. If making choices is itself a subjective good, the argument for forced choices is strengthened. But much of the time, especially in technical areas, people do not particularly enjoy the process of choice, and a large number of options becomes a burden. By contrast, a thoughtfully chosen default rule, steering them in sensible directions, is a blessing.

Conclusion

Our central empirical claim here has been that in many domains, people's preferences are labile and ill-formed, and do not predate social and legal contexts. For this reason, starting points and default rules are likely to be quite sticky. Building on empirical work involving rationality and preference formation, we have sketched and defended libertarian paternalism – an approach that preserves freedom of choice but that encourages both private and public institutions to steer people in directions that will promote their own welfare.

Some kind of paternalism, we believe, is likely whenever such institutions set out default plans or options. Unfortunately, many current social outcomes are both random and inadvertent, in the sense that they are a product of default rules whose behavior-shaping effects have never been a product of serious reflection. In these circumstances, the goal should be to avoid arbitrary or harmful consequences and to produce contexts that are likely to promote people's welfare, suitably defined.

References

Ayres, I., & Gertner, R. (1989). Filling gaps in incomplete contracts: An economic theory of default rules. *Yale Law Journal, 99*, 87–130.

Bateman, I. A., & Willis, K. G. (1999). *Valuing environmental preferences.* New York: Oxford University Press.

Benartzi, S., & Thaler, R. H. (1999). Risk aversion or myopia? Choices in repeated gambles and retirement investments. *Management Science, 45*, 364–381.

Benartzi, S., & Thaler, R. H. (2002). How much is investor autonomy worth? *Journal of Finance, 57*, 1593–1616.

Calabresi, G., & Melamed, A. D. (1972). Property rules, liability rules, and inalienability: One view of the cathedral. *Harvard Law Review, 85*, 1089–1128.

Calle, E. E., Thun, M. J., Petrelli, J. M., Rodriguez, C., & Heath, C. W., Jr. (1999). Body-mass index and mortality in a prospective cohort of U.S. adults. *New England Journal of Medicine, 341*, 1097–1105.

Camerer, C. F. (2000). Prospect theory in the wild: Evidence from the field. In D. Kahneman & A. Tversky (Eds.), *Choices, values, and frames.* Cambridge, UK: Cambridge University Press.

Camerer, C. F., & Hogarth, R. M. (1999). The effects of financial incentives in experiments: A review and capital-labor-production framework. *Journal of Risk and Uncertainty, 19*, 1–3, 7–42.

Richard H. Thaler

Centers for Disease Control and Prevention. (2003). *1991–2001 Prevalence of obesity among U.S. adults, by characteristics*: Retrieved May 6, 2004, from http://www.cdc.gov/nccdphp/dnpa/obesity/trend/prev_char.htm.

Choi, J. J., Laibson, D., Madrian, B. C., & Metrick, A. (2002). Defined contribution pensions: Plan rules, participant decisions, and the path of least resistance. In J. M. Poterba (Ed.), *Tax policy and the economy* (Vol. 16, pp. 67–113). Cambridge, MA: MIT Press.

Cropper, M. L., Aydede, S. K., & Portney, P. R. (1994). Preferences for life-saving programs: How the public discounts time and age. *Journal of Risk and Uncertainty, 8*(3), 243–265.

De Bondt, W. F. M., & Thaler, R. H. (1990). Do security analysts overreact? *American Economic Review, 80*(2), 52–57.

Dworkin, G. (1988). *The theory and practice of autonomy*. Cambridge, UK: Cambridge University Press.

Frederick, S. (2003). Measuring intergenerational time preference: Are future lives valued less? *Journal of Risk and Uncertainty, 26*, 39–53.

Frederick, S., Loewenstein, G., & O'Donoghue, T. (2002). Time discounting and time preference: A critical review. *Journal of Economic Literature, 40*, 351–401.

Friedman, M., & Friedman, R. (1980). *Free to choose: A personal statement*. New York: Harcourt Brace Jovanovich.

Grether, D. M. (1980). Bayes rules as a descriptive model: The representativeness heuristic. *Quarterly Journal of Economics, 95*, 537–557.

Johnson, E. J., Hershey, J., Meszaros, J., & Kunreuther, H. (1993). Framing, probability distortions, and insurance decisions. *Journal of Risk and Uncertainty, 7*, 35–51.

Jolls, C., Sunstein, C. R., & Thaler, R. H. (1998). A behavioral approach to law and economics. *Stanford Law Review, 50*, 1471–1550.

Jones-Lee, M., & Loomes, G. (2001). Private values and public policy. In E. U. Weber, J. Baron, & G. Loomes (Eds.), *Conflict and tradeoffs in decision making* (pp. 205–230). Cambridge, UK: Cambridge University Press.

Kahneman, D., & Frederick, S. (2002). Representativeness revisited: Attribute substitution in intuitive judgment. In T. Gilovich, D. Griffin, & D. Kahneman (Eds.), *Heuristics of intuitive judgment: Extensions and applications* (pp. 49–81). New York: Cambridge University Press.

Kahneman, D., Knetsch, J. L., & Thaler, R. H. (1991, Winter). Anomalies: The endowment effect, loss aversion, and status quo bias. *Journal of Economic Perspectives, 5*, 193–206.

Korobkin, R. (1998). The status quo bias and contract default rules. *Cornell Law Review, 83*, 608–687.

Kunreuther, H. (1996). Mitigating disaster losses through insurance. *Journal of Risk and Uncertainty, 12*(2–3), 171–187.

Loewenstein, G. F. (2000). How people make decisions: Costs and benefits of health- and retirement-related choice. In S. Burke, E. Kingson, & U.

Reinhardt (Eds.), *Social Security and Medicare: Individual versus collective risk and responsibility* (pp. 87–113). Washington, DC: National Academy of Social Insurance.

Madrian, B. C., & Shea, D. F. (2001). The power of suggestion: Inertia in 401(k) participation and savings behavior. *Quarterly Journal of Economics, 116*, 1149–1187.

Mill, J. S. (1972). On liberty. In H. B. Acton (Ed.), *Utilitarianism, on liberty, considerations on representative government*. London: Dent.

Morrison, E. R. (1998). Comment, judicial review of discount rates used in regulatory cost-benefit analysis. *University of Chicago Law Review, 65*, 1333–1359.

National Institute of Diabetes and Digestive and Kidney Diseases. (2001). *Understanding adult obesity*: Retrieved May 4, 2005, from http://win.niddk.nih.gov/publications/understanding.htm.

Okin, S. M. (1989). *Justice, gender, and the family*. New York: Basic.

Payne, J. W., Bettman, J. R., & Schkade, D. A. (1999). Measuring constructed preferences: Towards a building code. *Journal of Risk and Uncertainty, 19*, 243–270.

Qualified Transportation Fringe Benefits, 26 CFR Parts 1 and 602 (2001).

Redelmeier, D., Rozin, P., & Kahneman, D. (1993). Understanding patients' decisions: Cognitive and emotional perspectives. *Journal of the American Medical Association, 270*, 72–76.

Revesz, R. L. (1999). Environmental regulation, cost-benefit analysis, and the discounting of human lives. *Columbia Law Review, 99*, 941–1017.

Samuelson, W., & Zeckhauser, R. (1988). Status quo bias in decision-making. *Journal of Risk and Uncertainty, 1*, 7–59.

Schneider, C. E. (1998). *The practice of autonomy: Patients, doctors, and medical decisions*. New York: Oxford University Press.

Shiller, R. J. (2000). *Irrational exuberance*. Princeton, NJ: Princeton University Press.

Slovic, P., Kunreuther, H., & White, G. F. (1974). Decision processes, rationality and adjustment to natural hazards. In G. F. White (Ed.), *Natural hazards: Local, national, global* (pp. 187–205). New York: Oxford University Press.

Sunstein, C. R. (2001). Human behavior and the law of work. *Virginia Law Review, 87*, 205–276.

Sunstein, C. R. (2002a). *Risk and reason: Safety, law, and the environment*. Cambridge, UK: Cambridge University Press.

Sunstein, C. R. (2002b). Switching the default rule. *New York University Law Review, 77*(106–134).

Sunstein, C. R. (2004). Lives, life-years, and willingness to pay. *Columbia Law Review, 104*, 205–252.

Sunstein, C. R., Kahneman, D., Schkade, D., & Ritov, I. (2002). Predictably incoherent judgments. *Stanford Law Review, 54*, 1153–1215.

Thaler, R. H. (1991). *Quasi-rational economics*. New York: Russell Sage.

Richard H. Thaler

Thaler, R. H., & Benartzi, S. (2004). Save More Tomorrow™: Using behavioral economics to increase employee saving. *Journal of Political Economy, 112*, S164-S187.

Tversky, A., & Kahneman, D. (1973). Availability: A heuristic for judging frequency and probability. *Cognitive Psychology, 5*, 207–232.

Tversky, A., & Kahneman, D. (1974). Judgment under uncertainty: Heuristics and biases. *Science, 185*, 1124–1131.

Tversky, A., & Thaler, R. H. (1990). Anomalies: Preference reversals. *Journal of Economic Perspectives, 4*(2), 201–211.

VanDeVeer, D. (1986). *Paternalistic intervention: The moral bounds on benevolence*. Princeton, NJ: Princeton

Preference Change and Interpersonal Comparisons of Welfare[1]

ALEX VOORHOEVE

Introduction

Suppose that we agree that for questions of justice in a pluralistic society, we need a public standard of welfare. An appropriate public standard of welfare will have to meet the following two requirements. First, its conception of each person's welfare should, to the greatest reasonable extent, be something that each person can recognise as encompassing the things she wants for herself and as giving these things weights that reflect the relative importance she gives to them. Second, it should be sensitive to the fact that reasonable people hold conflicting conceptions of what constitutes an individual's welfare. It should therefore, to the greatest reasonable extent, respect neutrality of judgement by refraining from endorsing any particular conception of welfare as superior to any other.

In an influential set of essays, Richard Arneson (1990a, 1990b, 1990c) has argued that the following conception of welfare is ideally suited to these requirements: equate each individual's welfare with the degree of satisfaction of her ideally rational, self-regarding preferences. These are the preferences she would have on behalf of herself if she were to engage in ideally extended deliberation with full pertinent information, in a calm mood, while thinking clearly and making no reasoning errors (see Arneson 1990a, pp. 162–163).

[1] Earlier versions of this paper were presented at the Royal Institute of Philosophy conference on Preference Formation and Well-Being at St. John's College Cambridge in July 2004, in the LSE Choice Group Seminar in January 2005, and the ECAP 5 Workshop on Philosophy, Economics, and Public Policy in Lisbon in August 2005. I am grateful to those present at these meetings, and especially to Richard Arneson, Luc Bovens, Keith Dowding, Marc Fleurbaey, Christian List, Andrew Williams, and Jo Wolff for their comments. I also thank Richard Bradley, Roger Crisp, Michael Otsuka, and Serena Olsaretti for detailed comments on earlier versions of this paper. The Analysis Trust and the AHRB supported my work on this paper.

Alex Voorhoeve

(For simplicity, in what follows, I will use the term 'preferences', to refer to these ideally rational, self-regarding preferences.)

Arneson argues that this standard of welfare meets the two aforementioned requirements in the best way possible. It meets the first requirement, he argues, because it comes as close as possible to adhering to a person's own view of her welfare within the constraints set by the need to avoid the intuitively unpalatable move of considering something of value to her that she only considers to be so because of a lack of information or incomplete or erroneous deliberation (1990a, p. 163). It meets the second requirement, he argues, because it does not involve any commitment on the part of the state to a substantive view of what is good for individuals. As Arneson (1990b, p. 450) puts it: 'the good in this conception is an empty basket that is filled for each individual according to her considered evaluations.'[2]

In this paper, I will argue that the fact that people care about which preferences they have, and the fact that people can change their preferences about which preferences it is good for them to have, together undermine this case for accepting a preference satisfaction conception of welfare.

The paper is organised as follows. In section 1, I introduce three concepts of importance to the discussion of a preference satisfaction conception of welfare. First, a person's *preference type*, which encompasses all the things that determine how she would evaluate, after ideally rational and well-informed deliberation and from the perspective of her self-interest, her situation and her evaluative dispositions. Second, a person's *limited preferences*, which are her preferences over alternatives in which her situation differs whilst her preference type remains unchanged. Third, a person's *extended preferences*, which encompass her preferences over alternatives in which either her situation, or her preference type, or both, differ.

In section 2, I argue that the interest in having the preferences one wants to have is of central importance in human life, and that the preference satisfaction approach should therefore attempt to judge a person's welfare by the degree to which her extended preferences are satisfied.

In section 3, I argue that the possibility of a change in a person's extended preferences creates great difficulties for a measure of welfare based on the degree of satisfaction of a person's extended preferences. For if we evaluate a potential change in a person's

[2] See also Otsuka (2003, pp. 110–112).

extended preferences from the perspective of the degree to which her future preferences would be satisfied, then we do not adequately represent each individual's current interest in shaping her future preferences. If, by contrast, we evaluate a potential change in a person's preferences from the perspective of her current extended preferences, then we implausibly disregard the view of her own interests that she would have if the preference change occurred. In sum, it seems that any preference satisfaction measure will have significant drawbacks, since it will involve either neglecting individuals' current interests in shaping their future preferences, or, in their future, judging their welfare by a set of values which might be very alien to them.

In the final section, I suggest that this should prompt us to develop alternative measures of welfare. I suggest that one promising candidate is a substantive measure of welfare based on a list of goods and conditions that are recognised as valuable from the perspective of a variety of different conceptions of welfare.

1. Preference-based interpersonal comparisons of welfare

Let us start with a simple description of what is involved in preference-based interpersonal comparisons of welfare. For simplicity, I will limit the discussion to cases where, from the perspective of his self-interest, a person cares only about his own situation, and is indifferent to other people's situations and their attitudes towards him. Let us begin by introducing the notion of a *preference type*. A preference type encompasses all the things that determine how a person would evaluate, after ideally rational and well-informed deliberation and from the perspective of his own self-interest, his situation and his own evaluative dispositions. (From now on, I will drop reference to a person's evaluations being those he would have after ideal and fully informed deliberation and from the perspective of his self-interest, and take them to be so.) A person's preference type therefore tells us how he would rank each combination of his personal situation and evaluative dispositions, and also which evaluative dispositions he has. In a terminology which will shortly be introduced, this is equivalent to saying that two people have the same preference type just in case what I will be calling their 'limited preferences' and their 'extended preferences' are identical.

Let $\{A,B\}$ be the set of preference types consisting of artist's preferences (A) and banker's preferences (B). Let S be the set of all

Alex Voorhoeve

possible states of the world. A state of the world is a description of all relevant aspects of each person's situation, excluding each person's judgements and other evaluative dispositions. Let S be a state of the world in $\boldsymbol{S}$. Let I be the set of individuals and i be an individual in I. The set $\boldsymbol{S} \times I$ stands for the set of all pairs (S,i) with S in $\boldsymbol{S}$ and i in I. A pair (S,i) stands for 'occupying personal position i in state of the world S'. Let u^t be a Von Neumann and Morgenstern utility function defined on the set $\boldsymbol{S} \times I$, representing the preferences of a person with preference type t over combinations of occupying a person's position in a state of the world. It assigns a real number $u^t(S,i)$ to being in person i's position in state of the world S and is bounded both above and below.[3] Because this function only represents a person's preferences over (state of the world, person's position) pairs in which he has preferences of type t, I will refer to the preferences it represents as a person's 'limited preferences'.

Let v^t be a Von Neumann and Morgenstern utility function defined on the set $\boldsymbol{S} \times I \times \{A,B\}$. The function v^t represents the preferences of a person with preference type t over (state of the world, person's position, preference type) triples. It assigns a real number $v^t(S,i,t')$ to each triple (S,i,t') in the set $\boldsymbol{S} \times I \times \{A,B\}$ and is bounded both above and below. Because the function v^t represents how a person with preference type t would order a set of options that involve occupying various personal positions in various states of the world with various preference types, I will refer to the preferences it represents as this person's 'extended preferences'.

To write that $u^t(C,i)>u^t(D,i)$ means that, keeping his preference type fixed at type t, a person with preference type t will prefer occupying person i's position in state of the world C to occupying person i's position in state of the world D. To write that $v^t(C,i,A)>v^t(D,i,B)$ means that keeping his preference type fixed at type t, a person with preference type t will prefer occupying person i's position in state of the world C with preference type A to occupying person i's position in state of the world D with preference type B. By way of illustration, suppose Paul has artist's preferences. Suppose that in C, Paul is a struggling artist, and in D,

---

[3]   The fact that the utility function is bounded both above and below means that there exists some numbers a and b such that $a \leq u_t(S,i) \leq b$ for each S in $\boldsymbol{S}$. This means that in no case is being in person i's position ascribed a utility of negative or positive infinity. This assumption avoids certain decision-theoretic paradoxes that arise when utilities of negative or positive infinity are permitted. See Binmore (1991, p.112n12).

he is a successful banker. Then $u^A(C,Paul)>u^A(D,Paul)$ means that, keeping his artist's preferences constant, Paul prefers being a struggling artist to being a successful banker. This preference will be relevant to his choice of career, so long as his choice of career does not change his preference type. By contrast, $v^A(C,Paul,A)>v^A(D,Paul,B)$ means that, from the perspective of his artist's preferences, Paul prefers being a poor artist with his current artist's preferences to being a rich banker with banker's preferences. This preference would determine, for example, his choice between going to art school (which, let us assume, will maintain his artist's preferences and lead to a career as a struggling artist) and going to business school (which, let us assume, will lead to a preference change to banker's preferences followed by a successful career in banking). We can imagine he holds this preference because he believes that a life devoted to art is superior to one that is not, no matter how successful the latter is. He therefore values having his artist's preferences to such a degree that he would not want to be rid of them and have them substituted by banker's preferences (which, let us suppose, involve a desire to compete and succeed in the world of high finance and no appreciation of artistic values), even at the cost of being poor and unrecognised in the work he would do as an artist as opposed to wealthy and successful in the career he would choose if he were to acquire banker's preferences.

Both individuals' limited preferences and their extended preferences may differ. Suppose for simplicity that like Paul, Rob is a struggling artist in C and a successful banker in D. Suppose, further that Rob has banker's preferences, and that, keeping his banker's preferences constant, this means he would rather be a successful banker than a struggling artist: $u^B(C,Rob)<u^B(D,Rob)$. In addition, suppose Rob is committed to the competitive values that underlie his preference for banking, so that he would not accept an opportunity to acquire artist's preferences, especially not at the cost of then having to live as a struggling artist, so that $v^B(C,Rob,A)<v^B(D,Rob,B)$. In sum, in contrast to Paul, Rob believes it is worse to be a struggling artist with artist's preferences than to be a successful banker with banker's preferences.

It is worth noting that it is not necessarily the case that when individuals' preference types differ, both their limited and extended preferences differ. Two individuals with different preference types might have the same limited preferences, but different extended preferences, or the same extended preferences, but different limited preferences.

As an example of the former, consider the case of two gourmands who both enjoy exactly the same dishes to an equal extent: in environments in which they face only choices about what to eat, they will evaluate all options in exactly the same way, so that (at least in these environments) their limited preferences are the same. However, one of the two would prefer, if given the chance, to give up his taste for fine dining and develop a taste for music instead, so long as he would have an adequate opportunity to enjoy music with his new tastes. The other, by contrast, would not prefer to develop such tastes, so that their extended preferences are different.

As an example of the latter, consider two hedonists, who both rank all (state of the world, person's position, preference type) triples in the same way, viz. according to the pleasure they yield, so that their extended preferences are identical. However, one of them likes music, but takes no pleasure in eating, whereas the other takes no pleasure in music, but enjoys a good meal, so that their limited preferences differ.

Let us now turn to preference-based interpersonal comparisons of welfare. A preference-based standard of welfare involves making judgements about whether occupying Paul's position in state of the world C with preference type A is better, worse, or just as good as occupying Rob's position in state of the world D with preference type B. More precisely, let the function w be a Von Neumann and Morgenstern utility function representing this public standard of welfare. The function w then assigns a real number $w(S,i,t)$ to each triple (S,i,t) in the set $S \times I \times \{A,B\}$ and is bounded both above and below. This $w(S,i,t)$ stands for the value of occupying person i's position in state of the world S with preference type t. In attempting to determine these values with reference to a person's degree of preference satisfaction, we face two questions. First, whether we should use the degree of satisfaction of a person's limited or extended preferences in determining his welfare. Second, how we should evaluate options that involve preference change. I address the first of these questions in the next section, and the second one in section 3.

2. Extended preferences and welfare

As mentioned, people typically do not just care about having the world conform to their preferences; they also care about which values, aims, attachments, and therefore preferences they have. This interest in having the preferences one wants to have is, moreover, an important one. Considering people who could be said not to care, or not to care deeply, about their values and aims can illustrate this importance.

Consider first what the life would be like of someone who was completely indifferent about his values and aims. This person's life would be devoid of the kind of commitments and relationships that are a central part of most people's lives. This is evident in cases of commitments to moral ideals: being committed to a cause like eradicating world poverty, for example, involves more than having a particular pattern of desires connected to that cause, such as that it should be realised; it also involves wanting to maintain one's desire for its realisation. But is it also a feature of other commitments that are a central part of people's identity. Being committed to being an artist, for example, does not just involve trying to succeed as an artist, but also to want to maintain and develop one's appreciation of art.

Furthermore, deep friendship involves not just caring about one's friend, enjoying her company, and being ready to help her out when she needs help, but also being prepared to take steps to maintain these attitudes towards her. Similarly, being a loving partner involves not just desiring to share one's life with one's partner, desiring to see him do well, etc. but also to actively maintain and, when necessary, reinforce these desires (see Frankfurt (2004)).[4] In these cases, a person does not just desire to have certain preferences because having them would be instrumental to some other end that she has (eradicating world poverty, being a successful artist, furthering the welfare of one's friend or lover), but also because she regards these as the right preferences for her to have.

More generally, the life of someone who was completely indifferent about his values and aims would be devoid of a particular kind of agency: action directed not merely at shaping his environment to satisfy his desires, but also at shaping himself, in the sense of shaping his values and aims (see Frankfurt (1982, p. 83)). As a consequence, if his life showed any unity of purpose, it would not be the product of any action on his part intended to give his life any particular direction, but rather the product of causes in which he played no active part, or the unintended by-product of his actions.

---

[4] See also Voorhoeve (2003) for a discussion with Harry Frankfurt of his views on love.

Similar conclusions apply in the case of a person who, though she has preferences about which preferences she has, ranks her present and potential preferences only on the grounds of the ease with which they can be satisfied (see Dworkin 2000, pp. 292–293). Such a person would also lack the particular attitudes necessary for being substantively committed to any particular cause, relationship, or set of values. As a consequence, she would not purposefully shape her life and herself in accordance with the demands of such commitments.

In sum, the interest in having the preferences one wants to have is essentially the interest in one's ability to shape oneself and one's life in accordance with the demands of the causes, values and relationships to which one is devoted. Given the importance of this interest, we should attempt to base a preference satisfaction measure of welfare on the satisfaction of a person's extended preferences, since these represent both a person's interests in his situation and his interests in his preferences.

3. Preference change and the degree of satisfaction of a person's extended preferences

Let us now turn to a method for determining the degree of satisfaction of a person's extended preferences. Suppose there are four states of the world: one in which Paul is a struggling artist (C), one in which he is a successful banker (D), one in which he is an unsuccessful banker (E), and one in which he is a successful artist (F). For any Von Neumann and Morgenstern utility function, we are free to fix the zeros and units.[5] Once we do so, the utilities of all states of the world are fixed. In order to be able to interpret the number $v^t(S,i,t')$ as the degree to which occupying person i's position in state of the world S with preference type t' satisfies the extended preferences of someone with preference type t, we therefore proceed as follows. We set the value of what, from the perspective of type t is the best possible (state of the world, person's position, preference type) triple to one, and the worst triple to zero. For example, suppose that, from the perspective of his current artist's preferences, Paul would consider being a struggling artist with banker's preferences the worst possible triple,

---

[5] For an introductory discussion of Von Neumann and Morgenstern utility functions and their properties, see Binmore (1991, chapter 3).

and being a successful artist with artist's preferences the best possible triple. We then take $v^A(C,Paul,B)=0$, and $v^A(F,Paul,A)=1$.

The value of all other (state of the world, person's position, preference type) triples will then be determined as follows. We then take the number assigned to any other triple to be equal to the probability p that would render Paul indifferent between accepting that triple and a lottery with probability $(1-p)$ of ending up in his position in C with preference type B and probability p of ending up in his position in F with preference type A. In this way, each (state of the world, person's position, preference type) triple is assigned a number between zero and one, which we can call the degree to which this triple satisfies Paul's current type A extended preferences over (state of the world, person's position, preference type) triples. For example, if with artist's preferences Paul would be indifferent between being a struggling artist with artist's preferences and a lottery with a probability of 0.2 of ending up in his position in C with preference type B and a probability of 0.8 of ending up in his position in F with preference type A, then $v^A(C,Paul,A)=0.8$.

Now, we face a difficulty in deciding how to move from the degree to which each triple would satisfy Paul's current extended preferences to an assessment of how well off he would be if each of these triples were realised. The difficulty is that if we assess each triple by Paul's current, type A extended preferences, this assessment may differ from his own assessment of these triples once he is in the situation characterised by this triple. For when these triples involve a preference change to preference type B, then though Paul will now regard this change as making him worse off, once he has preferences of type B, he may regard this change in preferences as making him better off. For example, from the perspective of his current, artist's preferences, he might assign the situation in which he is a successful banker with banker's preferences a value of 0.3: $v^A(D,Paul,B)=0.3$. But if he ended up in this situation through a process of preference change that, from the perspective of his new preferences, he does not regard as in any way a bad one to have undergone, then we may suppose that from the perspective of his new preferences, he would assess this situation as the best possible one: $v^B(D,Paul,B)=1$. The question is, then, whether we should take Paul's pre-preference change, or post-preference change evaluation as determining his welfare in such cases.

Before we attempt to deal with this question, we should note that in order to assess the impact of a change in a person's extended preferences on his welfare, it is important to assess the conditions under which it takes place. If the preference change was a result of the subversion of Paul's cognitive capacities, or of coercion or oppression, or was a response to an unduly limiting environment, then this might discredit Paul's post-preference change view of his own welfare. I will assume, however, that all preference changes under consideration are not the result of the subversion of a person's cognitive capacities, of coercion, oppression, or unduly limiting circumstances. Preference changes of this kind can occur throughout people's lives; one might, for example, have artist's preferences and through contact with one's friends or one's social environment, or simply through the passage of time, find one's preferences changed to banker's preferences. I will also assume that from the perspective of preference types A and B, having had one's preferences change in this way is not viewed as a bad or a good thing in itself.

Now, the possibility of this change in an individual's evaluation of a particular (state of the world, person's position, preference type) triple means we have two possible ways of judging an individual's welfare by the degree of satisfaction of his extended preferences. The first is to equate the welfare level of each triple with the degree of satisfaction of the extended preferences that he has in that triple. The second is to equate the welfare level of each triple with the degree to which this triple satisfies his current extended preferences. I will discuss each method in turn.

The first method involves using the extended preferences of type A to evaluate a situation that involves Paul occupying his position in a state of the world with preference type A, and the extended preferences of preference type B to evaluate a situation that involves Paul occupying his position in a state of the world with preference type B. This would mean taking $w(C,Paul,A)$ to be equivalent to $v^A(C,Paul,A)$ and $w(C,Paul,B)$ to be equivalent to $v^B(C,Paul,B)$, and so on.

Doing so means that at every point in time, our standard of welfare will agree with each individual's own assessment of his welfare at that time. Moreover, this standard of welfare will always respect each individual's preferences over options that do not involve changes in his preferences. However, this standard will not always agree with an individual's pre-preference change assessment of the value of options that involve preference change. For this measure will count a change from a situation in which Paul is a struggling artist with artist's preferences to a situation in which he is a successful banker with banker's preferences as an improvement in Paul's welfare, since the degree of satisfaction of the extended preferences he has after the change is larger than the degree of satisfaction of his extended preferences before the change: $w(C,Paul,A) = v^A(C,Paul,A) = 0.8 < w(D,Paul,B) = v^B(D,Paul,B) = 1$. But from the perspective of his current, artist's preferences, Paul will disagree with this judgement.

It follows that this measure does not adequately represent Paul's interest in having the preferences he wants to have: it will not consider the goods and conditions that enable him to sustain his preferences, or develop them in the direction he wants, as contributing to his welfare, unless his sustaining or developing these preferences will contribute to a higher degree of satisfaction of whatever preferences he ends up having. For example, so long as Paul has artist's preferences, this measure will regard the resources and conditions that help him sustain or reinforce his artist's preferences as of less value to him than the resources and conditions that would lead him to develop banker's preferences, when the latter could be more easily satisfied. Given the importance of the interest in shaping one's tastes, values and aims in the direction one wants, this represents a severe drawback of this version of the satisfaction measure of welfare.

The second method assesses each (state of the world, person's position, preference type) triple from the perspective of his current preferences. To illustrate this method, suppose again that Paul's current extended preferences are those that go with type A. We regard these extended preferences as determining the welfare of all future (occupying Paul's position in a state of the world, preference type) triples. We would then take $w(C,Paul,A)$ to be equivalent to $v^A(C,Paul,A)$, $w(C,Paul,B)$ to be equivalent to $v^A(C,Paul,B)$, and so on.

This method obviously represents Paul's current interests in his future preferences. However, it does so at the cost of not always respecting Paul's post-preference change extended preferences. Suppose Paul's preferences at time 0 are artist's preferences. Suppose further that we take the degree of satisfaction of his extended preferences at time 0 as the measure of his current and future welfare. Then we will evaluate a change from a situation at time 0 in which he is a struggling artist to a situation in which at time 1 he is a successful banker as making him worse off. As noted, after this change, Paul will disagree: at time 1 he will regard his new situation as the best possible one. Now, suppose this change does take place, and at time 1 we can present Paul with an opportunity to change his preferences back to artist's preferences at time 2. From the perspective of Paul's extended preferences at time 0, this would be an opportunity to increase his welfare. But from the perspective of his extended preferences at time 1, taking this opportunity would make him worse off. By making his preferences as time 0 normative throughout these periods, we would not be respecting his judgements at time 1. We thus can represent Paul's interests in his future preferences at time 0 only at the cost of disregarding his extended preferences at time 1 (including, of course, his interests in his future preferences at that time).

Now, in some cases of preference change, we might have reason to regard a person's initial preferences in sequences of this kind as normative; an example might be a case in which the preference change between time 0 to time 1 was a result of the subversion of Paul's cognitive capacities, or of coercion or oppression, or was a response to an unduly limiting environment. But we have assumed that the process of preference change was not of this sort. In such cases, it does not appear appropriate to judge Paul's welfare at time 1 from the perspective of his very different extended preferences at time 0: this would be judging his welfare by a set of values that he no longer holds.

Though I cannot discuss all possible methods of dealing with the case of preference change that fall within the family of possible preference satisfaction measures, it seems that all possibilities that involve a compromise between these two approaches will suffer from some combination of the drawbacks of these two methods. For example, consider determining a person's welfare in a given period by the degree of satisfaction of a weighted average of the extended preferences he has over that period, with the weights determined by the relative amount of time he holds certain preferences.[6] This would involve both limiting the degree to which a standard of welfare represents a person's interest in his future preferences, and assessing his welfare at some points in time by a set of values which he no longer holds. It would, for example, imply that if Paul had has artist's preferences for 30 years, and then developed banker's preferences later in life, then (re)developing his taste for art by enrolling in evening classes of art appreciation would improve his welfare even if he had his banker's preferences for 10 years, and saw no value at all in taking these classes.

[6] Something akin to this possibility, though without the use of the distinction between limited and extended preferences, is discussed by Richard Brandt (1979, pp. 247–253) and Arneson (1990a, pp. 162–167). See also the following footnote.

In sum, it seems that any preference satisfaction measure will have significant drawbacks, since it will involve either neglecting individuals' current interests in shaping their future preferences, or, in their future, judging their welfare by a set of values which might be very alien to them.[7]

4. A substantive conception of welfare?

This conclusion should, I believe, prompt us to consider alternative measures of welfare. In closing, I would like to outline one approach that strikes me as worth pursuing. This is to construct a public conception of welfare from a list of goods and conditions that can be recognised by people with divergent values as generally important constituents of a good life (see also Scanlon 1991). Some of its constituent elements will be broad categories that can be realised in different ways by people with different values, such as developing one's capacities, leading the life one wants with family

[7] It may be of interest to note how my discussion of the difficulties which preference change creates for a preference satisfaction measure differs from Brandt's. Brandt (1979) also argues that the possibility of preference change undermines the case for a preference satisfaction measure of welfare. His discussion differs from mine, however, in not making use of the distinction between a person's limited and extended preferences. This distinction is, I believe, crucial to the problem. For not just any change in a person's preferences generates a problem for a preference satisfaction metric. A change in a person's limited preferences is not sufficient to undermine the preference satisfaction measure; what is required is a change in a person's extended preferences. To see this, consider the case of a hedonist, who ranks all (state of the world, person's position, preference type) triples on the basis of the pleasure they yield for her. Suppose that, at time 0, she wants to celebrate her birthday at time 2 with a dinner in her favourite fish restaurant rather than in a steak house, since her current limited preferences are for fish over meat, and she does not expect to undergo a preference change between now and time 2. However, suppose she does undergo a change in her limited preferences, so that at time 2 she prefers to dine in a steak house. So long as this is a change in her limited preferences only, we have no difficulty assessing the welfare of these two options. For we can assess the welfare associated with the four options (eating fish at time 2 with a taste for fish), (eating meat at time 2 with a taste for fish), (eating fish at time 2 with a taste for meat), and (eating meat at time 2 with a taste for meat) from the perspective of her unchanged extended preferences, that is to say, by equating the welfare of each option with the pleasure it yields.

and friends, job satisfaction, and achieving success in one's main endeavours. It will also include more specific goods like health, leisure, and wealth, which are generally judged to be important elements of a good life. Our discussion also teaches us that this list should include goods and conditions that generally enable people to maintain or develop the tastes, values, and aims they want to have.

By including categories, goods and conditions that are valuable from the perspective of different views of the good life, this list accommodates both the diverse views of the good life that are held within a population, and the different views of the good life that a person may have during his lifetime. The standard objection to a conception of welfare of this kind is that by using the same list of goods and conditions to assess everyone's welfare, and by using the same weights for these goods and conditions in each person's case, it fails to fully respect each person's view of their own welfare. The force of this objection depends on the assumption that there is an alternative measure of welfare—the preference satisfaction measure—which *does* fully respect each person's view of their own good. But our discussion makes clear that given the possibility of change in a person's extended preferences, no form of the preference satisfaction measure can fully respect each individual's judgements of her own welfare. It may be, therefore, that a substantive conception of welfare of this kind meets our first requirement (to respect, to the greatest reasonable extent, each person's view of their own welfare) because this just *is* the furthest we can go towards respecting each person's view of their own good.

A standard of welfare of this kind also respects our second requirement of neutrality of judgement (see Scanlon 1991, pp. 39–40 and Otsuka 2003, pp. 110–112). For, in attempting to accommodate to the greatest extent possible different views of the good life, it is constructed without the assumption that any particular conception of the good or set of conceptions of the good is the right one to the exclusion of others. In sum, the difficulties that the possibility of change in a person's extended preferences causes for a preference satisfaction conception of welfare render a substantive conception of welfare more attractive.

References

Arneson, R. (1990a) 'Liberalism, Distributive Subjectivism, and Equal Opportunity for Welfare', in *Philosophy and Public Affairs* 19, pp. 158–194.

Arneson, R. (1990b) 'Primary Goods Reconsidered' in *Noûs* 24, pp. 429–454.

Arneson, R. (1990c) 'Neutrality and Utility' in *Canadian Journal of Philosophy* 20, pp. 215–240.

Binmore, K. (1991) *Fun and Games*. Lexington, Mass: D.C. Heath.

Brandt, R. (1979) *A Theory of the Good and the Right*. Oxford: Oxford University Press.

Dworkin, R. (2000) *Sovereign Virtue*. Cambridge: Harvard University Press.

Frankfurt, H. (1982) 'The Importance of What We Care About', reprinted in his *The Importance of What We Care About*, Cambridge: Cambridge University Press, pp. 80–94.

Frankfurt, H. (2004) *The Reasons of Love*. Princeton: Princeton University Press.

Otsuka, M. (2003) *Libertarianism Without Inequality*. Oxford: Oxford University Press.

Scanlon, T. (1991) 'The Moral Basis of Interpersonal Comparisons', in *Interpersonal Comparisons of Well-Being*, eds. Jon Elster and John Roemer. Cambridge: Cambridge University Press, pp. 17–44.

Voorhoeve, A. (2003) 'Harry Frankfurt on the Necessity of Love', in *Philosophical Writings* 23, pp. 55–70.